Harry Pearson was born and brought up on the edge of Teeside. He is the author of eight works of non-fiction. *The Far Corner – A Mazy Dribble through North-East Football*, was runner-up for the William Hill Prize and has been named as one of the Fifty Greatest Sports Books of All Time by both the *Observer* and *The Times*. He wrote a weekly sports column in the *Guardian* from 1996 to 2012, and won the 2011 MCC/Cricket Society Prize for his book about Northern club cricket, *Slipless in Settle*. He lives in Northumberland.

'At last Constantine has found a biographer capable of telling his magnificent story – Harry Pearson has written a beguiling work that does full justice to this wonderful sportsman and most honourable of men' Peter Oborne, *Daily Mail*

'An excellently researched and sensitively handled account of Constantine's life and impact beyond the game. He was "a 'Champagne cocktail' cricketer – effervescent but with a kick" and half a century on, his story has lost none of its fizz' ESPN.com

'Harry Pearson is an author with an aversion to uninteresting sentences. *Connie* is a constantly engaging study' Giles Smith, *The Times*

9071

D0270822

Also by Harry Pearson

The Far Corner
Racing Pigs and Giant Marrows
A Tall Man in a Low Land
Around the World by Mouse
Achtung Schweinehund!
Dribble!
Hound Dog Days
Slipless in Settle
The Trundlers

CONNIE

THE MARVELLOUS LIFE
OF LEARIE CONSTANTINE

HARRY PEARSON

ABACUS

First published in Great Britain in 2017 by Little, Brown
This paperback edition published in 2018 by Abacus

1 3 5 7 9 10 8 6 4 2

Copyright © Harry Pearson 2017

A CIP catalogue record for this book
is available from the British Library.

ISBN 978-0-349-14039-1

Typeset in Baskerville by M Rules
Printed and bound in Great Britain by
Clays Ltd, Elcograf S.p.A.

Papers used by Abacus are from well-managed forests
and other responsible sources.

Contents

Introduction

Any cricket fan growing up in Lancashire or Yorkshire during the sixties and seventies would have heard of Learie Constantine, known affectionately, and almost universally, as Connie.

The great West Indian all-rounder had played his last competitive match, for Windhill in the Bradford League, a few years after the end of the Second World War; his greatest days had been before it started. Yet people spoke of Connie's deeds as if they had happened yesterday, as if they had seen them, as if they had been old enough to have seen them. Little footage of Connie exists, and even if it had, in those pre-internet days we would have had no access to it. Yet Connie's whirlwind fast bowling, cavalier batting and magical acrobatics in the field remained vivid decades after he had played his last meaningful match, so imprinted on the collective consciousness of cricket followers across the northern counties it seemed that, if you closed your eyes and really tried, you could see him, front foot down the wicket, back knee on the turf, heaving a decent-length delivery over the midwicket boundary, bouncing across the street beyond, scattering the queue outside the Odeon.

Born in rural Trinidad in 1901, Connie was the most dynamic all-round cricketer of his age. When he signed to play as professional for Nelson in the Lancashire League in 1929, he became one of the highest-paid sportsmen in Britain, and one of the country's first black stars.

Constantine established the blueprint of Caribbean cricket: bowling fast and short, batting audaciously and fielding with such athleticism John Arlott thought 'he must be made of springs and rubber'. As Jamaican prime minister Michael Manley observed, 'He brought the nature of West Indies cricket to the world: good-natured aggressiveness, extrovert exuberance, panache.'

Few who saw Connie in action would ever forget the experience. Playing for the West Indians against Middlesex at Lord's in 1928, the Trinidadian smashed a century in fifty-nine minutes, including one blow off the back foot that flew over cover point and ricocheted off the Father Time weather vane on the roof of the old Grand Stand. The future British prime minister Alec Douglas-Home (then Lord Dunglass) was in the crowd that day. Close to half a century later he would still recall the shot as 'prodigious'.

Cricketers and cricket writers lined up to acclaim him. Sir Neville Cardus called Connie 'a genius' and 'the most original cricketer of recent times'. Sir Pelham Warner wrote that 'Next to Donald Bradman, Constantine is the greatest "draw" of any living player,' while Raymond Robertson-Glasgow rated him 'The most exciting cricketer of his generation'.

What makes this praise all the more astonishing is that in his entire career Connie played in just eighteen Tests and a meagre 119 first-class matches. Connie never much cared for figures or averages (he thought they led to cautious play), and perhaps that is just as well, for his own are not impressive. In Tests he took fifty-eight wickets at 30.10 and hit 641 runs at 19.42, with a highest score of 90. In first-class matches his 439 wickets came at 20.48, his runs at 4475 runs at 24.05. He scored five centuries and ten fifties. Compared with other great all-rounders, this is a moderate return. So how did Connie come to engage the imaginations of so many, to be spoken of as a genius? Showmanship was part of it, star quality, charisma, an ability to apparently defy the laws of gravity and play havoc with conventional notions of time and space. Connie was a man not of days, but of brief golden moments that stayed in spectators' memories long after the context surrounding them had faded into blankness: a cartwheeling catch, a lightning-fast yorker that splintered a stump, a lofted back-foot drive that cannoned off the pavilion fence. He turned matches in an hour with bravura hitting, a spell of hostile pace interspersed with cunningly disguised slower deliveries, or in a split-second with a panther-like pick up and throw that saw the key opposition batsman stranded in mid-pitch. Connie played some cricket in India, at the invitation of a wealthy maharajah. What sort of fee might he have commanded in the Indian Premier League, had it been around in those days?

Connie came into my life shortly after his own had ended. It was 1972. I was eleven. In the early seventies, cricket in England was, by and large, an attritional affair occasionally enlivened by men who had followed in Connie's footsteps: Clive Lloyd, Garry Sobers, Keith Boyce, Alvin Kallicharran. During long afternoons at Acklam and Scarborough watching Richard Lumb ('The Pudding', as my father, a Lancastrian, always called him) and the sacred Geoffrey Boycott advancing the score by glacial increments

my head was often filled with daydreams of the players of
bygone eras I'd read about in books borrowed from the
village library: Prince Ranjitsinhji, Gilbert Jessop, Arthur
Wellard and Connie. They were far more colourful than
reality. But then so was the North Sea.

I read Connie's autobiographies, *Cricket and I* and *Cricket
in the Sun*. The tone was avuncular, ebullient, and perhaps
a little bumptious. If Connie had done something amazing, he did not gloss over it, but told you so in a style that
suggested leaping and cries of jubilation. I had Connie's
coaching manual for young players, a gift from one of my
father's colleagues at British Steel. In games in the garden
I tried to put into practice his lessons. Connie favoured the
unorthodox and his techniques were soon knocked out of
me by the MCC coach who came to our school once a week
and drew chalk outlines on the playground to show where
our feet should be. It was the sort of coaching Connie railed
against for churning out mediocre cricketers. In my case,
that was not true. I aspired to mediocrity.

Over time Connie slipped from my mind, replaced by
the cricketers who enlivened my later teenage years – Jeff
Thomson, Tony Greig, Michael Holding. He came back
into my life a few years ago when I was writing *Slipless
in Settle*, a book about cricket in the northern leagues. In
Lancashire, Connie still loomed large in the minds of supporters. Indeed, it would be as hard to meet a cricket fan
in East Lancashire who had not heard of him as it would
be to locate an Argentinian who is ignorant of the name
Diego Maradona. We live in an age when events and
people are forgotten ever more quickly, which makes the
longevity of Connie's reputation all the more extraordinary.
In large part it was built far from the traditional arenas of
cricket, in the Lancashire League. As his friend and fellow

countryman C. L. R. James wrote, 'Constantine is not a Test cricketer who plays in the Leagues. He is a League cricketer who plays in Tests.'

Connie signed to play at Nelson for financial betterment – professional cricket barely existed in Trinidad. But though he was always conscious of money, there was another reason too. The West Indies was a divided society, and white people ruled it. For black people like Connie there was no chance of social advancement. His father's position as an overseer on a small cocoa plantation was the highest to which he could aspire. No black person could be put in a position where whites might have to defer to them. Playing for Trinidad and the West Indies, Connie always served a white captain. There were other, less publicly obvious, slights to black cricketers in their homeland. It transpired, for instance, that visiting MCC tour parties were invited to post-Test dinner-dances at which only the white members of the West Indian team were present. That the MCC players had no idea this was the case was revealed to Connie in Jamaica when Jack Iddon, whom Connie knew well from playing alongside him in various charity matches in Lancashire, remarked that he would 'see you at the dance later'. This was the life of black cricketers in the West Indies in those days – heroes on the field and uninvited guests off it.

C. L. R. James commented, 'He revolted against the revolting contrast between his first-class status as a cricketer and his third-class status as a man. The restraints imposed on him by social conditions in the West Indies had become intolerable and he decided to stand them no longer.' In England opportunities were open to Connie that were closed to him in his homeland.

Connie's impact on northern life spread well beyond the cricket field. In his spare evenings he toured Lancashire, giving lectures in town halls, mechanical institutes and working men's reading rooms about the West Indies and its inhabitants. 'Nearly all the prejudice I have ever encountered,' he would later write, 'was based on ignorance.' It was a situation he did his best to rectify.

Constantine battled prejudice and ignorance with charm and dignity – 'firm but free of acrimony', John Arlott would note. He maintained a sense of humour, often in difficult circumstances. His performances when fielding on the boundary at Nelson's away fixtures, during which he would converse with the crowd in mock Lancastrian, provoked almost as much delight as his cricket.

In Nelson, Connie shone by example, on the field and off it. Unlike many professional cricketers he did not lie in bed until late in the morning, nor was he reluctant – as some were – to help in the coaching of the youth-team players. Nelson was a town of nonconformists and self-improvers; Constantine's lifestyle and work ethic was admired there. The local newspaper went so far as to describe him as 'the ideal citizen'.

At Nelson's Seedhill ground Connie's legend grew so great that even fifty years after he had left the Lancashire League and entered the House of Lords he remained the measure by which all other professionals were judged.

During Connie's years in the Lancashire League other great names from Test cricket arrived to challenge him, including the great Indian all-rounder Amar Singh, and Australian Test stars Arthur Richardson and Alan Fairfax, as well as English stalwarts such as Fred Root, Nobby Clark and George Macaulay. Aside, briefly, from Amar Singh, none ever did eclipse Connie.

Hundreds of West Indian cricketers would follow his path into northern league cricket, first contemporaries such as

George Headley, Manny Martindale and Edwin St Hill, and then the post-war generation of Sonny Ramadhin, Frank Worrell, Everton Weekes and Clyde Walcott. In the sixties, seventies and eighties there was barely a West Indian Test player who had not played league cricket. Even giants of later decades such as Courtney Walsh had spent seasons in their youth swaddled in sweaters beneath grey skies. They played in Lancashire and Yorkshire, Durham and Northumberland, and in Scotland too. Would they have come without the example of Connie to follow? Would they indeed have been invited, had it not been for his glowing example?

Connie's life outside cricket was also influential. He worked tirelessly throughout the war as a welfare officer, helping newly arrived workers from the Caribbean, and playing charity cricket before huge, sport-deprived crowds. Though he struggled to keep himself out of mainstream politics and did not enjoy the experience when he was finally pulled in, his brave campaigning work on racial equality would pave the way for the 1965 Race Relations Act. He became a barrister, was appointed an MBE and later knighted, and became the first black person to sit in the House of Lords. He appeared on *This Is Your Life* and *Desert Island Discs*.

Life was not always plain sailing. He had a bitter feud with Walter Hammond that lasted a decade; found himself embroiled in the Bodyline controversy; was accused of having 'communist sympathies' by some sections of the British media because of his outspoken views on racial discrimination; quit his seat in the Trinidad Legislative Assembly after becoming disillusioned over repeated and unfounded allegations of corruption; and was forced to give up his post as Trinidad's High Commissioner in London after falling out with prime minister Eric Williams. In the sixties Connie became an establishment figure, sitting on the Race Relations Board and the Board of the BBC. He was mocked in *Private Eye* for perceived pomposity and accused of arrogance by others, while many West Indians felt disappointed by what they saw as his preference for life in England over that in the Caribbean. To some, he would remain a 'black white man'.

Over time, the verdict on Connie's political life has been kinder and the strength of his legacy more widely recognised. For many, though, it is the game of cricket, which Connie loved and which never seemed to let him down, which carries his name forward. He had been there at the birth of the West Indies as a Test nation, playing his part in the often uneven struggle against England and Australia in a side that was too often, by his own estimation, more mob than team: inexpertly led, ineptly administered and selected by criteria that often saw the best players omitted for reasons of race or politics.

All that changed after Connie's retirement from playing. He saw Frank Worrell become the West Indies' first black captain – a breakthrough for which he had campaigned for decades – and the former colonies emerge as one of the major forces in the world game. He would not live to see their rise to dominance under Clive Lloyd, nor their slide back from seeming invincibility into the chaotic vulnerability he had battled so hard to raise them from. Certainly the West Indies could do with his galvanising and inspirational presence now.

Cricket has changed massively since I first read about Connie, sitting in my bedroom in North Yorkshire, the John Player League on the television, Peter Sainsbury bowling to Brian Bolus. It is more exciting, attacking and dynamic. It is almost as if the game has finally caught up with him at last. Yet to this day, on the benches of grounds across the north of England, and likely in Port of Spain too, you will find old men who will react to the mention of some brilliant prodigy of our era with a sniff and a shake of the head, and the words, 'He's not a patch on Connie.'

Chapter 1

Sipping Nectar with the Gods

It was just before lunch on 18 March 1935, the fifth day of the final and deciding Test, that Jackie Grant fell heavily on the damp outfield while chasing a shot from Walter Hammond and twisted his ankle. The West Indies captain knew straight away that he could not continue. His team had fought hard for four days at Sabina Park and in the weeks before that too, struggling to overcome an England side packed with tough old county pros and gifted amateurs from the universities. They had rallied after a shattering first Test defeat in Barbados, tied things up in Trinidad and now, in Jamaica, were within touching distance of their first-ever victory in a Test series. Before he hobbled back to the Sabina Park pavilion, Grant called his team around him, exhorted them to do their best and told them that, in his absence, the team would be captained by his fellow Trinidadian Learie Constantine.

The message was delivered matter-of-factly, yet it carried great import. Connie was the most experienced, charismatic and popular player in the team. Yet in a system in which leadership was inextricably linked with class, education and, ultimately, race, it was a call that Connie must have thought would never come, even temporarily. Grant had attended Queen's Royal College and Cambridge University. He was privileged, and white. Connie was neither. Though he was fêted around the world for his prowess and his sportsmanship, neither counted when it came to the captaincy of the West Indies.

Yet while the elevation was no more than Connie's due, Grant deserves a little credit for his action. Had he observed the strictures of the society he had been raised in he would surely have passed the reins to his younger brother, Rolph. Certainly it is impossible to imagine that, in similar circumstances, England's amateur captain Bob Wyatt would have handed over command to an experienced and popular professional such as Patsy Hendren – and, as we shall see, he didn't.

Connie was a man for the big moment, a master of the match-changing hour. As Grant limped from the field, the caretaker captain immediately went on the offensive. England had no chance of winning; the West Indies needed just seven wickets for victory. Hammond, one of the world's greatest batsmen, and the classy and experienced Les Ames were at the wicket. Rain clouds were building. A storm seemed guaranteed before close of play. For the home side, time was running out . . .

When the MCC touring party had arrived in the Caribbean – after a particularly rough crossing from Avonmouth on the banana boat SS *Cavina* – nobody would have anticipated such dramas. Not in England certainly. The West Indies were the newest Test-playing nation and had hardly distinguished themselves on tours of the British Isles and Australia. There had been flashes, and most would agree that the Caribbean islanders were in all likelihood better than fellow fledglings New Zealand, but still the feeling prevailed that the MCC had been a little hasty in promoting them, and most around the counties agreed with Maurice Tate, the doughty and popular Sussex all-rounder, who had concluded that 'Only matches against Australia can really be counted as Tests.'

One English observer who would have taken issue with that assessment was the man tasked with captaining the MCC in the Caribbean. Warwickshire's Wyatt was a tough, shrewd cricketer, a gentleman who at times played with the gritty no-quarter-asked-none-given attitude of a pro. Wyatt had come up against the West Indians many times and considered the prevailing opinion of them to be wrong. In his view, the West Indies were not to be taken lightly, especially at home. The England skipper believed that the MCC had underestimated the strength of West Indies cricket and selected a touring party accordingly. Right from the outset he had misgivings about the task facing him. For while a batting line-up featuring Walter Hammond, Les Ames, Maurice Leyland, Patsy Hendren and Jack Iddon looked strong enough, and Eric Hollies and George Paine provided decent spin options, the fast bowling appeared underpowered. Wyatt himself could swing the ball both ways at medium pace, Hammond was nippy for a few overs and Big Jim Smith of Middlesex, a nineteen-stone slab of a man, could be relied upon to deliver over after over of the sort of nagging seam-up that was the default setting of the English county pro, but the only genuinely quick bowler in the party was Ken Farnes, a tall, wavy-haired amateur from Essex. Farnes was fast enough to have caused controversy by bowling Bodyline in the 1933 Varsity Match, pinging the ball off various Oxford batsmen's chins, but he

was suffering from a variety of niggling injuries and certainly did not seem capable of carrying the attack on his
own. Wyatt had travelled west with a sense of foreboding,
keeping up his spirits – and irritating the always-irascible
Hammond – by playing 78s on the wind-up gramophone
he had brought with him.

By contrast, the West Indians were more optimistic.
The domestic game was in good fettle. George Headley
could now be placed alongside Hammond and Don
Bradman in the top rank of Test batsmen, while the fast
bowling trio of Connie, Manny Martindale and Leslie
Hylton was potent enough to prey on the nerves of even
the toughest opponents. There were high hopes for Rolph
Grant, recently returned from England, who had just
struck the highest score ever recorded by a West Indian
on the matting wicket at Port of Spain. With promising
wicketkeeper-batsman Cyril Christiani and the leg spin of
Ellis 'Puss' Achong, they could at least allow themselves a
little optimism.

There was a feeling too that West Indian cricket was
becoming a little more professional, particularly when it
came to selection. The days when the team was picked to
save travelling costs and appease local fans had thankfully
passed. (In 1930, the Test in Port of Spain had featured
no fewer than eight Trinidadians, while the one at Sabina
Park a couple of weeks later had seen the same number
of Jamaicans taking the field.) The policy of selecting a
local captain for each Test had also been abandoned. Yet a
degree of chaos remained, and it touched Connie.

The all-rounder had spent the autumn of 1934 coaching in India. When he arrived home in Nelson in
mid-December after a long sea voyage via the Suez Canal,
he found a telegram waiting for him from the West Indies

selectors, inviting him to take part in the forthcoming series. Connie was taken aback, having apparently been given no previous indication that he might be picked and having therefore presumed that he would be spending the winter with his family in Lancashire. The invitation had arrived too late for him to have any chance of getting back to the Caribbean for the first Test. Nevertheless, he elected to accept it and booked his sea passage to Trinidad, arriving several weeks after the MCC party.

Wyatt's party had arrived in Barbados on 27 December. They were warmly greeted by the locals and by Patsy Hendren, the Middlesex batsman having travelled to the Caribbean ahead of his team mates to play, coach and referee football matches. The amiable Hendren, a gifted all-round sportsman who played on the wing for QPR and Manchester City, was hugely popular in the West Indies and – according to Wyatt – there were any number of small boys around the islands who had been named in his honour.

The Englishmen enjoyed the sunshine and fresh winds of Barbados, and the happy nonchalance of the Barbadians themselves. At the Kensington Oval the nets were damp and lively, the ball jumping and turning alarmingly, though Hendren seemed untroubled, amusing the locals by continually straight-driving balls onto the roof of the pavilion.

With Connie still on his way across the Atlantic, the West Indies were unable to select their first-choice side for the opening Test. Jackie Grant was named captain. His side batted: Roach, George Carew, Headley, Charles Jones, Derek Sealy, Jackie Grant, Rolph Grant, Hylton, Christiani, Achong and Martindale. Carew, Rolph Grant, Hylton and Christiani were all making their Test debuts. Jones had played a single Test five years before. Headley

had just completed his first, highly successful season in
the Lancashire League with Haslingden. Luckily – unlike
Connie – the great Jamaican had no commitments to
detain him and was able to return to the Caribbean as soon
as the board's invitation arrived.

The game began in English conditions of dark skies and
heavy rain. The wicket was damp – a 'real pig', Farnes
thought – and the game was one of the most sensational
in the short history of West Indies cricket. Wyatt won
the toss and inserted the West Indies. Farnes bowled at
his fastest and the first five West Indies wickets fell for 31
runs. Headley alone was master of the situation and batted
with bravery and style before falling for 44 – run out by
Christiani. When Farnes tired, Paine and Hollies took over
and the home side were dismissed for 102, Headley run out
for a brilliant 44 that confirmed Bradman's view that he
was the best bad-wicket batsman in the world game.

West Indies small total was put into context when
England batted. With Martindale and Hylton both bowling fast the visitors struggled to 81 for five at close of play.
But for a plucky 43 from Hammond, it might have been
far worse. No play was possible until tea on the second
day. When play did recommence, two England wickets fell
quickly, prompting Wyatt to declare 21 runs behind. It was
a bold decision designed to give his bowlers another go on a
wicket that seemed likely to get better, provided no further
rain fell.

The pitch was treacherous and Grant responded by sending his tail-enders in first, in the hope that they could keep
things going until conditions had improved. The plan came
to nothing. Big Jim Smith found the perfect line and length
for the wicket and sent back Martindale, Achong and
Rolph Grant with only four on the board. Christiani and

Hylton – who always chewed a toothpick when batting – shored things up and the West Indies were 33 for three at the close, ten of the runs coming in extras.

More rain fell during the night, soaking the uncovered wicket and preventing play from commencing until late in the day. The West Indies attempted to consolidate their position but lost three wickets for 18 runs, including Headley for a duck. At tea Grant made a move even bolder than that of Wyatt and declared, setting England just 73 to win – still the lowest target ever set by a declaration.

Some saw Grant's decision as adventurous, others as so rash as to border on the foolish. In his defence the wicket was still borderline unplayable, and with Martindale and Hylton at their best England were soon struggling at 49 for five. Martindale in particular bowled brilliantly, in a spell that Farnes considered 'as fine a piece of fast bowling as you could ever wish to see'. Once Martindale tired, however, the West Indies had no real back-up. If only Connie had received the telegram sooner, things might have been different. As it was, Hammond, who had survived a number of near-misses early on and rarely looked comfortable against the rising ball, found the going much easier against the home side's second-string attack. With Wyatt batting with commendable solidity the pair took England to within five runs of victory, at which point the Gloucestershire man stepped down the wicket to the flagging Martindale and drove him for six, a magnificent hit that provided a fitting end to an extraordinary match.

In the aftermath of defeat Grant was widely criticised by the home supporters. Wyatt recalled seeing people pointing him out in the street as 'the man who lost us the Test match'. The England captain was more charitable, concluding that in the circumstances Grant's decision was the correct one and that he had come as close to winning the match as anyone might have expected.

England, meanwhile, celebrated the win in high style at Bridgetown Aquatic Club. Wyatt, who was usually a teetotaller, downed a huge rum punch then astounded everybody by doing a backward somersault off the high diving board.

The following day the MCC party left Barbados for Trinidad on board the SS *Venezuela*. Connie would be waiting for them.

They arrived in Port of Spain to a climate that was hotter and more humid than that of Barbados. While they amused themselves by visiting the Angostura distillery, listening to local calypso musicians singing songs about the Graf Zeppelin and the recent nuptials of the Duke and Duchess of Kent, and bathing in Macqueripe Bay (where Les Ames surprised the rest of the party by learning to swim at the ripe old age of thirty), Connie was practising in the nets and reacquainting himself with his Trinidad team mates. He had not played for the island since turning out against the MCC in 1930. The Inter-Colonial Tournament still barred professionals, a short-sighted policy that, as outside observers noted, forced the best and most ambitious cricketers such as Constantine to leave the Caribbean, depriving local youngsters of their example and expertise.

Connie also needed to familiarise himself with the new batting surface at the Queen's Park Oval. The wicket was still matting laid on fine-grained mud that had set like concrete, but the original coconut matting, which Connie had played on in his youth, had now been replaced with jute. The coconut matting had produced vicious bounce and cut, while the jute (which Wyatt thought looked like string) lay flatter and played more like turf. For Connie, used by now to the wickets of the Lancashire League, adjusting to the man-made surface was as much an issue as it was for the English visitors.

Despite the new surface, Connie was looking forward to the forthcoming matches. The Queen's Park Oval was one of his favourite grounds. He loved the hard, sun-baked outfield, the yelling and wild betting of the Trinidadian fans and the encouragement of those 'barefoot people who have paid good money'. The crowd were Connie's inspiration wherever he played, but here on his home soil he felt the power of their support most keenly. He knew they desperately wanted him to succeed. Other players might have counted this as pressure. To Connie, it was a pleasure to be revelled in.

The first tour match began in perfect conditions, the scarlet blossoms in the shrubbery around the pavilion contributing to the scene. Farnes, who had spent the previous evening dancing with American ladies from a visiting cruise liner to the accompaniment of a rumba band, found it all delightfully picturesque.

Wyatt won the toss and elected to bat. When Connie came out onto the field he was greeted with enthusiastic cheers from a large and lively crowd. He opened the bowling for the home side. There were to be no heroics. The MCC batted sensibly and made 348. In Trinidad's reply a debutant named Arthur Maynard made an unbeaten 200 and once he had reached that milestone Grant declared with Trinidad 23 in front. Maynard was the first West Indian to score a first-class double century in Port of Spain. According to Farnes, Maynard's performance created such local interest that it was 'made the subject of a speech of political propaganda in favour of the separation of Trinidad from the British Commonwealth of Nations'. It did little for

Maynard's career, however. When the twenty-five-year-old was not picked to play in the Trinidad Test he was reportedly so disappointed he retired from first-class cricket with a batting average of 208 and concentrated on playing football instead. It was the sort of sudden, sad ending to a career that would blight Caribbean cricket throughout the era.

The MCC crawled to 200–6. Wyatt then declared, leaving Trinidad the task of scoring 178 in eighty minutes to win. They could not manage it, though Connie, coming in at number three, thrashed 25 in ten minutes, including consecutive sixes off the notoriously niggardly slow-left armer Paine. The second of these blows went straight over the fence into Elizabeth Street, a prodigious hit. Connie's contribution had been small statistically, but his presence had given his team and the spectators a massive psychological lift. With the great all-rounder in the side anything seemed possible.

Trinidad's second match with the tourists was another tightly contested affair. Connie bowled faster than he had in the first match, and produced one bumper that bounced so high it flew over the leaping wicketkeeper's gloves and smacked into the sightscreen. Farnes was impressed, since the wicketkeeper was standing well back. In Trinidad's first innings Wyatt swung the ball both ways and reduced the home side to 42 for six. Connie and his brother Elias now came together at the wicket – it was the first time they had played together, a touching moment for them both. Connie took a fraternal interest in his younger brother's career and was constantly urging the selectors to give him his chance at a higher level, sometimes to a degree that suggested filial loyalty was clouding his judgement. Batting in a manner Wyatt thought 'calm, unforced and unorthodox', Connie produced an amazing display of hitting, including some prodigious sixes, and finally fell for 68. The rest of the match was rain-affected, though a series of MCC batting collapses served to confirm Wyatt's mistrust of the surface and his side's ability to cope with it. It would affect his approach to the forthcoming Test.

Connie duly took his place in West Indies side. His presence helped refocus a team still a little shell-shocked after the events in Barbados. Oscar Da Costa was also brought into the team, with Clifford Roach – who would not play international cricket again – and George Carew the men to miss out. The Australian Test cricketer Arthur Richardson, who was coaching on the island, was asked to stand as one of the umpires, despite having no experience in the role. Connie knew Richardson from the Lancashire League, where the Australian had been enjoying a successful spell, and they'd played together in various benefit matches. This familiarity, as we shall see, would be of little help to the West Indies.

The weather was hot and rather humid, and after the shocks of the two previous games Wyatt set out simply not to lose this match. On winning the toss, he inserted the West Indies. It was a defensive decision, one that placed the onus on the home side. With the matting surface remaining true throughout the match, it would allow him better to determine whether to pursue victory or settle for a draw. Wyatt was emphatic that he had consulted other members of the party before making his decision – a fact that suggests he was criticised for it in the English press.

The first day's play was uneventful to the point of dullness. Their selection reshuffle had left the West Indies short of opening batsmen, so when Wyatt won the toss and put in the home side Grant sent out wicketkeeper Christiani and

Charles Jones to do the job. The makeshift pair failed. True to Wyatt's intentions, England bowled defensively, particularly the slow left-armer Paine, who went round the wicket with an offside field to contain Headley, and switched to over the wicket with a packed leg-side field to confound Derek Sealy.

The policy worked, with Headley out for a scratchy 25, while the normally aggressive Sealy became bogged down and crawled to 92. He fell to Wyatt, who was making the second new ball wobble about in the air. The skipper then also dismissed Rolph Grant and Puss Achong.

When Connie came to the wicket Wyatt spread the field to prevent fours. In an attempt to overcome this tactic Connie played some extraordinary shots, moving across to the on-side and pulling balls from well outside off stump away to square leg. Though he failed to make contact on a number of occasions, when he did, the ball went racing to the boundary as if fired from a howitzer. His unorthodox approach saw him race to 73 not out as the home side closed the day on 284–9.

The following morning, with Martindale as a more-or-less silent partner, Connie added a further 17 to his score, but with a first Test century within reach sliced a shot high into the air off Jim Smith and was caught in the slips by Hendren for 90. 'It was just one of those days when people like Smith, Paine, Farnes [actually the Essex paceman was not playing – deemed unsuitable for the matting, he was left to watch from the pavilion] and Wyatt look easy, and the ball is always in the right place as the bat goes flashing through the sunny air.' Such was Connie's modest assessment of an innings Wyatt thought one of the most extraordinary he had ever seen in his life, and also one of the luckiest.

Smith and Wyatt both bowled well, but England were missing Hollies, who had a thigh strain, and soon regretted leaving out Farnes. Since the West Indies had spent a day and a bit compiling a total of 302, Wyatt and his men were relatively pleased with events. However, any feelings of security were quickly blown away. With Connie, Martindale and Hylton extracting bounce off the jute and Rolph Grant fielding brilliantly at short leg, England soon found themselves in trouble at 23–5. Connie grabbed the first wicket, that of Townsend, lbw, and celebrated exuberantly – vaulting over the stumps as the batsman trudged off.

Wyatt considered it one of the best sustained spells of pace bowling he had ever witnessed – not as quick perhaps as Larwood and Voce at their most hostile, but fast and accurate, and, with Connie now producing the odd cunningly disguised slower delivery, extremely difficult to play against. Watching from the stands the schoolboy Jeff Stollmeyer, a future West Indies captain and opening bat, found it a fearsome sight, the thought of facing such bowling sending shivers down his spine.

The first five English wickets fell for 23. Hendren and Iddon slowly pulled things around, Iddon making a patient 73 and Hendren scoring 41. Errol Holmes continued the good work and was 41 not out when close of play came with England 200–8. The following morning Rolph Grant got amongst the wickets with his bowling and when England were all out they trailed by 44. Grant finished with three for 68. Martindale conceded just 26 runs in seventeen overs. However, he fractured a finger on his right hand fielding and was forced out of the attack.

Despite having a small first-innings lead on a low-scoring track, the West Indies did not force the pace, batting sensibly and reaching 150–3 by the close. Headley was the mainstay of the innings, though he was not at his best and had a lucky escape when Hammond dropped him in the slips.

Despite the fact that there were just three sessions left of the match, the West Indies spent the final morning batting in a slow, methodical manner. Headley, still struggling for form, was trapped lbw by Jim Smith for 93 (it is a mark of Headley's unflappable temperament that this was the only time in his Test career that he was dismissed in the nineties). Connie and Rolph Grant attempted to ginger things up late on, the two Trinidadians smashing 31 and 38 not out respectively despite a widely spread field. When Connie fell, Grant and Da Costa then pushed the score rapidly along, adding 55 quick runs.

At lunch, Jackie Grant told Farnes he intended to carry on batting. Farnes thought the West Indians had been annoyed by England's defensive tactics and were doing so 'in a fit of pique'. Farnes underestimated Grant. His remark had been a deliberate piece of disinformation. Grant had every intention of declaring during the interval – he just wanted to do so as late as possible to disrupt the preparation of the England batsmen.

Wyatt's side started the fourth innings needing 325 to win in 210 minutes. Some observers, Farnes amongst them, felt England should have chased the runs. Wyatt, however, was determined to put safety first and, having told his men to play out time, he sent in the defensively minded Farrimond to open with Townsend. Out on the field Connie thought Wyatt's decision mystifying. Not that he much cared: the situation was tailor-made for him. The result of the Test had come down to a few hours of focused endeavour. He looked around at the stands packed with adoring fans, felt the hot sun on his back and was so charged with energy and confidence he 'felt as if I could throw the ball as high as the moon'.

When Farrimond fell early, he was replaced by Paine, another player noted for his belt-and-braces approach to batting. He was out for 14, hit wicket. Townsend at least showed some enterprise striking a six off Achong, but when he tried to repeat the shot he was caught at deep gully. The big-hitting Jim Smith, promoted up the order, was soon run out. And now there was Hammond. After making just a single in the first knock he came in with a stern look on his face that Connie recognised from previous encounters. The great batsman was determined to put away his flashy and fluid strokes and save the game for his side. Connie bowled to him with 'the loving care a mother gives to her child'. He fed Hammond full deliveries on off stump to tempt the flashing drive. The Englishman resisted, for a while, but then went after one that cut back in off the wicket and bowled him through the gate. He had made 9. In ninety minutes England had lost five wickets in amassing 71 runs. Wyatt's tinkering with the batting order had handed the initiative to his opponents. The momentum was now with the West Indies. The crowd in the ground, and hanging from the trees outside, knew it. As Hammond's stumps were knocked back they howled and cheered until it seemed to Connie the sky trembled.

The West Indians were, to Farnes's mind, 'right on their toes', sensing victory and needled by Wyatt's obvious defensive tactics. Martindale came out after tea and bowled despite his broken finger. He took the first over. Connie bowled the second to England's captain. Wyatt was obdurate and determined, but his opponent was irresistible. The third ball was Connie's quickest. It pitched on middle

stump and moved away, catching Wyatt's edge, and flew
'like a meteor' into the slips, where it was brilliantly caught
one-handed by Headley. Hendren contrived to get himself
run out. Leyland came out to join Ames with the situation
desperate and the crowd boiling with excitement. Fifteen
minutes remained; three wickets were needed.

Leyland and Ames were as reliable a pair of county
pros as could be imagined. They stuck to the task. Connie
decided to soften them up and pinged a couple of bouncers past Ames's chin. Richardson called Jackie Grant over
and warned him that if it continued he would bar Connie
from bowling again. Fearful of losing one of his most potent
weapons, the West Indies skipper removed Connie from
the attack, much to the bowler's exasperation and the ire
of the crowd. It appeared an over-reaction from the novice
umpire. Connie would later deduce that the trauma of the
infamous Bodyline tour had left a mark on Richardson, and
that he had determined to stamp leg theory out even where
it did not exist.

The frenzied atmosphere seemed to get to the normally
phlegmatic Ames. When Hylton bowled him a full toss the
Kent player played it tamely into the hands of Achong at
short leg. In came the reliable Lancastrian Iddon. He fell
second ball.

Holmes, fresh from his first-innings 85, was last man in.
Seven minutes remained. The vociferous crowd of eleven
thousand – the largest in West Indies history – had fallen
utterly silent.

The England vice-captain played out the remainder
of Hylton's over. Connie's spell of cooling off did not last
long, and now he returned to the attack with renewed and
furious intent. Leyland, a Yorkshireman who more-or-less
embodied the word 'doughty', was on the receiving end.

With some difficulty he played out the over. Holmes then safely negotiated a maiden from Hylton. The clock ticked on. One over remained.

Connie took the ball and advised umpire Victor Guillen, standing in his first Test, that he was changing from bowling over the wicket to going round it. The first delivery was fast and straight, the next aimed a little outside leg stump, the third swinging away to tempt Leyland into a rash drive. The Yorkshireman refused the bait. The fourth ball was Connie's slower delivery; the hand dragged slightly over the ball at the last moment to arrest its flight. It pitched wicket to wicket, rose. Leyland offered no shot and was struck high on the pad. The entire ground erupted in one massive howled appeal that – Connie thought – could be heard in Los Angeles. Guillen hesitated for a second, then raised his finger.

According to Hammond watching from the pavilion, 'Every tree instantly deposited all it had. The crowd rushed the pitch and chaired the winners off to the accompaniment of such shouting as I have seldom heard.' Constantine was carried off the field on the shoulders of the gleeful West Indian fans who slapped his back and patted his head and yelled and laughed. Resistance would have been futile, and besides, Connie admitted, he loved the experience. 'It was one of those moments when one sipped nectar with the Gods,' he would recall later.

Like Grant before him, Wyatt was widely blamed for the defeat. His defensive tactics had handed the initiative to his opponents and allowed the West Indies to get on the front foot. Wyatt accepted a degree of the criticism, but after making a veiled complaint about the umpiring – the dismissal leg before of Leyland to a delivery bowled from around the wicket had vexed him and left Leyland dumbfounded – he laid the blame squarely at the feet of his batsmen who, with the exception of Oxford University's David Townsend, had performed deplorably in the second innings.

The West Indies had won by 217 runs. In England's second knock Hylton took three for 25 and Connie picked up three for 11. With his two brilliant innings, and his incisive pace bowling, whatever part Wyatt's decisions had played in the home side's victory, Connie was the hero of the hour.

It was a demoralised MCC party that sailed for Georgetown. Nor did British Guiana do much to raise their spirits. The players went through their usual routine of nets, sightseeing, dancing and dinners, but the city and its scenery were uninspiring, Farnes comparing the views of Georgetown to 'washing day somewhere on the outskirts of Manchester' before concluding that, on the whole, it was perhaps better than certain quarters of Birmingham.

Wyatt, meanwhile, was tormented by a local cricket fan named Daddy Bell, who hung a coffin bearing a photo of the England skipper from a tree and claimed to have put a spell on him that would bring him ill fortune. Wyatt was promptly struck in the ribs by a Farnes bouncer during a net session and had to go to hospital for an X-ray. Worse was to follow for the England captain.

After the feverish excitement of the first two encounters, the third meeting of the international sides was an oddly lifeless affair. The West Indians brought in Ken Wishart and James Neblett, both locals who had done well in the tour matches. Neblett had toured the British Isles in 1928 but, like Wishart, was making his Test debut. Neither man would earn a second cap. Da Costa and Achong were the pair who made way. The bespectacled Arthur Richardson again took on umpiring duties. Wyatt won the toss and elected to bat. Heavy rain then fell, preventing play from starting until a quarter to four. On a damp and unresponsive wicket England's progress was grim. They were finally all out for 226 just after tea on the second day. Paine top-scored with 47, but only the mighty Smith seemed like he wanted to shake the game out of its torpor. One huge drive struck off Connie flew over the sightscreen and into the trees beyond, scattering the spectators who were sitting in them. Hammond later said it was the best hit he'd ever seen. Hylton was the pick of the bowlers with four for 27, though as Connie commented the painful crawl of England's batting owed more to their mindset than the quality of the West Indies bowling. When the home side batted they struggled against the leg breaks of Hollies. Wyatt again set defensive fields and ordered his bowlers to focus on line and length. Runs came in sluggardly manner, Headley ignoring or padding away dozens of leg-side deliveries from the persistent Paine. Wishart made a half-century but took more than four hours to get to it. Hollies finished with seven for 50 as the West Indies were bowled out for 186, 42 adrift. With just over a day remaining there appeared little chance of a result, but stranger things had happened already in the series, and when Connie sent the first three English batsmen back to the pavilion with just 9 runs on the board it seemed like another extraordinary result might be conjured. Wyatt – despite problems breathing due to the bruising to his ribs – put a stop to such ideas, scoring 71, and Hendren helped him along the way. With two hours remaining, Wyatt declared, setting the home side 203 to win. The target would have required huge risk-taking on a slow and lifeless wicket, and with the series at 1–1 Grant decided not to go after the runs. The match ended in bad light, much to the relief of everybody involved.

The MCC tour party spent two weeks in Jamaica, though to the obvious frustration and annoyance of one or two of the party twelve of those days were spent playing cricket. By now the long stretch away from home and the constant travelling had started to take its toll on the tourists.

More worryingly for Wyatt, as the final winner-takes-all Test approached, his side was beset by a series of mishaps. In the first tour match Jamaica's Groves took a big swing to leg and struck wicketkeeper Farrimond on the head with his follow through, knocking the Lancastrian unconscious and putting an abrupt end to his tour. Hammond and Iddon both tore leg muscles, while Hollies's old leg strain recurred and he was forced to leave the field. Farnes was troubled by a neck injury. Maurice Leyland, meanwhile, had suffered one of the most bizarre sporting injuries of all time, when a British sailor to whom he had just told an amusing anecdote gave him a hearty slap on the shoulder, sending the Yorkshireman tumbling off his chair. The fall damaged Leyland's back so badly he was bedridden for several days. Like Farrimond, his tour was over.

On the eve of the Test, Farnes (who had been suspended from 'a gibbet' by a blind local osteopath in an attempt to cure his neck problems), Hammond, Hollies and Iddon were all passed fit, though none were able to train or practise.

While the tourists were aching and jaded at the end of a long tour, the West Indies were in confident mood. For the first time, they felt they had the beating of their Test opponents. Headley was back to his best, while Connie and his pace colleagues were nodding in approval at a Sabina Park track that was so hard, smooth and lacking in grass it was

said you could see your face in it. The West Indies selectors
clearly saw pace as the key and added Dickie Fuller, a big,
raw Jamaican with a slinging action, to the attack.

Anticipation levels were dangerously high all across the
Caribbean. When Connie and the rest of the team arrived
in Kingston they found the whole city nattering inces-
santly about the match. Crowds began to assemble early
on the morning of the first day. Reggie, the most famous of
Jamaica's fans, took up position outside Sabina Park almost
at daybreak, twirling his trademark colourful umbrella and
assuring passers-by that 'We're going to win at a common
canter, a common canter.'

Grant won the toss and his batsmen, high on the expectation of the five thousand in the crowd, launched into the
England attack in a style that had calypso cricket stamped
all over it. Headley was at the wicket early. Christiani kept
him company until after lunch, when he was out to Paine.
It was the last wicket to fall that day. Headley ('Graceful,
swift, exact,' as Connie put it) went on to make 270 not out,
a Test record for his country. He batted superbly, hitting
thirty fours and giving just one chance, spilled by Farnes.
Derek Sealy with 91 and Rolph Grant 77 ensured a massive total. With the England bowlers tired and demoralised,
Connie strode in. He was by his own estimation 'happy
from the ground up' and didn't care who knew it. In whirlwind innings filled with wristy cuts, flashing drives and the
occasional improvised heave, he thrashed 34, including
two huge sixes, allowing Grant to declare at twenty past
four. The total of 535–7 was a record for the West Indies,
and ended England's chances of winning the game and the
series.

The following day's *Jamaica Gleaner* was inspired by
Connie's brief but devastating innings to offer the following

encomium: 'Some of his work is essentially of Constantine's exclusive manufacture, there being no necessity for taking copyright or forbidding imitations. Will we ever again have a player like this?'

In light of the fact that a Jamaican had just made the highest score in West Indies Test history, this was praise indeed.

Fired up by their batting success and with only a short time until the close, Connie and Martindale tore into the England batting. Martindale, in particular, bowled at a ferocious pace – 'far faster than he had ever done before', in Farnes's view. His fourth ball pitched only slightly short of a length, rose sharply and at speed. Wyatt played a normal defensive stroke, and saw the ball whizz past his wrist before it struck him in the face. 'It was like being hit by a sledgehammer ... down I went like a felled bullock.' 'You could hear the crack all over the field,' said the watching Farnes. The England skipper was carried from the field spitting blood, his jaw fractured in four places.

The sight of their captain – celebrated for his bravery and skill in playing pace – leaving the field dazed and bleeding can hardly have done anything for the English batsmen's confidence. Hammond visited Wyatt in the treatment room, where bloodied towels were strewn about the floor, and left ashen-faced.

Martindale and Connie both bowled at express speed, but on the fast wicket they resisted the obvious urge to overdo the short-pitched stuff. Connie continued to vary his pace cleverly, occasionally producing a brilliantly disguised googly without any apparent change in his action. Errol Holmes took over the captaincy in Wyatt's absence. The dashing Surrey amateur determined to play a captain's innings, but was bowled by Martindale with a delivery so fast he later told Wyatt that the first he knew of it was when he heard it collide with the stumps.

Yelled on by nine thousand fans, Martindale picked up two wickets more, while Connie got the vital scalp of Hammond, deceived by a slower one and driving uppishly straight into the bucket-like hands of Hylton at cover. England had lost four wickets for just 26 runs. Hendren survived till the close, but on returning to the pavilion told Farnes that his first ball from Connie had whistled by him 'like a bullet'.

Arthur Richardson was no longer on umpiring duty, but if he, or anybody else, was questioning the legitimacy of Martindale's delivery, Holmes was on hand to put them straight. Wyatt's injury, he said was, 'caused by a ball which was, in the opinion of all the MCC members, perfectly fair, and bowled by a man we all consider to be one of the fairest fast bowlers playing the game today'. It was a gracious statement, and given the bile that had been spouted about short-pitched bowling during previous series, a welcome and level-headed one too.

After the excitement of the final session, the following day was an anticlimax. In bright sunshine and a slight breeze, with a ball that had by now lost much of its shine and bounce, the West Indian pacemen struggled to reproduce the electrifying performance of the previous day. Connie, Martindale, Hylton and the beefy Fuller gave it everything. The crowd shouted and cheered and bet on each ball. Reggie declared that a West Indies victory was so assured it was already in the history books. Yet Ames and Hendren would not be budged. Indeed, Ames seemed to be enjoying himself, collaring the bowling, setting the scoreboard numbers flicking rhythmically. Connie clean-bowled him with a snorter that knocked his middle stump out of the ground, but the umpire had called 'No ball!' before Ames launched his airy drive.

Jackie Grant switched the bowling regularly. Gave the pacemen rests, brought them back at opposite ends. Nothing seemed to work. Then his younger brother returned to the attack, the only slow bowler in the West Indies team. Hendren, on 40, went to chip him into the outfield, hit the shot harder than he'd intended – and straight to Ivan Barrow in the deep.

It was a breakthrough, but the West Indies could not capitalise on it. Iddon and Ames took the score from 90 to 254, Ames making a century on the way, despite having to use a runner after a bad bout of cramp, and Iddon batted competently to reach his fifty. The pair appeared to be easing England towards a draw, but with Ames on 126 Connie intervened. Fielding at silly mid-off he flung himself full length to catch a slashing drive one-handed with his arm outstretched. For a moment Ames stared at him in incredulity, then gave a rueful shrug. The crowd rose to the Kent batsman as he walked off the field; it had been, Connie thought, 'the sort of innings to which every cricket lover's heart goes out, sound, steady, fast, with never a chance, pulling his side out of the pit of despair'.

With Ames gone, England fell to pieces. Smith aimed a swipe at a Connie straight one that seemed designed to send the ball to Cuba, but missed it completely and lost his off stump. A couple of overs later Iddon got tangled up trying to farm the strike and went lbw to Mudie, and Connie brought things to a close clean-bowling Farnes, who looked like he'd rather be back at the osteopath's.

With England 264 behind and Wyatt unable to bat, Grant elected not to fool around. He asked the visitors to follow on. There was half an hour, plus three sessions of play, left, on a fast track that was starting to deteriorate. The West Indies players looked up at the sky. Dark clouds had rolled in as the game progressed, but surely rain would not rescue England now.

Once again England tinkered with the batting order. Iddon came out to open with Townsend. Urged on by the crowd, Connie and Martindale hurtled to the stumps, exerting every muscle, every ounce of strength. Maybe they tried too hard. The half-hour passed without a wicket. Fourteen runs were scored. The next day was Sunday, the rest day. Rain fell, but there was not enough of it to save England. In fact, it only made things worse for them.

When play began at eleven o'clock on Monday, the usually glassy Sabina Park strip had turned sticky. Connie bowled the first over to Iddon; he had dropped his friend in the first innings and it made him more determined than ever to get him out this time around. The first two deliveries were looseners, the third was quicker. Iddon did not get forward fast enough. The ball cannoned off his pad: lbw. Next over, Martindale produced one that broke back into Townsend and flattened his middle stump. Hendren joined Hammond. The two saw off Connie and Martindale. Mudie came into the attack. Connie moved in at silly mid-off, until he was just a few yards from the bat. He had studied Hendren closely. He knew the shots he favoured. Sure enough, the Middlesexman went to push one gently through the off side, it was in the air for only a split-second but that was enough, Connie hurling himself forward to scoop it up a few feet from the bat. And then Jackie Grant slipped on the wet outfield and Connie took charge.

With rain clouds closing in, he acted decisively. Elated by the unexpected turn of events Connie brought himself on to bowl, and in his first over had Ames – who alongside a thunderstorm seemed England's last hope – caught at silly mid-on by the athletic Rolph Grant, who got to it just inches above the ground.

As if to prove his almost magical powers, Connie then decided that he and Martindale should change ends. To effect the switch he brought on Sealy for an over of his occasional medium pace. The innocuous Sealy promptly trapped acting captain Holmes in front of the stumps, one of only three wickets he would claim in his eleven-Test career.

As trouble raged at the other end, Hammond soldiered on. It was after lunch and he had made 34 when Martindale produced another blazing delivery to clean-bowl him off an inside edge. The broad-shouldered, bandy-legged pace-man followed that delivery by smashing two of Jim Smith's stumps clean out of the ground with a ferociously quick yorker, and having Farnes caught at the wicket for a duck. It was just after two o'clock. England had no hope, but Paine resisted bravely, scoring 10 runs in a last-wicket stand with Hollies.

Connie brought himself back into the attack. Hollies cracked a short ball to the boundary and took a couple more off the next. Connie charged in again; Hollies aimed to drive through the covers but mistimed it. Martindale, alert and predatory, pouched the catch. It was all over. England had been bowled out for 103, giving the West Indies victory by an innings and 161 runs. Martindale had taken seven wickets in the match for 84 and Connie six for 68.

As the players left the field the rain began to fall, prompting Errol Holmes to remark, 'I see that the rain has come just a little too late for us.'

The crowd gathered outside the pavilion and called for

their heroes, Headley, Martindale and, of course, Connie, to come out onto the balcony. When they did they were rousingly cheered. Their team had proved to the world that their elevation to Test status, so long held in doubt by the major cricket powers, was merited. The visitors had been handicapped by Farnes's persistent neck and ankle injuries, by Smith's inability to find his best form and Wyatt's negative tactics. Yet the fact remained that an England side not too far below full strength had been defeated by a team that was simply better than they were.

For Connie, leading the side in that final push for victory was sweet indeed.

The match and the series had been a personal triumph. He had batted with dashing belligerence, bowled with brio and skill, and fielded with his characteristic fiery genius. His personality and charisma had shone throughout, boosting the morale of his team mates. Little wonder the *Jamaica Gleaner* described him as 'the most attractive personality in cricket the West Indies ever had'. Moreover, it was Connie who had piloted the side to victory on the final day. Unsurprisingly, this was something that he particularly cherished. That night he attended a reception given by the Governor of Jamaica and afterwards fell asleep dreaming of the jubilant, encouraging roars of the West Indian spectators. Though Connie did not know it, it was the last time he would ever be cheered on by his home crowd. For he would not play a competitive match in the Caribbean again.

Chapter 2

A Cushion for the Life Ahead

Connie was born on 21 September 1901 in Petit Valley, near Diego Martin in Trinidad's north-west peninsula. Diego Martin was founded by the Spanish, but in the 1780s the original settlers were joined by groups of French planters and their slaves fleeing from unrest in the Windward Islands. It was the French who gave Connie's village its name.

The land around Diego Martin was fertile and easy to cultivate. Hemmed in by mountains, the hillsides were wooded with immortelle trees, which looked like grey spectres decorated with orange flowers. The valley faces west towards the narrow strip of sea, clouded with silt from the Orinoco River, which separates Trinidad from the South American mainland. When the British seized control of the island in 1797 they found the land around Diego Martin the most profitable in Trinidad. By that time the population was almost entirely French: twenty-six families and more than a thousand slaves working estates of sugar cane and coffee. The biggest estate belonged to the Begorrats, a wealthy slave-owning family who built the area's first

Roman Catholic church. The priest who served in it was awarded the title Protector of Slaves. Catholicism would be Connie's faith for most of his life.

When slavery was abolished in 1834 the plantations were thrown into disarray. Many of the freed slaves simply walked away and settled wherever land was available. The labour shortage resulted in an influx of indentured Indian workers and free Africans from Sierra Leone. They arrived to work on the sugar plantations, but shortly sugar gave way to a new crop: cocoa.

The region was ethnically diverse, as was Trinidad itself, but racial demarcations that could be traced back to the early years of the island's development still ran deep. Connie's maternal grandfather had been born a slave, so had his paternal great-grandparents. Connie's parents, Lebrun and Anaise (usually called Anna), had been born into freedom, but their opportunities were still prescribed by their skin colour. A white elite ruled Trinidad, supported by lighter-skinned negroes. The Constantines had dark skin, which put them at the bottom of the island's pecking order. For them opportunities for professional or social advancement were strictly limited.

Connie's background was, by his sometime friend C. L. R. James's assessment, that of neither a pauper nor a prince. But his family were, if not quite West Indian cricket royalty, then certainly members of its aristocracy. There was first-class cricket on both sides. Lebrun Constantine would tour England; so would Connie's maternal uncle, Victor Pascall. Another uncle, St Croix Constantine, was a celebrated local player. Even in those days women's cricket was taken seriously in Trinidad and Anna was, by her son's estimation, a wicketkeeper good enough to play for an English county.

The first West Indian inter-colonial match was played on the Garrison Savannah, Barbados, in 1865, nine years before Lebrun was born. Barbados's opponents were British Guiana. The two teams played each other twice, each winning a game. In 1871 an attempt to organise a triangular tournament in Georgetown foundered when Trinidad were let down by a shipping company and were unable to travel.

After a lapse of nine years, Barbados made an attempt to revive the triangular competition, inviting Trinidad and British Guiana to play matches on the island. British Guiana rejected the invitation, claiming players were unable to obtain leave from work – a problem that would beset the competition for decades and cause Connie problems on several occasions. Trinidad refused to go alone and so the idea came to nothing.

In 1891 the long-mooted competition was finally played in Bridgetown. Trinidad lost to British Guiana and were then slaughtered by Barbados, who defeated them by an innings. Barbados won the tournament. The final match was supposed to be between the champions and a combined side, but such was the poor standard of the Trinidadian team that Charles Wyatt, the British Guiana captain, refused to pick any of their players for his starting XI.

The success of the 1891 series encouraged the colonies to place the inter-colonial on a regular footing. All the colonies subscribed to pay for a fine silver trophy – the Inter-Colonial Cup – which would be presented to the winning team. The next tournament was played at Saint Clair, Port of Spain, in 1893. Owing to the objections of Barbados and British Guiana, it was decided that the competition would be open only to white players, a rule that was enforced for the next ten years. Most of Trinidad's best bowlers were ineligible because of the colour bar and the team, made up almost entirely of players from the elite Queen's Park Club, were again battered by Barbados. Since British Guiana had failed to send a team, Barbados then agreed to play a representative Trinidad team including players of African and Asian descent; among them was Lebrun Constantine.

Lebrun – generally referred to as Old Cons – had learned cricket in an unorthodox manner. Brought up on a cocoa plantation in Diego Martin, he had fallen in love with the game at an age when most boys were falling in love with girls. He had fashioned his first bats from coconut branches and used an orange for a ball. A man of resourcefulness and winning charm – characteristics his most famous son would inherit – Lebrun was not put off by the lack of a cricket club anywhere within walking distance. He marked out his own field, laid his own wicket and organised his own team. They began playing matches against nearby villages such as Petit Valley and Four Roads. In 1894 he took his team across the hills to play in a competition in Port of Spain, carrying off first prize. Lebrun's performance caught the eye. He was a hard-hitting and not strictly orthodox batsman (considered by *Wisden* to be second only amongst West Indians to the more polished Harold Austin), particularly strong on the leg side, a decent medium-pace bowler and a superb slip fielder. If pressed, he could also keep wicket. Over a career of fifty-six matches he scored 2433 runs, took forty-six wickets and ninety-five catches and stumpings. C. L. R. James said he was 'the most loved and respected cricketer on the island', a figure sufficiently part of the popular consciousness for V. S. Naipaul to name a character in *A Way in the World* after him. Not that this did much to alter Lebrun's social standing. Professionalism was still frowned upon in the Caribbean, and he barely earned a penny from cricket during his twenty-five-year career. Working on a cocoa plantation for an unusually liberal employer, Sidney Smith (later Connie's godfather), who promoted him to overseer, a job normally reserved for white men, Lebrun was still poorly paid for his labours, and despite the acclaim afforded him as a cricketer he was still not allowed to vote.

In 1895 a team of English amateurs visited the Caribbean, led by Robert Slade Lucas of Middlesex. His team was not a strong one, but won one, drew one and lost one against Barbados, easily defeated Antigua and St Kitts, and then St Lucia, before losing a one-day match to St Vincent. In Trinidad they won a twelve-a-side match against Queen's Park before being easily beaten by the colony side for whom Joe 'Float' Woods and Archie Cumberbatch – both black professionals – bowled effectively. Lebrun was also part of this victorious Trinidad team. Slade Lucas was impressed by what he had seen, and *Wisden* commented that the sides in the Caribbean had been 'well up to the standard of good club cricket in England'.

In January 1897 two English touring sides arrived in the Caribbean. This created something of a furore since one was led by Lord Hawke, who regarded the second party, under Arthur Priestley, as interlopers. Hawke had in fact ordered Priestley – who had been invited to tour by the cricket authorities in Barbados – to stay in England. Priestley bravely refused to bow to his lordship's demand. A complex itinerary designed to keep the two sides from ever being in the same colony at the same time was drawn up. On the one occasion their paths did cross the two captains steadfastly refused to speak to each other. The entire affair might have made a Gilbert and Sullivan opera. Lord Hawke would pop up repeatedly during Connie's career.

A bombastic autocrat who has over the passing decades come to seem more and more like a satirical creation, Lord Hawke was a good deal less funny to those who encountered him at the time. Indeed, Connie would compare him to Hitler.

Whatever bad blood there was between the visiting skippers, the twin tours marked a turning point in West Indian cricket. Hawke's team contained many top-class players, including Henry 'Shrimp' Leveson Gower, Hugh Bromley-Davenport, Christopher Heseltine and the Trinidad-born Pelham 'Plum' Warner. Warner was a contemporary of Lebrun, but had learned his cricket in quite a different manner. The son of Charles Warner, the Attorney General of Trinidad, he had been educated at Harrison College, Barbados (an elite school that also produced Harold Austin, George Challenor and scores of later West Indian cricketers) and Rugby, and was by now one of the stars of the Oxford University team. Though he would go on to captain England, Plum Warner would always think of himself as a West Indian and take a keen interest in the development of the game in the Caribbean. A man of great decency who believed passionately in the gentlemanly virtues (though that didn't preclude the rumours that he was Gubby Allen's biological father), Warner would write joyfully about Connie and become one of his greatest and most public admirers.

Hawke's side began their tour in Trinidad, where they were undone by the brilliant bowling of Woods and Cumberbatch. Woods took 10–67 and Cumberbatch 8–91 as Trinidad won by five wickets. Hawke's team would lose only one other match on the tour, an indication that – when they had all their players available to them – Trinidad now had a formidable side. Leveson Gower was certainly impressed. The bowling in Trinidad, he said, was of a much higher class than they encountered elsewhere in the Caribbean, with 'Cumberbatch and Woods, both of them very fast and Woods especially so'. He thought 'the fielding of our opponents was excellent; coloured men especially seldom miss a catch and can throw very well', and recalled that Lebrun Constantine 'batted and fielded well'.

Cumberbatch and Woods were the leading black professionals of the era. The careers of both illustrate the problems facing non-white cricketers in the Caribbean during the early years of the game's development there. Cumberbatch, a lively right-arm bowler who could make the ball lift from just short of a length, was born in Barbados but, unable to make any inroads as a cricketer on his home island, moved to Trinidad and took a job as a groundsman at Queen's Park. In 1899 Cumberbatch moved briefly back to Barbados, then went to play in Jamaica, before returning to Trinidad again. Excluded from the Inter-Colonial Tournament, he played little first-class cricket. Cumberbatch's opening partner, Woods, is generally regarded as the first in the line of West Indies quick bowlers. He generated real pace off a short run, his delivery stride culminating in a fierce stamp of his front foot. Like Cumberbatch, Woods was born in Barbados, but left his home to play as a professional in British Guiana and Trinidad. Witnesses believe he may have been the fastest bowler in the world during his peak years, but like Cumberbatch his colour meant he rarely got an opportunity to test himself in regular first-class competition. That both men were bowlers is notable: this was generally the allotted role for black players, as it was for working-class professionals in England. Bowling was hard physical labour. White West Indians preferred the more graceful and less sweaty business of batting. That Lebrun Constantine should achieve fame as a batsman was, as C. L. R. James observes, something of a blow to the status quo.

On this point, Leveson Gower also had some pertinent observations. Noting that Trinidad – unlike Barbados and British Guiana – included 'coloured men' in the team, he commented, 'In the competition between the three islands every other year for the Inter-Colonial Cup, all coloured men were then excluded and consequently Trinidad did not do as well as might have been expected, for her coloured professional bowlers were the backbone of the team in those days.' While not wishing to enter 'into a discussion about the advisability of such a course', Leveson Gower did note that on the smaller islands, where 'coloured men played as a matter of course in the teams', all sections of the population were 'much more enthusiastic about cricket'.

'It was obvious to us when we were touring these beautiful palm-clad Islands so long ago that a new force was being liberated in the world of cricket by the keenness of the players there,' Leveson Gower would recall. He was to play his own small part in ensuring that West Indian cricket progressed.

Hawke's side was strong, but Priestley's was arguably the better on paper, containing as it did a man who was one of the great stars of the era – Andrew Stoddart – and the brilliant Australian all-rounder Sammy Woods. Yet they struggled. The visitors' game against Queen's Park was spoiled by rain, though spectators got to see Stoddart at his best, the batsman making 108 not out. Priestley's team then took on a combined West Indian XI at the same venue. This was the first time the West Indies had fielded a

'national' side at home. The team was skippered by Aucher
Warner, one of Pelham's many siblings (he had seventeen)
and a future Attorney General of Trinidad, and included
Lebrun alongside Harold Austin, Clifford Goodman – con-
sidered the finest West Indian cricketer of his time – and
Cumberbatch.

The West Indians won a hard-fought match by three
wickets; Austin scored 75 and Lebrun hit 38 in the first
innings and 45 in the second. Goodman and Cumberbatch
did the damage with the ball.

In the next match against Trinidad, Priestley's team
were bowled out for 33 – Cumberbatch and Woods the
destroyers – and the home side romped home by ten wickets. In the return, Lionel D'Ade scored 140 not out for the
colony, and with Woods returning match figures of 11–115
Trinidad again won comfortably.

Lord Hawke had been as impressed by what he saw
as Leveson Gower, and called for the West Indians to
be invited to England to play against the counties. Lord
Hawke generally got what he wanted, and the first West
Indian tour party duly arrived in 1900, though without its
appointed captain Harold Austin, who had to go off and
fight in the Boer War instead. Aucher Warner replaced
him, though he went down with a bout of malaria and
played only half-a-dozen matches. Woods was picked. But
Cumberbatch had been left behind for reasons none could
fathom, and not for the last time the selectors decided
against bothering with a specialist wicketkeeper, allocat-
ing the duties to two part-timers: George Learmond of
British Guiana and Lebrun. The absence of Cumberbatch
would further widen Old Cons's duties. He became
an effective fast-medium bowler during the tour and
gradually abandoned his position behind the stumps and

moved to point, where his catching was said to have been exceptional.

The tour began disastrously, with the West Indians hopelessly outclassed at Crystal Palace by W. G. Grace's short-lived London County side. As the tour went on the schedule of playing cricket six days a week exposed the players' lack of fitness and their inability to maintain focus. They lost heavily to Worcestershire and were slaughtered by Warwickshire. However, the team rallied against Lord Harris's MCC side at Lord's. The MCC batted first and made close to 400. When the tourists batted they were routed by Grace and followed on 189 behind. The West Indians were 132–8 when Tommie Burton joined Lebrun at the wicket. Perhaps relaxing now that defeat seemed inevitable, Burton and Constantine batted as they might have done back at home, playing their shots, attacking the bowling. In sixty-five minutes they added 162, a speed of scoring which, even in those days of faster over rates, was considered prodigious. Constantine finally fell, stumped jumping down the wicket, for 113, the first century by a West Indian batsman in England. Plum Warner thought it a 'dashing and faultless display'. Nevertheless the MCC won by five wickets.

Tommie Burton, Lebrun's partner in that bludgeoning attack on the MCC bowling, had been born to a white father and black mother in Barbados but, like Woods and Cumberbatch, quickly realised that his colour counted against him on his home island and moved to British Guiana. A medium-pacer, he was much admired in England for his immaculate line and length and subtle variations in pace, and had a yorker that proved too much even for WG, who fell victim to them twice. In the tour match with Norfolk he took eight wickets for 9 runs as the

home side were bowled out for 32 in their second innings.
Burton's career would end unhappily and prematurely
when he was sent home from the 1906 tour after refusing
to oil the bats and clean the boots of the white members of
the side, tasks the black players were expected to perform.
He never played first-class cricket again, and later moved
to Panama.

Lebrun batted well again in the meeting with Gloucestershire, hitting a half-century in the second innings, though
his efforts were overshadowed by those of the extraordinary
Gilbert Jessop, who made 157 in an hour against a tired
attack. At one point 'The Croucher' belted five fours in an
over from Woods. Warner recorded the reaction to Jessop's
onslaught: 'The black members of the team were so amused
that they sat down and shouted with laughter at the unfortunate bowler's discomfiture.' Connie would later criticise
the West Indians for not playing as a team; this perhaps was
an early indication of the problem.

To try to restore confidence after this shellacking, Plum
Warner joined the party and played in the next game
against Leicestershire, who were defeated by an innings
thanks to a century from Plum and 159 by Charles
Ollivierre. Lebrun contributed a useful 41. West Indians
were heavily beaten at Nottingham despite Lebrun's not-
out 50, and – more humiliatingly – fell to an innings defeat
against Wiltshire. Lebrun top-scored in both innings, but
that was hardly a consolation.

It had been a tour of ups and downs, with downs
predominating. Five matches were won, eight lost, four
drawn. Even against weaker county sides the West Indians
had struggled. Only Woods and Burton – the two pros –
seemed capable of getting wickets. The assessment of the
visitors' skills by the English press was withering, though

the West Indians' fielding was generally exempt from criticism. Ollivierre, the black middle-order batsman from Saint Vincent who had begun his career playing for Trinidad alongside Lebrun, did make sufficient impression to be invited to stay behind. He went on to play professionally for Derbyshire and in the Yorkshire leagues. He never returned to the West Indies, dying in Pontefract shortly after the end of the Second World War. Another of Lebrun's Trinidad team mates, Sydney Smith, a white all-rounder, also moved to England and played for Northamptonshire. In the case of Ollivierre, at least, there was inspiration for a young black cricketer eager to make a living from the game.

The issue of race could not be ignored. An article in *Boys' Own* commenting on the racial mix of the tourists and drawing attention to the colour bar that operated in West Indian cricket suggested that 'On the return home, many of the islands must have found themselves in a very awkward position over the matter. If, for instance, any of the coloured players are good enough to represent the team in an international match, it is difficult to see how they can be refused opportunities of playing at home.'

The black players on the tour also found life off the field to be freer in England than it was at home. The tour manager, W. C. Nock of Trinidad, reported how they had 'very quickly fallen into English ways' and that 'they lived in the same hotels [as the white players] and were treated exactly like the white members'. Such a situation would have been unthinkable in the Caribbean then, and would remain so for many years.

Lebrun returned to Trinidad and married Anna. He had enjoyed the tour. He'd scored 610 runs and finished second in the batting averages behind Ollivierre. He'd also made a friend: a chatty, cheerful Irishman named Learie. His first child, born twelve months after his return from England, would be named in the man's honour.

The fifth Inter-Colonial Tournament was played at the Bourda, Georgetown, in 1901. As *Boys' Own* had predicted, in the wake of the tour the rule banning non-white players had been lifted (though professionalism remained outlawed) and so Lebrun was at last able to take his place in a Trinidad side. Perhaps unsurprisingly the island – now at full strength – won the tournament for the first time.

In 1902 a touring party captained by Richard Bennett and predominantly made up of undergraduates – amongst them Bernard Bosanquet, inventor of the googly – arrived from England. Though a youthful outfit, they defeated an all-Trinidad team twice in twelve-a-side matches, but a West Indian select side that met them in Port of Spain trounced them by 111 runs.

In 1905 Lebrun was joined in the Trinidad side by his brother-in-law Victor Pascall, a slow left-armer and a decent lower-order batsman. Later that season the West Indies had their first real trial of strength on home turf when Lord Brackley toured the Caribbean with a very strong side that included English professionals for the first time. After playing matches in Jamaica and Barbados, Brackley's side met a West Indies XI in Bridgetown. Lebrun was not selected – but since only one non-Barbadian was, this was hardly surprising. The final leg of Brackley's tour was in Trinidad. The visitors lost the match against the colony for whom Cumberbatch was again in splendid form, taking thirteen wickets for 57 in the match. A second game against a West Indies XI also took place. The team was skippered by Bertie Harragin, and featured Lebrun along with

Cumberbatch. The game swung back and forth. The West Indies batted last, needing just 159 to win. Lebrun scored a sparkling 56 and the home side seemed to be coasting to victory, but when he fell the innings went to pieces and the tourists snatched a tense victory by 4 runs. Old Cons again featured in the next match as Trinidad beat the tourists by five wickets. This time his second-innings knock of 47 not out saw his side home.

The 1906 Inter-Colonial Tournament, held in Port of Spain, was seen as a trial series for the forthcoming tour to England. In the final, Trinidad and Barbados went toe-to-toe in an epic battle that saw Trinidad give away 51 extras in Barbados's second innings, and eventually lose.

The fine performances by the West Indies against Lord Brackley's team raised hopes that this tour party would perform better than the first one had. The team was captained by Austin, a superb batsman and, as C. L. R. James put it, 'the natural captain of the West Indies for as long as he chose to play'. The side included batting prodigy George Challenor – then just eighteen years of age – and fellow Barbadian Percy Goodman, considered one of the best players in the West Indies despite carrying more flesh than a cricketer would normally elect to bear in a hot climate (fittingly, perhaps, the rotund Goodman played for Pickwick Cricket Club). Dr John Cameron, whose son John would play alongside Connie on the 1939 tour, was also in the party, as well as Sydney Smith. Cumberbatch was picked this time, but he was past his best, as was Burton, who also made the party.

Lebrun had also been selected, but initially turned down his chance to go on the trip because he could not afford the time off work. The rest of the party had sailed without him before a white merchant, Michael Maillard, learned of what had happened and gave Lebrun the funds to pay for his trip. A motor launch was hired and Old Cons, armed with a bag filled with hastily assembled kit, was able to board the ship as it passed the Bocas Islands.

London County had ceased to exist, but W. G. Grace was still a formidable figure in the capital and led his own XI against the visitors in the opening match at Crystal Palace. The West Indians' matches had now been granted first-class status, but that looked premature when they tumbled to defeat by 247 runs in two days. Lebrun was one of the few players who emerged with their reputation enhanced, coming in at number four and smashing 89 in spectacular style. The fact that five West Indian batsmen were run out in the match suggests some problems in that area; this would persist for many years and was indeed mentioned by Bradman as a failing when Connie and his team mates toured Australia some twenty-five years later.

Lebrun again did well against the Minor Counties, hit two half-centuries against an England XI at Blackpool, put on 126 in sixty-four minutes with Sydney Smith in the clash with South Wales in Cardiff and scored 68 in fifty minutes against Scotland in Edinburgh. Against a strong Yorkshire side that included Wilfred Rhodes, he scored 79 in the first innings to help his team record a memorable 268-run victory. Lebrun scored 92 and 50 in the next match against Leicestershire, batting well in partnership with Challenor, but the tourists were defeated by 24 runs. He opened with Challenor in the final first-class match against Northamptonshire and the pair posted a fifty partnership for the opening wicket at more than a run a minute to help secure a convincing win. Two more friendly fixtures were played; in the last of which, Lebrun is said to have hit 111, though no records exist of where the fixture took place, or against whom. In total Lebrun scored more than a thousand runs in all matches, a mark also achieved by Smith and Challenor. In first-class games he hit seven fifties. He had frequently been pressed into service as a wicketkeeper and added four stumpings to his eighteen catches.

Once again the British press were sniffy about the visitors, with Austin's field placings a cause of some merriment. The ground fielding was criticised too, though Challenor was thought to have done well in whichever strange position the captain placed him.

On his return to Trinidad, Lebrun was promoted to overseer of the whole of Smith's plantation. The Constantine family moved to Cascade, near Maraval (now one of Port of Spain's most expensive suburbs).

Connie was now four and loved the life his father's new appointment had brought: 'As children we never wanted for anything . . . There was always something to eat. We could go hunting for meat, we kept pigs, chickens and goats, and there was fruit and vegetables.'

Connie was aware, however, that not everyone was so fortunate. He would recall how some estate workers' children were reduced to stealing food and that if his father, normally so strict, caught them he would let them go with no more than a lecture. When Connie quizzed his father on why he did not punish these children in the same way he might his own, Lebrun replied that it was because theft was the only means they had of preventing starvation. It was a message Connie took to heart. He would always be thankful for what he had, while at the same time remaining sharply aware of how quickly and easily it could disappear. Later in life he'd be criticised by some of his team mates for his apparent absorption with money.

Those who spoke of him in that manner were generally from wealthier backgrounds. Connie was not greedy; he was just determined to ensure his family's financial security.

In 1911 the first MCC side toured the West Indies. In order to get in shape for the massive event, the West Indian authorities organised two Inter-Colonial Tournaments instead of the usual one. In the first, at Port of Spain, Lebrun hit 116 against British Guiana to help his side to an innings victory. In the final against Barbados he failed with the bat, but took 6–17 in the visitors' first innings to help his side to a 215-run win. The next tournament took place in British Guiana. Percy 'Tim' Tarilton starred for Barbados, who defeated Trinidad in the final.

As a batsman it seems that Old Cons had much in common with Connie. He was self-taught, his game improvised to suit his talents. He was particularly noted for a peculiar variation of the hook shot. As Connie described it, 'Off the fastest bowlers he would move the right foot over to the off-side and hit across the line to square leg; but more often than not he would move the right foot back a little. Stoop forward, put his head behind the line of the ball and flick the ball over his left shoulder to the fine-leg boundary using the right wrist.' It was the sort of spontaneous improvisation for which generations of later West Indies batsmen would be noted. Not that things always worked out. Connie would recall a boyhood Saturday when his father returned home early from the game, a bandage round his head. Asked what had happened by his anxious wife, Old Cons replied simply, 'I missed one.'

Arthur Somerset, who had toured the West Indies as a member of Lord Brackley's XI, led the MCC party. The tourists included in their ranks the Trinidadian Sydney

Smith as well as the youthful Middlesex medium-pacer Jack Hearne and the eccentric all-rounder George Brown of Hampshire.

Despite the presence of these two future stars, Somerset's team was weaker than Lord Brackley's. This became apparent right from the start when they were routed by Barbados, who beat them twice, by an innings each time. In the first representative game in Bridgetown, Barbados provided ten of the starting XI. The tourists rallied to win the game by five wickets. In Trinidad they were defeated twice, apparently struggling on the coconut matting. They drew one and tied one in Jamaica (the first tied match in West Indies first-class matches), beat British Guiana twice and drew with a representative XI in Georgetown.

The message from the tour was plain to the MCC: if they wanted to avoid the sort of reverses they had suffered in Bridgetown and Port of Spain, they would have to send much stronger touring parties in future.

In 1912–13 the MCC returned, once more under the captaincy of Somerset. The side was much stronger. Alongside previous tourists Smith and Tom Whittington were Albert Relf, 'Razor' Smith and Arthur Jacques, the Hampshire in-swing bowler. The tourists defeated the West Indian XI by seven wickets at Bridgetown, but again found it much tougher on the Trinidad matting, losing by an innings and 6 runs. The backbone of the West Indian innings was a big century by Harry Ince of Barbados. Considered the finest left-handed batsmen the Caribbean had produced, he would sadly be unable to reproduce his best form in England, but that tour was some way off.

While his father was establishing himself as one of the leading figures in West Indian cricket, Connie was developing his own game. From the age of three he had been seen parading up and down outside the family home with a bat in his hand. Shortly after Connie turned six, Lebrun returned from work one day with a strip of coconut matting. With the help of his family Old Cons rolled out a base of clay until it was hard and flat and laid the matting on top of it. Now that the Constantines had their own wicket, Lebrun could start teaching his children to play the game. Soon passers-by were regularly treated to the sight of Connie, his younger brothers Osmund, Rodney and Elias, sister Leonora (who Connie claimed was the most talented young player in the family), mother, father and assorted uncles engaged in hard-fought matches that lasted until darkness fell.

Lebrun was at the forefront of these games. Connie's love and admiration for his father shines through in everything he said and wrote about him, but there is little doubt that Old Cons was a tough teacher. He bowled at his children at full tilt, 'just as he bowled at inter-colonial batsmen, or veterans from England'. The ball rose sharply on the coconut matting and the youngsters learned to take evasive action or, better still, to follow their father's dictum and use the bat for what it was meant to do – hitting the ball. It was a lesson Connie carried with him all his life. When others complained of short-pitched bowling he would counter them with his father's phrase.

Old Cons took a relaxed attitude to batting, allowing the youngsters to develop their own styles while emphasising the need to always hit the ball as hard as possible. As a batsman, he taught them always to look for a vacancy in the field, even if that vacancy is in the air.

When it came to bowling he was more rigid, demonstrating the correct grip for various deliveries, stressing the importance of a side-on action and high arm. If batting was about timing and eye, bowling was a task of plans and stratagems. Connie would always be a natural batsman and – however fast – a cerebral bowler.

Old Cons was also very clear on the importance of fielding. Here, concentration was the key. Connie would later recall that vigilance was essential; anyone who missed a catch or failed to make a stop could expect a rap on the head. 'My father knew the dictum that genius is one-tenth inspiration and nine-tenths perspiration,' he would write.

Even when no ball was available, fielding could be practised, Connie and Elias regularly turning washing up into an impromptu session by throwing the crockery and cutlery at one another. Woe betide them if anything was dropped. Parental discipline was tough, the rap around the head always waiting for a miscreant.

Lebrun was a strict taskmaster but the warmth and pleasure of the family cricket matches would stay with Connie all his life. 'A happy childhood is one of the greatest defences a man can have against the world,' he said, adding that the joy of those days under the Trinidadian sun 'served as a cushion, I am sure, for the sterner life which was ahead for all of us.'

Connie attended the government elementary school at St Ann's on the outskirts of Port of Spain and was soon playing in practice matches with boys three or four years his senior. At twelve he transferred to St Ann's Roman Catholic High School. Here he came under the influence of the headmaster, Andrew de Four, a cricket coach who believed in trusting ability above age. Within two years Connie was captain of the First XI. Like Lebrun, de Four encouraged Connie to hit the ball hard. He too was a hard taskmaster, once banning his school captain from cricket for a month after he was out for a duck twice in a row.

Under Connie's captaincy the team thrived, losing just once in two years and then to an elite school whose arrival in full whites utterly demoralised the St Ann's XI, who played in khaki shorts and black boots, before the game had even started. It was a small lesson in psychology and a grim reminder of the real world, one far removed from the happy matches under the palms with his family.

C. L. R. James would later teach at St Ann's, and one of his pupils was Osmund Constantine. Watching the son of Old Cons in action filled him with envy at the ease with which he could strike the good-length ball through the covers. Osmund might have gone on to become a fine cricketer, but sadly he was to die young.

Connie was never a particularly diligent pupil, his head already filled with cricket. Though his mother and father both urged him to pursue his studies, he failed to get any of the college scholarships on offer and, in 1917, quit full-time education at the age of fifteen. Too young to join the West India Regiments then fighting on the Western Front, Connie found work as a law clerk in the firm of Jonathan Ryan in Port of Spain. He nursed some hope of becoming a lawyer. In that he may have been inspired by one of the Constantines' neighbours in Petit Valley. Emmanuel Mzumbo Lazare was the son of immigrants from Guadeloupe. He lived in a large house called Lazdale, with a tree-lined garden and running water. He was also active politically, adopting an African middle name to show pride in his racial heritage and was heavily involved with the Pan-African Congress. A noted campaigner for the underprivileged, it was by Lazare's initiative that Emancipation Day, celebrating the abolition of slavery, became a public holiday. Lazare was also a successful solicitor and a barrister – one of the first black men to emerge into the professions in Trinidad. For black people hoping for advancement, he was a shining example.

As much as he might think of the law, Connie's real commitment was to cricket. Clerical workers finished at the early hour of four o'clock which gave him time to practise, usually in the nets with his Uncle Victor.

As a child, Connie had been chubby and ungainly. 'A thickset, rather slow boy,' said James, who first encountered him around 1911. It was an appearance exacerbated by his clothing, which generally consisted of baggy khaki shorts and a shirt made 'from a kind of flour bag'. As he grew to his full height, however, Connie became lithe, coordinated and quick across the ground. He was a high-class schoolboy sprinter and a decent footballer, dribbling down the wing with speed and skill.

Encouraged by de Four, Connie had adopted his father's hard-hitting all-action batting style, his bowling was medium pace but with the promise of more to come as his physique matured, and his fielding was already a thing of wonder. To the concentration drilled into him on the matting wicket at home had been added anticipation and an acrobatic athleticism. Though much would be made in the British and Australian press of Connie's 'natural gifts', he had in fact worked hard to achieve most of them. His speed in the covers was improved during his time as a law clerk by covering his frequent trips from Ryan's law offices to the courts at a sprint, sometimes throwing and catching an orange as he went. To paraphrase Gary Player, the harder Connie practised the more natural ability he got.

Connie's entry into adult cricket began when he was selected to play for Shannon Cricket Club (still known in those days as Victoria) Second XI – an appearance that required him to purchase his first set of whites. In his third match he came to the wicket and in a display of bravado thrashed fifty in just over an hour as his side reached 72 in a rain-affected match.

Cricket was as rigidly divided along racial and class lines as everything else on Trinidad. The wealthy white cricketers played for the Queen's Park Club, which had its headquarters at the Queen's Park Oval, a ground that Leveson Gower considered 'Magnificent ... With a comfortable pavilion, some waving palms, and the blue mountains in the distance, it was all one could wish to see.' As C. L. R. James commented, it would have been far easier for a black cricketer such as Connie to become a member of the MCC than it would for him to play for Queen's Park. Stingo Cricket Club, by contrast, was the leading club for working-class black cricketers (Archie Cumberbatch and Joe Small both played for Stingo), while Maple served the lighter-skinned middle-class blacks. Shannon was a club for the black lower middle classes, the natural home for the Constantines. Old Cons ruled the club as he had the family cricket games. His players did not dispute umpiring decisions and always walked when they knew they had nicked one.

Nor would Old Cons tolerate any nonsense from the opposition. When the Queen's Park Club insisted on employing a match official he believed to be biased in their favour he demanded the umpire be changed. When Queen's Park refused, Old Cons led his team away. It was a brave action to take against a side that belonged to Trinidad's ruling class, but when it came to cricket Old Cons acknowledged no social distinction. The world at large might be unjust, but on the cricket field higher standards prevailed.

Shannon played their matches on the Savannah, which the visiting Ken Farnes described as a 'flat expanse of yellow grass-covered land' enclosed by the rails of the race course. 'In the centre a lonely group of palm trees and on the far side beyond the Governor's residence the high hills of the northern part of the island'. By night the fast bowler found the Savannah 'aloof and eerie', and claimed that locals refused to walk across it under full moon for fear that 'a tree of evil purpose' would 'trip them over with its roots'.

Whatever the truth or otherwise of Farnes's tales, during the season – which in Trinidad often lasted for eight months – the Savannah was home to more than thirty cricket fields, which were used by clubs and schools. Conditions were not ideal: the lonely palm trees gave little shade and the roughly mown outfields made ground fielding hazardous (Connie would be delighted when he encountered his first properly prepared outfield at the Bourda in Georgetown), while the coconut-matting wickets made batting difficult against any bowler who could spin or cut the ball.

It may not have been Lord's or even the Queen's Park Oval, but Shannon's makeshift ground produced some of the best cricketers on the island and the club's games, played over two weekends with two innings per side, were regularly watched by four-figure crowds. The games were noisy affairs. Connie would recall the partisan fans calling out encouragement or yelling insults, the excited betting – a feature of any game involving West Indian sides, one spectator calling out his wager, another taking up the bet and a third party handed the wagered cash – the drinking and the laughter. Unlike some sportsmen, Connie never lost sight of the importance of the supporters, revelling in their applause, laughing at their jokes, nodding in approval at their moments of wisdom.

Shannon had its own playing style, characterised by fierce determination, guile and diligence. James wrote that the cricketers of Shannon played 'as if they knew that they represented the great mass of black people on the island. By their play they said: "Here on the cricket field, if nowhere else, all in the island are equal – and we are the best men on the island."'

Lebrun was skipper of the first team. He had always been reluctant to allow players to come into the side at too young an age, fearing that the toughness of the competition at that level might leave a permanent dent in their confidence, or spoil them for good. Despite his father's reservations, Connie came into the Shannon first team when he was eighteen. He joined another young player of talent in the starting XI, Wilton St Hill. A batsman of great grace, St Hill also had immense self-confidence, impressing Connie by going out to bat against the formidable George John with a cigarette in his mouth, taking guard and then keeping the fast bowler waiting while he finished his smoke. He then smacked John's second delivery to the boundary for four with a languid flick of the wrists, compounding the big man's irritation.

Compared to schools cricket, the competition in club cricket was daunting. In 1921 Connie found himself lining up for Shannon in what was the fiercest of all the local cricket derbies: the clash with Stingo. Stingo's opening bowler was the same George John who had been so cockily dismissed by St Hill. He was one of the fastest bowlers of his era, comparable to Gregory or Larwood – neither of whom were to be faced on coconut matting laid on clay.

Influenced perhaps by Connie's cricket pedigree as much

as by anything he had so far achieved, cricket fans around Trinidad had started to speak of him as the new George John. It was a grave exaggeration of his bowling talent, for at that point Connie was barely above medium pace and, by the assessment of James, who batted against him for Maple, offered 'stuff to which one could play forward with confidence'. George John was not amused. A good-natured man off the field, like future generations of Caribbean pacemen John was transformed into a snarling brute once he had a ball in his large hand. He determined to teach the Shannon youngster a harsh lesson.

Coming in first wicket down, Connie felt the tingle of nerves running down his spine. He arrived at the crease and took his guard. John tore in. His third ball was a real snorter and knocked Connie's stumps all over the place. The old George John sent the New George John on his way with the comment, 'You ought to be at school instead of coming here worrying big cricketers.'

The next time the two men met Connie changed his approach. He had been overawed in that first encounter, timidly and unsuccessfully attempting simply to guard his wicket. This time he went out determined to bat as his father instructed. John clean-bowled him again, middle stump, but not before the young upstart had carted 67 at better than a run a minute. From then on Connie would never go to the wicket simply to defend, but always to take the attack to the bowlers. He shared that attitude with many of his team mates. Like latter-day Australian sides, Shannon played hard, aggressive cricket. It might have been entertaining and spectacular, but they did not do it for fun. Shannon's players took the game seriously: as far as they were concerned, there was no such thing as a friendly match. The side's fielding was notably brilliant,

James claiming that any player who dropped a catch was looked upon 'as a potential fifth columnist'. Like many of the great West Indian cricketers who would follow him, Connie was a genial man, but he had an inner toughness and a will to win that was undeniable. A head-high bouncer might be followed by a broad and friendly smile, but it was no less dangerous for that. Anyone who mistook amiability for softness or lack of commitment was making a big mistake. During one match Connie became seriously ill with a fever. Called on to bat with his side eight wickets down, he stumbled, dazed and delirious, out to the middle in his work shoes. Barely able to hold the bat, he was out first ball, but his determination to contribute was indicative of the ethos of Shannon Cricket Club.

Connie never underestimated the debt he owed to Shannon. The lessons taught to him by his team mates about principled behaviour, honesty and endeavour stayed with him throughout his life. He played cricket joyously, but always aimed for excellence, and nothing annoyed him more than to find himself in the company of men who did not share his attitude. With the West Indian touring parties that seemed sadly inevitable, since some of the cricketers were there not on merit but because the social order called for it. It was a situation that would rankle with Connie throughout his career.

Chapter 3

The Chilly Embrace of the Mother Country

The Great War ended on 11 November 1918. Though more than fifteen thousand West Indians had left the Caribbean to serve on the front line, the carnage of conflict had barely impinged on Connie's daily life. One consequence of the war would have an impact, however. In 1918, the men of the West India Regiments discovered that the white regiments they had been serving alongside had been given a pay rise, while they had not. The mutiny that followed in the port of Taranto in southern Italy would lead to the forming of the Caribbean Association, and one of the first direct appeals for home rule in the West Indies.

While there was no direct link between the West Indian cricketers' quest for Test status and the growing political movement, there is little doubt that for black cricketers the two things would become inextricably linked. To have a national team that competed on equal terms with England was a clear step towards independence. Connie would play his part, both as a player and a politician. First he had to establish himself as a player of the highest calibre, a task that at times appeared to be beyond him.

Top-class cricket returned to the West Indies in 1920, when Trinidad travelled to Barbados to play two matches in a goodwill series. Barbados won the first match by an innings, despite aggressive bowling from George John. In the second match Barbados were even more dominant. Tim Tarilton hit an unbeaten triple hundred, George Challenor posted a century and Barbados captain Austin declared on 623, a West Indies record. Demoralised by the task ahead, Trinidad tumbled to 131 all out. Following on, they were propped up by Wilton St Hill, who scored 95, and the mercurial Joe Small, who cut and pulled his way to a rapid century, but even the impressive second-innings total of 461 could not save them from another humiliating innings defeat.

In September 1921 the mighty Barbados travelled to Port of Spain for the resumption of the Inter-Colonial Tournament. After the crushing defeats they had inflicted on their hosts the previous winter they had every expectation of retaining their title. They were in for a shock.

Before the Trinidad team were selected, a series of trial matches were arranged. To Connie's surprise his father, who in twenty-five years had barely missed a match, absented himself from the games pleading work pressure. Connie was nineteen and as self-absorbed as any teenager. It was only later he'd come to realise that his father had deliberately stepped aside to increase his son's chances of selection. All-rounders in the same mould, it seemed unlikely a place would be found for them both; Old Cons sacrificed his for his son. It was a selfless gesture and one Connie would come to appreciate even more as his own career began to wind down: 'It is so much harder to do when one is old enough to know there will not be many more chances – if one gives one's place to a youngster,

perhaps none. Much, much harder! He was a grand sportsman, if ever there was one.'

Trindad's captain was Bertie Harragin, a batsman,
army major and all-round athlete who also held the West
Indies record for throwing the cricket ball. Unusually for
a member of Trinidad's white establishment, the Major
seemed to have not the slightest concern about colour and
spoke to everyone he met with the same politeness and easy
charm. By now Harragin was well into middle age, but
he was still a commanding figure and had a keen eye for
cricket talent. Connie did little in the trials save for making
a brilliant left-handed catch in the slips, but Harragin
decided he was worth a place in Trinidad's twelve-man
squad, and his word counted. Without him, it's unlikely
Connie would have got a place.

The week leading up to the tournament was filled with
anticipation. In Port of Spain people seemed to talk of
nothing else. At work and in the street Connie was quizzed
about his prospects. Determined to avoid a situation that
would see him pacing nervously around the pavilion for
hours before play, he decided to arrive as close to the start
as possible. The local press said that would be at noon, so
Connie turned up at Queen's Park Oval at a quarter to. To
his horror he found the match had actually started at half-
past eleven, and that he had been left out of the XI in his
absence.

Humiliated and embarrassed, Connie sat and watched
as Harragin and his men routed British Guiana by an
innings and 80 runs. He would never be late for a match
again.

The Major was clearly a forgiving sort and picked
Connie to play in the final against Barbados, his first-class
debut. The hosts batted first on the matting wicket and

were all out for a disappointing 174, with Connie, coming
in at eight, dismissed for a duck – one of seven wickets for
pace bowler Herman Griffith. The Barbados side was one
of the hardest-hitting in Caribbean history, and might have
been expected to post a total that would ensure victory.
Opening batsmen Challenor and Tarilton ('the Hobbs and
Hammond of that day', in Connie's estimation) came out
to bat. They had scored a few runs when Tarilton edged a
delivery from Victor Pascall and Connie, who had anticipated the outcome by moving slightly to his right at slip,
pouched the catch. The crowd roared with delight. Perhaps
their enthusiasm got to Connie, for when Challenor prodded at another one and the ball flew to Connie he went to
celebrate the catch prematurely, throwing it into the air
before he had it under control and failing to grab it again
when it came down. The yells of the crowd 'turned into a
terrific groan', Connie recalled, 'and I had to face Major
Harragin at the end of the over'. The former Army officer's
summary was blunt and to the point. 'It taught me never to
do it again. I have larked about with catches many times,
but never again dropped one that way.'

Barbados struggled to adapt to the surface, leaving
Trinidad with an unexpected lead of 18 runs. Connie had
opened with his Uncle Victor and bowled tidily to finish
with two for 44 off twenty-one overs. There were frequent
rain interruptions when Trinidad batted again, and they
had made 266–5 when Barbados's captain, Tarilton,
announced that his side had to leave and catch the boat
back to Bridgetown. The Trinidadians argued that the
match should be played to a conclusion; their opponents
were adamant that a passage was booked and could not be
changed. It was the first draw in the history of the tournament and meant that the visitors retained the trophy. Some

were annoyed, but Connie saw the sense behind Tarilton's decision – why lose if it was avoidable?

The 1922 Inter-Colonial Tournament was played at Georgetown. The competition aroused intense interest throughout the Caribbean, as the third West Indian tour of England had been arranged for the following summer. Form shown in the matches in British Guiana that September would play an important role in determining who would be selected. Connie was again selected, and travelled to South America with his team mates. It was the first time he had ever left the island. There was little chance of him becoming homesick, however, as his father, not far from his fiftieth birthday, and Uncle Victor were also in the Trinidad twelve.

In the elimination game Trinidad defeated British Guiana in a hard-fought match. Connie was chosen to open the batting and made 14 in both innings of what was a very low-scoring match. Set a small total to win, the home side were cruising to victory thanks in the main to Clarence Hunter. So sure were British Guiana of victory that the Trinidad fielders noticed the ground staff putting up posters offering the public the chance to come and see them practising for the final. This display of hubris spurred the visitors on to great efforts. Hunter was dismissed for 52 and the batting duly fell to pieces amidst crowd disturbances provoked by a series of contentious umpiring decisions. With policemen posted around the boundary, Trinidad sneaked home by 29 runs.

It was the game that shaped Connie's career. He had always fielded in close catching positions, but with Joe Rogers, Trinidad's regular cover, having been dropped, he found himself moved into the outfield. Here his athleticism, speed across the ground and sure hands were an obvious asset, and it soon turned out that he had a hard and accurate throw too – on the first morning he ran out a Guianese batsman with a direct hit. True to his nature, Connie did not simply stop there. He practised at every opportunity until he could strike the stumps from thirty yards, throwing with either hand. He also improved his speed of pick-up by dropping pieces of paper on the ground and retrieving them, working out how far he could lean and stretch without losing his balance. Within a few months he was the finest cover fielder in the Caribbean, and matched by very few outside it.

In the final, Trinidad won the toss and batted. The experiment of Connie opening was abandoned and he went in at his more natural position of eight. His father was one above him in the order. Things began badly when Wilton St Hill was run out for a duck, and with Griffith and Teddy Hoad bowling well wickets continued to tumble. Connie was dismissed for 6, his father for 17 and Trinidad were eight down for 200. Enter Uncle Victor. The slow left-armer was not noted as a batsman, but he came to his team's rescue, hitting 92 in rapid time. George Dewhurst, the wicketkeeper, also made a half-century and number eleven, Cyril Fraser, in the team for his leg spin, scored a remarkable 69 not out to help Trinidad reach a very respectable 359. The momentum of the match seemed to be with Trinidad, but Tarilton and Challenor then put on 174 for the first wicket, left-hander Harry Ince caned 151 and the record total posted at the Kensington Oval two years earlier was surpassed as Barbados reached 673. A plainly demoralised Trinidad offered little resistance in their second innings and Barbados won comfortably without the need to bat again.

Despite the defeat, Connie had enjoyed his experience in

Georgetown. Playing with his father had brought him great joy and the standard of the outfield at the Bourda – far superior to that at the Queen's Park Oval – had delighted him. His athleticism in the field during the two matches did not go unnoticed, and when the twenty-one-year-old was – to the surprise of many, for his performances in first-class matches had been so modest as to have avoided attention – named in the tour party for England, the captain of the side, Harold Austin, made it clear that Connie owed his place to his new brilliance at cover as much as to his potential with bat and ball.

Like Harragin, Austin was a shrewd judge of cricketers and a powerful influence in Connie's development. An excellent tactician, he had been a superb middle-order batsman – probably the best in the early years of West Indies cricket. He was also a great admirer of Old Cons. Now forty-seven, it was clear that he would not be able to play in every match on what was sure to be a gruelling tour. Captaincy duties on the field would therefore often fall to vice-captain Karl Nunes. Nunes was a white Jamaican left-hander who'd attended Dulwich College, where he topped the batting averages in 1911, scoring 770 runs at an average of 59. It was the sort of thing that impressed the West Indies selectors, and it was plain to many that he was being groomed as Austin's successor.

The team's undoubted star was George Challenor, the Barbadian often described as the 'father of West Indian batting'. A tall front-foot player in the English public-school tradition, Challenor had attracted headlines since his teenage years. On the 1906 West Indian tour of the British Isles he had struck a century against Nottinghamshire and 90 in a match against Scotland. When the MCC visited Barbados in 1912–13 he hit centuries against them in successive matches. Some of the MCC players who faced him on that tour considered him the equal of the Australian Victor Trumper, at that time regarded as the best batsmen ever to have played against England.

Challenor was joined on the 1923 tour by Tim Tarilton, his opening partner for Barbados. The pair were almost as prolific in the Caribbean as Percy Holmes and Herbert Sutcliffe were in county cricket, and had once scored seven hundred runs between them in matches against British Guiana and Trinidad. While Challenor was the more dazzling strokemaker, some – including C. L. R. James – thought Tarilton more reliable.

Also in the tour party was the thirty-two-year-old barrister Cyril 'Snuffy' Browne, a Barbadian all-rounder; Small of Trinidad, a forceful and stylish batsman who bowled medium-pace off-breaks that were particularly effective on damp or sticky wickets; Maurius 'Maurice' Fernandes of British Guiana, a handy middle-order batsman noted for being more of a 'sticker' than most of his team mates; and Harry Ince, the dashing Barbadian left-hander who drew fanciful comparisons with Frank Woolley. The team's main spinner would be Victor Pascall.

Wicketkeeping duties fell to portly and avuncular George Dewhurst, who was widely regarded as the best stumper in the West Indies even by those from rival colonies (though not by C. L. R. James, who thought Piggott, who played for Stingo, should have been picked instead), while the burden of fast bowling would be carried by the muscular, big-framed George John. The man who had once given Connie the jitters was now approaching middle age and his pace was much diminished, though he could still be fiery when the mood was on him.

Born and raised in Barbados, paceman George Francis

owed his place on the tour almost entirely to Harold Austin, whom he had bowled to frequently in the nets while working as a groundsman in Bridgetown. Francis had not played in a single first-class match and his selection ahead of the better-known Herman Griffith caused a kerfuffle, with C. L. R. James vociferous in his criticism of his fellow countryman's omission. As with Connie, however, Austin's instinct was to be proved correct.

Joseph Holt of Jamaica was another contentious pick. Already in his late thirties, his record in the Inter-Colonial Tournament was unimpressive, and he had not played a first-class match since 1911. His presence was at least partially explained by a quota system, which limited the number of players who could be picked from any one colony.

Clarence Hunter (British Guiana) and off-spinner Raymond Phillips (Jamaica) made up the remainder of the party. To the outsider, the selection process appeared haphazard to the point of being almost arbitrary, but as Connie pointed out later, the absence of first-class matches made selecting younger players a matter of educated guesswork.

The party arrived in Bristol aboard the SS *Intaba*. It was April and the mother country – as the West Indians thought of it – was at its greyest. Connie had enjoyed the voyage and the thought of seeing England filled him with excitement. Like most of the population of the Caribbean, he had formed a bright and glorious picture of Britain. But in the bitter aftermath of the First World War the reality was not quite as splendid. 'I recall miserable journeys in freezing rain, from one damp hotel to another, dressing rooms with their own private chills laid on, and afternoons in the field when it was impossible to pay attention because one kept thinking about overcoats,' he recalled. He found the British reserved and unwilling to engage in conversation unless absolutely cornered, and Sundays were stiflingly dull. With only thirty shillings a week living expenses there was little chance of the players indulging themselves either. On the boat over they had made elaborate plans for adventures in London's West End: visits to theatres, picture houses and music halls, and sight-seeing expeditions. Money prevented them from making any of it come true. Nor did the MCC lay on anything by way of greeting. The shivering tourists were on their own. Connie filled the time playing practical jokes, writing letters home to his new girlfriend, Norma, and lying in bed wrapped in all the blankets he could find.

The West Indians had last toured England in 1909 and there was a feeling that in terms of establishing a reputation they were pretty much starting from scratch. The opening match of the tour was at Fenners against a strong Cambridge University side that featured a youthful Gubby Allen. It was an inauspicious beginning. The West Indians were bowled out for 117, to which Connie contributed a valuable 23 not out, one of only four batsmen who made double figures. Connie and his Uncle Victor then took eight wickets between them. Connie's 3–51 were his best first-class figures so far. But with Claude Ashton hitting 92 and George John too frozen to offer much help, the students built up a big first-innings lead. When the West Indies batted again Connie was dismissed for a duck. Austin did his best, despite suffering from a cold, and made a half-century, but the target set was far too low and the University knocked the runs off for the loss of just one wicket. A match that had been scheduled to last for three days was done and dusted in two.

Things improved dramatically in the next match, at Hove, where the West Indians faced a powerful Sussex

team led by Arthur Gilligan. George Francis made his
first-class debut and impressed everyone watching. The
Barbadian had a dramatic, bustling action that culminated
in a great leap, which some writers felt should be accompa-
nied by a yell. Generating fearsome pace through the air
and off the pitch, he twice ripped through the home side's
batting to finish with ten wickets. Challenor top-scored.
Connie made 18 and 1, and took two wickets in the first
innings. The tourists won by 23 runs.

Against the MCC in a rain-affected match, Victor
Pascall again outshone his nephew, taking 6–77. A draw
was unfair on the home side, who had only needed two
more wickets to secure victory when another downpour
brought a premature end to the fixture. By now a singular
problem had presented itself to Connie and his black team
mates: they could not tell the white English players apart.
The difficulty was so acute that at times they believed that
a batsman they had dismissed earlier in the day had come
out to bat again, and would mutter indignantly to one
another about it. It took Connie some years to get over the
idea that sharp practice had been at play.

At Southampton, the tourists were confounded by a
splendid innings by Phil Mead and the medium pace of
Alec Kennedy, who took 11 for 101 as Hampshire secured
victory by 144 runs. Connie was one of Kennedy's victims,
dismissed for a duck with a cleverly concealed slower ball.
Perhaps Connie's ebullience suggested big-headedness to
the Scotsman, for he sent him on his way with the words
'Not so good, eh?' Afterwards Connie sat in the pavilion
and studied the bowler's technique, eager, as he would
remain throughout his career, to improve. In the second
innings Kennedy got him again, but had to fight longer for
his wicket this time. Connie was hugely impressed by the

way the bowler had used guile and cunning to trap him, luring him into a false stroke through a series of innocuous deliveries. 'That is cricket cunning – the battle of skill against personality. It is what every great bowler has to learn, and it taught me quite a lot that I sedulously applied later.'

The second victory of the tour was secured in fine style. Oxford University declared on 390–6, but consistent batting saw the tourists get to within two runs of that total. Connie made the most eye-catching contribution, hammering eleven fours and a six on his way to 77 in sixty-five minutes, inspired by the supercilious remarks of some undergraduates in the pavilion who evidently found high comedy in the idea of uneducated black men playing the summer game.

The pitch at the Parks was, Connie thought, 'perfect, far different from the matting wicket on which I had played nearly all my cricket.' Nonetheless, Oxford were skittled out for 178 and, with Challenor making a cultured century, the West Indians romped home by eight wickets. A much weakened Essex team were then beaten by three wickets, Challenor making 101. Next came wins over minor counties: Durham at Darlington – Challenor again outstanding in a low-scoring match – and Northumberland at Jesmond. Decent crowds turned up at all the venues, Warner commenting that 'The West Indies enjoyed immense popularity for they played the game in a delightfully happy and enthusiastic manner.'

With four straight wins behind them, morale was high amongst the visitors, but then typical English summer weather curtailed matches against Derbyshire and Northamptonshire, depriving the West Indians of practice. A lack of match sharpness cost them against a powerful

Lancashire side at Old Trafford. Despite defeat, it was the batting of Joe Small and his unorthodox and at times cheeky innings of 94 and 68 that most caught the imagination of spectators. It also impressed the canny Cec Parkin, who remarked that Small was the best batter he had bowled against all season.

All through the tour, no matter what the problems, Connie was improving his game. For the first time he was able to study great players whose performances he had read about in the newspapers back in Trinidad. He watched the elegant Frank Woolley in action, made careful note of the subtle bowling technique of Essex's medium-pacer Johnny Douglas, and marvelled at the unhurried craftsmanship of Jack Hobbs.

Yorkshire were the most admired team in the Caribbean, and Connie recalled how in playground games the boys would all want to pretend to be the White Rose county. His first game against the real thing did not disappoint. Yorkshire, Connie saw, had the very thing he'd so loved about playing for Shannon: they were not stylish, but they were, to a man, 'bulldog fighters ... never defeated until the last ball was bowled'. They were 'a real fighting team, welded together, cunning, steady,' he would note. Though he makes no comparison, it seems certain that the West Indians displayed nothing like the same dogged determination. And how could they, for as Connie records one of their most famous white players was once heard to remark of his black team mates, 'We play and worship and eat together, but, of course, we don't mix socially.' And that was one of the problems

The last three matches of the tour provided a fitting climax to the three-month adventure. Kent won at Canterbury after the West Indian batting failed comprehensively, but both

Norfolk – against whom Challenor made a century and John took 11–75 – and Worcestershire were easily beaten. Before the latter game, Worcestershire's amiable pro, Fred Root, generously demonstrated the art of bowling inswingers to Browne. The West Indian then showed how well he had mastered the skill by clean-bowling his teacher with one in the first innings.

The final game was against H. D. G. Leveson Gower's XI at Scarborough. The festival team was a formidable one; Leveson Gower himself thought it of Test standard. Jack Hobbs opened the batting with Greville Stevens. Ernest Tyldesley, Johnny Douglas, Wilfred Rhodes, Percy Chapman, Frank Mann, Percy Fender, Frank Gilligan and Cec Parkin, along with Leveson Gower, made up the rest of the side.

It was the West Indians' most severe test of the tour, and they rose to it. Batting first they struggled in typical seaside conditions against a miserly and expert attack and were all out for 110. Gaining help for their swing from the moist coastal air, John and Francis bowled brilliantly and only Tyldesley's battling 97 prevented a rout. As it was, the home team closed just 108 runs ahead, Austin drawing praise from his opposite number for his astute handling of his attack.

Alas, the West Indian batting again failed and they set Leveson Gower's men a paltry 31 to win. So confident of victory were the Englishmen that the middle- and late-order batsmen had all changed into their street clothes ready to depart to the train station when the final innings began. What followed was to have momentous consequences for West Indies cricket. Hobbs and Stevens had both taken singles when Hobbs pushed one gently into the hands of Austin off the bowling of Francis. It was a simple catch, but the veteran skipper spilled it. Undeterred, Francis tore in again and soon had Hobbs trapped lbw for two and Stevens magnificently caught by John. Douglas and Tyldesley had edged the score to 14, when the Lancastrian snicked one from John straight to Browne in the slips. In the dressing room, the waiting batsmen changed back into their whites. Rhodes came in. The great Yorkshire all-rounder survived two confident lbw shouts, but was then caught by Dewhurst for a duck, while John clean-bowled Chapman for two. For a moment it seemed that the visitors were going to pull off an extraordinary victory, but the pugnacious Douglas survived another clamorous lbw appeal and along with Percy Fender nursed the Englishmen to a shaky victory.

'The West Indians were cheered to the echo' by the Yorkshire crowd, Leveson Gower wrote. And though the final innings had lasted just one hour and ten minutes, he noted it as a turning point in the Caribbean game: 'I had very little doubt that as a result of this match West Indies cricket would be considered worthy of Test status in the future, and so it proved ... the 1923 match at Scarborough was the dawn of a new era for the West Indies.'

Connie agreed: 'We felt we had put the West Indies far on the road to parity with England, Australia and South Africa. Much was still to be done, but we had laid a true foundation.'

Though Challenor hit six first-class centuries and finished third behind Hendren and Mead in the first-class averages, and had good support from the obdurate Fernandes and the mercurial Small, the West Indians had generally batted far below what was expected of them. Tarilton, Nunes, Holt, Austin and Ince had accomplished very little.

Browne and Pascall had done well with their spinners, taking seventy-five and fifty-two wickets respectively, but the quick bowling was what had impressed most. Bowling aggressively, with speed and bounce, John and Francis earned comparison with the devastating Australian duo Gregory and McDonald. Francis topped the bowling averages with eighty-two wickets at under 16 apiece.

Connie had put in some good spells with the ball too, taking thirty-seven wickets, but he had batted erratically, apparently unable to distinguish between being bold and being rash, to score 425 runs, many of them with shots *Wisden* described as 'unorthodox to the point of spontaneous invention'. His main contribution had come in the field, where he had taken eighteen catches; his athleticism in the covers and brilliant work at short leg and in the slips was a source of wonder to English crowds used to the more sedate movements of the county circuit. Warner already regarded Connie as one of the finest fieldsmen in the world game, and years later his chief memory of the tour would be 'A piece of fielding by Constantine: stopping a hard hit at cover-point, he threw the wicket down at the bowler's end, and, racing across the pitch, backed up the ball that ricocheted off the stumps!'

Wisden was equally enthusiastic, remarking that 'In the deep he picked up while going like a sprinter and threw with explosive accuracy.' Connie was already well on the way to earning his nickname Electric Heels.

England's best cricketers, Jack Hobbs, Herbert Sutcliffe and Patsy Hendren, recognised Connie's raw talent and marked him down as a youngster to watch. Hobbs even gave him a spot of coaching. By the end of the tour Connie was almost as big a draw to paying spectators as Challenor. His achievements were much more modest than those of the great batsman, but there was something about him. Connie had presence, an easygoing charm, and an undeniable charisma. The eyes of the crowd were drawn to him even when he wasn't doing much. He was a star.

On the tour, the West Indians had played twenty-one first-class matches; they won six, lost seven and drew the remainder. It was not an outstanding performance, but they had been sufficiently impressive in key matches for the MCC to give them the go-ahead to form a regional organising body and make an application to join England, Australia and South Africa as a Test-playing nation.

It was little wonder, then, that the team arrived home in September to be met by a brass band playing 'See, the Conqu'ring Hero Comes'. Though the tour might not have been the unqualified success such a welcome suggests, it had sparked massive interest across the Caribbean and created an unprecedented enthusiasm for the game. 'We returned home elated,' Connie recalled. 'We had shown the world that the West Indies could produce cricketers as good as any. That was the great thing.'

The West Indies Cricket Board of Control was established in 1926, partly through the endeavours of Harry Mallett, a former Durham all-rounder and ex-chairman of the Minor Counties Cricket Association, who had been manager of the West Indian tour party in 1906. Mallett had been sent out to the Caribbean by the MCC to help organise the game. He would manage the West Indies tour parties to England in 1928 and to Australia in 1930–1.

The 1924 Inter-Colonial Tournament was held at Bridge-town. Barbados retained the Cup in a competition notable for its low scoring. Small batted well in the elimination game to see Trinidad through to the final. In this, Challenor scored 114, but the game was dominated by pace bowlers. For the home side, Herman Griffith showed what

the West Indians had been missing when they left him out
of the tour party by returning match figures of 10–77, while
in the second Barbados innings Connie bowled quicker
than he ever had before and took 8–38. He was generally
not at his best, however, but weighed down by worries about
work.

Connie had returned from the 1923 tour determined to
focus on cricket. He would have liked to stay in Trinidad,
but there was still no professional cricket on the island,
nor was there a system, such as existed in Australia and
would later in Pakistan, to support amateurs by employing
them in sports shops, insurance companies and the like,
effectively as public relations figures. England was the only
place where Connie could make a living from the game.
Old Cons's team mate Charles Ollivierre had managed it,
and the brilliant Joe Small had been approached and asked
if he would like to stay on in England at the end of the 1923
tour – he had turned down the chance, daunted perhaps by
the enormity of the move. If Connie got such an opportunity he was certain he would grab it. As *Wisden* would later
observe, the tour had opened his eyes and he 'recognised
the game as his only possible ladder to the kind of life he
wanted'. Juggling playing cricket with a full-time job had
always been a burden. He had left his job as a law clerk,
frustrated by the obstacles placed in the way of any black
person hoping to progress to becoming a solicitor or barrister, and apparently feeling that the struggle was affecting
his game. After a miserable period of unemployment
during which he was forced to live on handouts from his
father, Connie found temporary work in the civil service,
first in the registrar's office of the Supreme Court and then
in the Education Department. The nature of his position
left him in an awkward situation when it came to asking

for leave to play cricket. There was little chance of making either of the jobs permanent; such work was reserved for men with lighter skin, as Connie would later record bitterly: 'To put it plainly, if two men went for a job or were being considered for the Test team and one was black and the other only brown-skinned, superior ability in the black man would not get him the job or the place – no, not once in a thousand times.'

Fearful he might lose his job, Connie initially turned down the invitation to play for the West Indies XI against the MCC at Georgetown. Harold Austin, by now a senior figure in the Barbados parliament, intervened, securing leave for Connie on full pay. It was proof of the esteem Austin had for the Constantine family, but the fact it had been a Barbadian rather than a member of the Trinidadian ruling elite who had acted was duly noted. Connie, it seemed, was undervalued in his own country.

In 1925 Jamaica started to take a more prominent role in West Indies cricket, sending a side to Barbados for a series of goodwill matches. They were not yet competing in the Inter-Colonial Tournament, however, which that year was played at Port of Spain. Once again the coconut matting undid the Barbados batsmen and Trinidad claimed the Cup by defeating the holders in the final by 13 runs.

Trinidad held on to the title by defeating British Guiana in Georgetown the following October. Many of Barbados's best players were now past their prime, but Browne showed his all-round class by scoring 102 and taking 13–135 in the elimination match, though he still finished on the losing side. The final between the hosts and Trinidad was a hard-fought affair. Needing 182 to win, Trinidad had struggled to 162 when Connie joined his Uncle Victor at the wicket ninth man in. Batting with singular introspection, Connie helped push the score forward to 177, but then lost Pascall. Ben Sealey, batting surprisingly low in the order, came in and together he and Connie knocked off the remaining runs to secure victory by a couple of wickets.

The MCC tour of the Caribbean, which began in October 1925, was to be a final examination of the West Indies' Test credentials. In England, a certain degree of scepticism remained. Good results for the home side were a necessity, if they were to reach the game's highest level.

The touring party was led by the Honourable Freddie Calthorpe, captain of Warwickshire. Though hardly the strongest squad England could have assembled, it had enough quality to provide a stiff test. The West Indies would find themselves up against players such as Percy Holmes, Yorkshire's jaunty opening batsman; his county team mate Roy Kilner, one of the finest all-rounders in England, who would die while still in his prime from a mysterious fever contracted while playing for the Maharajah of Patiala's XI in India; Wally Hammond, already high on the list of the world's greatest batsmen; sharp-witted Warwickshire wicketkeeper-batsman Tiger Smith, who would later serve as a Test umpire in the Caribbean; off-spinner Ewart Astill, who would take close to 2500 wickets for Leicestershire during a long career and become one of the first professionals to captain a county side; Lionel Tennyson and Leonard Crawley were both dashing aristocratic strokemakers; and guile would be added to the attack by Fred Root of Worcestershire. Root had happily helped Browne develop his in-dipper during the 1923 tour, but on the field he was tough and miserly. He had created his own brand of leg theory bowling when playing for Derbyshire before the First World War. The ploy involved bowling in-swingers aimed at leg stump or slightly outside it to a packed leg-side field. Root had developed the idea largely because he felt Derbyshire – less wealthy than most of their rivals – needed to redress the balance in some way. He varied the inswing with the occasional well-disguised leg-cutter.

The opening representative match was played in Bridgetown. Connie was not selected for this, the first game played by the West Indies rather than the West Indians. The news was a bitter blow to him, especially since he had received a letter earlier that autumn from the Barbados Cricket Association, asking if he would be available for the fixture. Five other Trinidadian players – Pascall, Small, John, Dewhurst and St Hill – had received similar letters. That they were all selected to play only made things worse for the young all-rounder. He must have felt rejected and forgotten about, his notion of playing professionally looking ever more like some childish dream.

The match was drawn. Tropical rainstorms interrupted play. Hammond made 238 – then the highest score by an Englishman in the Caribbean – and Root bowled his inswingers and cutters effectively to take eight wickets in the match as the home side battled hard to avoid defeat between the weather breaks. Root would later comment that the wickets in the West Indies were more dramatically affected by rain than any he had previously encountered. 'The best wickets are like a feather bed, true, easy and comfortable, but a tropical storm instantly invests them with more danger and devil than I have seen anywhere else.' It was a judgement Bob Wyatt would come to agree with.

In Trinidad, the MCC played two games against the colony and the second match with the West Indies. Here, an incident took place that would create a feud between two of the era's greatest cricketers that lasted for almost a decade.

Connie had met Wally Hammond during the 1923 tour. They were of comparable ages and both played the game in the same dynamic manner. Connie believed they had become friends. Yet when he greeted Hammond warmly in Trinidad the Englishman acted as if they had never met. Connie felt snubbed. It seemed to him that Hammond, a middle-class amateur influenced by the prevailing attitudes of West Indian society, had decided it was beneath him to socialise with black people. Connie wrote, 'We'd been good pals in England. Now I got the strong impression that though I was good enough for a morning's fun in England, things were not quite the same where the colour bar was more pronounced.'

Connie 'swore by all the Gods to make [Hammond] regret that day', and for the rest of the tour, whenever the Gloucestershire all-rounder came to the wicket the Trinidadian greeted him with a volley of bouncers. 'I had the ball whizzing round his ears. Wally didn't look happy so I sent down a few more, with my mind no doubt lingering on his frozen expression and the coldly casual rebuff to my eager greeting when he came off the boat.'

Whether Hammond actually meant any harm by not reciprocating Connie's greeting is hard to determine. He was a man whose style of cricket – dashing strokeplay, hostile bowling, loose-limbed cover fielding – seemed at odds with his introspective and at times brooding personality. One of the most celebrated English sportsmen of his era, he remained an enigma even to those who played with him; one Test colleague recalled a ten-hour car journey across Australia during which Hammond spoke just once, and then only to ask his companion to watch out for a petrol station, while another asked to summarise his character simply remarked, 'He liked a shag.'

While it is very possible that Hammond's failure to respond in kind to Connie's warmth was down to the Englishman's reserve, it is equally easy to see why Connie might have felt slighted. In the fashion of the day, neither man chose to openly address the other about his feelings, and so a matter that might easily have been resolved instead festered. In this, at least, there was fault on both sides. Hammond was never an easygoing man, as his bitter disputes with Don Bradman and Charlie Barnett (amongst others) attest, and his temperament was not helped by health and financial worries. If he had treated Connie poorly that day in Port of Spain he made amends in later years, writing sympathetically of the hardships Connie and his black team mates had endured: 'Constantine himself, on his first tour of England, had to stay in bed at hotels a good deal of the time because he simply had not got enough pocket money ... But he did get to England and because cricket in his homeland could not support him, he had to stay here. I know he liked League cricket and League cricket loved him. But I can't help wondering how much higher the standard of West Indies cricket would have been if the two Constantines, George Headley and other West Indians who have gone into the League had been able to live at home and teach the young to bowl and bat.'

On the issue of the West Indies captaincy, Hammond was equally supportive, commenting that when representative sides had met in wartime cricket the West Indies 'could not have had a better captain or a more inspiring player to lead them'. In 1954, when Constantine applied for a post as a legal adviser to Trinidad Leaseholds Ltd, he gave Hammond as a referee. The former England captain took upon himself to write personally to the chairman of the company, Simon Vos, who was a friend of his.

All that was for the future. For now, the contests between the two were carried out with marked hostility, at least on Connie's part.

In the first of the matches against the colony, Calthorpe's side were bowled out for 278. Hammond and opener Hugh Dales, a County Durham-born amateur who played for Middlesex, both made half-centuries. Connie failed to impress with the ball – the damage was done by George John, who took 5–54, and Wilton St Hill's younger brother Edwin, who picked up three wickets with his medium-pacers.

Trinidad replied with 259 thanks in the main to a century from the veteran Andre Cipriani – a barrister from British Guiana – who had played against the MCC sides Arthur Somerset had brought to the Caribbean before the First World War. Much to his annoyance, Connie fell to Hammond who, bowling at a rattling pace, took six wickets.

When the MCC batted again they reached 198–6 before the match ended. Connie opened the bowling with John and took 1–38, his victim predictably Hammond.

The second game was also drawn. Trinidad batted first, making 173. Hammond was again the main danger, taking 5–39 with short, concentrated bursts of genuinely quick bowling. Joe Small scored 57 and Connie contributed too, making 29. In reply the MCC struggled to 143 with Connie again failing to make an impression, taking 1–22. Victor Pascall was the pick of the bowlers with 3–20. Trinidad pressed home their advantage in the second innings, scoring 270–7. Connie was run out without scoring. Wilton St Hill made a century batting with genuine flair even against Kilner, who took six wickets with his slow left-armers. St Hill's range of offside shots and elegant late cuts and leg glances impressed the former England captain Lord Harris, who was watching from the pavilion. Harris, who had been born in Trinidad, would later opine that St Hill was the best West Indian batsmen he had seen.

Any hopes Trinidad had of forcing a victory were slowly squashed by resolute batting from the visitors, who were 177–3 when the game ended. Connie made no inroads with his bowling, Pascall taking all of the wickets that fell.

For the representative match at Port of Spain the West Indies selectors made a number of changes. Dewhurst, Connie and Archie Wiles came in for Cecil Nascimento, Tim Tarilton and Teddy Hoad. The Barbadian Wiles was a competent middle-order batsman who would make his Test debut at Old Trafford in 1933, three weeks shy of his forty-first birthday.

The West Indies won the toss and batted first on the man-made surface. Root believed that Challenor 'was among the five best batsmen in the world on turf', but 'he hated the very name of matting'. This assessment was quickly borne out when the Worcestershire medium-pacer got the great man caught and bowled for a duck. After that the side struggled hard to eventually post a reasonable total of 275. Wicketkeeper Dewhurst made 55 and Snuffy Browne 74. Connie fell for seven – one of Kilner's three victims.

Hammond had again bowled fast and a series of bumpers directed at Austin clearly aggravated Connie. He was determined to exact revenge by directing a similar barrage at the MCC's own, equally rickety, skipper. When Calthorpe came to the wicket Connie duly sent the ball whizzing round his ears. Watching in the stands, even C. L. R. James – a man of marked revolutionary tendencies – was horrified. Fearing that a direct hit on the MCC's aristocratic leader's head might signal a sudden end to

Connie's career, he and a group of friends rushed to see the bowler during the tea interval. "'Stop it, Learie," we told him. He replied: "What's wrong with you? It's cricket.'" James informed Connie bluntly that to injure so prominent a figure would result in a huge row from which the Trinidadian was unlikely to emerge victorious. Connie continued to argue the point, but in the end 'he saw what we were driving at ... and loyally kept the ball out of harm's way'. Connie was, James concluded, a rebellious man, riled by the iniquity of the system, yet one who was, in the final analysis, sensible enough only to fight battles he had some chance of winning.

The MCC batted comfortably despite the eccentricities of the surface and Connie's ire. Holmes scored a sprightly 65 and Frank Watson of Lancashire 74 as the tourists finished their innings 44 runs ahead. Browne followed up his half-century by taking three for 108 in thirty overs, but Connie could only manage a single wicket.

The West Indies did well in the second innings, making 281 all out. Connie struck 18 before falling to Astill, whose six wickets cost 67. Wiles top-scored with 75.

The MCC looked to have a tough task on their hands batting last and chasing over 200 with time running out, but they made light of it, knocking off the runs with five wickets to spare. Holmes, Hammond and Smith all contributed; Connie took the wicket of Holmes with a typical piece of brilliance, bowling a well-disguised slower ball, then racing down the wicket to catch the mistimed defensive shot a few feet in front of Yorkshireman. He finished with match figures of two for 57.

Despite his minimal contribution so far, Connie was selected for the West Indies' next meeting with the MCC, in Georgetown, his involvement eventually ensured by

Austin's intervention (Connie would later comment that without the Barbadian he might not have had a cricket career at all, and there is much in that). While Connie was retained other changes were made, Fernandes, Neblett and Wight coming in for Wiles, Pascall and John. The switches strengthened the batting at the expense of the attack. Barbadian James Neblett was a professional who bowled neat and tidy medium pace and was a decent left-hand bat, while Vibart Wight of British Guiana was a firm striker of the ball who could also keep wicket and would, surprisingly, be appointed vice-captain when the West Indies toured the British Isles in 1928.

The West Indies won the toss and elected to bat. Challenor and Dewhurst put on 127 before Dewhurst fell for 54. Fernandes, Small and Neblett all failed and Challenor eventually perished for 82. The innings was revived by Browne coming in at number eight, who struck a century despite having to retire at one point after being struck by a rising delivery. He got good support from St Hill, who batted beautifully for 72. When St Hill was finally dismissed Wight came in and scored a rapid 90 as he and Browne added 173 for the seventh wicket. Connie struck 13 before falling to the canny Root and the West Indies closed on 462.

The MCC looked to be going along nicely in reply, but then Connie struck to remove Holmes when the Yorkshireman looked well set on 53 and, despite a half-century from Watson, the tourists were all out for 264.

The West Indies enforced the follow-on. Connie at last found his form, dismissing Holmes for 47, Smith for 17, Hammond for 1 and Astill for 51, but a gallant 57 not out from Lionel Tennyson and a late rainstorm saved the match for the visitors, who finished on 243 for eight. Connie finished with four for 54, which was enough to take him to the top of the averages for the series.

The visit to British Guiana was not a happy one for Wally Hammond. At some point during his time in Georgetown, he was bitten by a mosquito. The bite turned septic and then gangrenous, and by the time the party sailed back to England the Gloucestershire player was perilously close to losing a leg. (That, at least, was the official line: Hammond's biographer, David Foot, has claimed the illness was actually syphilis, something that plagued the cricketer for the rest of his life.)

Despite putting up a decent display against the visitors, the West Indian administrators concluded that improvements could and should be made. The job of selecting the team – previously in the hands of whichever authority was hosting the match – would be handed to the West Indian Cricket Board of Control. From now on the side would, allowing for considerations of race, be selected purely on merit.

The ban on professionals continued, however, which meant that George Francis missed the 1927 Inter-Colonial Tournament in Bridgetown. In the qualifying match Barbados slaughtered British Guiana thanks to a remarkable display of batting that saw them reach 771–9, the highest score ever made in the West Indies. They met holders Trinidad in the final. The game ran from 24 January until 2 February, and Connie would later describe it as the most extraordinary match he ever took part in. The home side won the toss, but then struggled to 175 all out. Trinidad made better use of the traditionally fine Bridgetown wicket: Small hit a century, Wiles broke the tournament record by scoring 192, Ben Sealey made 98 not out and the innings closed with Trinidad 384 ahead. No side in cricket history had ever come from so far behind to win a match, but Barbados opened in extraordinary fashion, Challenor and Tarilton putting on 292 for the first wicket. Tarilton was out for 120, but Challenor strolled on, breaking all records to reach 220 – an innings Connie considered the finest he saw in his life. Hoad scored 174 not out as Barbados surpassed the record they had set earlier in the tournament, declaring on 726–7. The innings had knocked the stuffing out of the Trinidadians and they were bowled out for 217 to lose by 125 runs. Of the 1677 runs scored in the match, Connie had contributed just 24; nor were his match figures of three for 220 anything to be proud of. Yet such was his character that he was able to take delight in the achievements of others, even on the opposing team, and he would later write glowingly of the batting of Challenor, Tarilton and Hoad.

Connie was, it is true, in a happier frame of mind than he had been for several years. Unable to secure a permanent role in the education office, he had gone to work in the oilfields in the south of the island. He found a job as clerk with Trinidad Leaseholdings, the company that had built the Point-a-Pierre oil refinery, and was paid eight pounds a month. The prospects of advancement were still limited. According to Michael Manley, the administrative staff in the Trinidad oil industry was divided along racial lines, with only those who were white, or light-skinned, allowed to rise above a certain level. The upside was that Connie's new employer, H. C. W. Johnson, a white South African, took a keen interest in his clerk's cricketing career and allowed him leave to play on half pay. It was a small turning point in Connie's professional life. A major one was just over the horizon.

Chapter 4

A Man of Steel Springs and India Rubber

With their first official Test series approaching, the West Indies made an effort to ensure the party to tour the British Isles was the strongest possible. A series of trial matches were arranged in Barbados that would draw the cream of Caribbean cricketers. It was a good plan – at least in theory.

In the first trial match in Bridgetown, a combined Trinidad and British Guiana team played against a Barbados and Jamaica XI. The game was remarkable. The side from the southern colonies scored 378 in first innings thanks to St Hill's 144 and 84 from the relatively unknown Colin Roach. Small and Pascall then bowled beautifully, ripping through the powerful northern colonies' batting line-up and dismissing them for 59. Forced to follow on, the Barbadians and Jamaicans rallied slightly, with Challenor batting with his customary elegance, but it was too little too late and they lost by an innings and 132 runs.

The second match was a twelve-a-side game between teams captained by Tim Tarilton and Archie Wiles. Wiles's XII won the match largely because of a sporting declaration by Tarilton. Neblett and Wight took the batting honours, while Connie shone with both bat and ball, striking a sprightly half-century and taking five for 32.

The final trial match was another twelve-a-side affair, between Barbados Born and the Rest of the West Indies. The game was a high-scoring draw. For Barbados, Hoad made 153, Bartlett 93 not out and Tarilton 93 and 71. For the Rest, Wight made a century while Rae, St Hill and Small all did well. Connie had bowled extremely fast and fielded with his usual brilliance, but his batting had been erratic and even the supportive Austin deemed it necessary to offer a cautionary word about being more responsible in future.

Two months later, in February 1928, Lionel Tennyson arrived in Jamaica with a touring side that included Phil Mead and the fearsome left-arm pace bowler Nobby Clark. Jamaica proved too strong for them, winning two of the matches easily and drawing the other. The sensation of the games was an eighteen-year-old batsman, George Headley. Described by one of the visitors as 'bow-legged and bright-eyed', Headley made 50 in even time in the second innings of the first match, eventually falling for 72. The youngster's cutting, pulling and hooking was of such quality that the crowd started calling him J. K. Junior in reference to the big star of Jamaican batting, John Kenneth Holt. (Since John Holt had a son called J. K. Holt Junior, who would also play for the West Indies, it was fortunate the nickname didn't stick.) In the next game, at Melbourne Park, Headley did even better, striking a double century. The experienced Tennyson rated him very highly, saying, 'I have seen Trumper and McCartney bat, but I do not think that when they were as old as George Headley they could have been any better.'

Sadly for Headley, the West Indies selectors had already chosen the tour party. Karl Nunes, Austin's vice-captain from 1923, was made captain – an uncontroversial choice as far as the ruling class were concerned, though Connie was singularly unimpressed. Vibart Wight was named as vice-captain, though he had no experience of leading a first-class side.

As well as Nunes, Jamaica provided Martin, the leg-spinning all-rounder Oscar Scott (known to everyone as Tommy) and Ernest 'Big Man' Rae, a forceful batsman who could also keep wicket and bowl leg-breaks. Five Barbadians were selected: Challenor, Francis, Griffith, Hoad and Bartlett. Tarilton had done well in the trials, but the combination of his age and his failure to adapt to English conditions in 1923 counted against him. From Trinidad came Connie (some thought a little fortunately), Roach, Small and St Hill, and from British Guiana Fernandes, Snuffy Browne (who had moved to Georgetown to practise law) and Neblett.

The party had plenty of experience, but there were several clear weaknesses. Leaving aside the ongoing leadership issues, Challenor was forty and, though game, was past his best, while the man viewed as his successor, St Hill, had no experience of English conditions. More damagingly, there was no specialist wicketkeeper in the seventeen-man squad – Nunes, Rae or Wight were expected to take turns behind the stumps as required. There was also a preponderance of old legs and dimming eyes. With the exception of Connie, this was one of the poorest fielding teams ever to come out of the Caribbean. The catching was almost comically substandard and the ground fielding that had thrilled English crowds in 1923 was now aspiring to mediocrity.

With a makeshift wicketkeeper and a dearth of decent

slip fielders, the major strength of the squad – its pace bowlers – would be undermined. Connie, Griffith and Francis were all genuinely fast; Small was also nippy. The constant fumbling of catches would do little for their morale or for their team's chances of winning matches. Indeed, after the tour Nunes would tell Warner 'that had he possessed a Chapman and Hammond in the slips the England totals in the three Test matches would have been cut in half'. A frustrated Connie would likewise speculate as to what might be possible if he could field slip to his own bowling.

The West Indies were unfortunate to arrive in Britain on one of those rare occasions when the England team were the best in the world. Captained by Percy Chapman – a player whose shrewd leadership and acrobatic fielding Connie greatly admired – they had a formidable batting line-up, with Hobbs and Sutcliffe opening, followed by Wally Hammond, Douglas Jardine and Ernest Tyldesley. The pace attack was led by the expert seamer Maurice Tate and the ferociously quick Harold Larwood, while the slow bowling was provided by 'Tich' Freeman, a diminutive leg-spinner who, on the dry, fast wickets of what was to prove a long, hot summer, would break all records by taking 304 first-class wickets.

Connie knew the tour was his big chance to realise his ambition of becoming a full-time professional. When Austin had told him he had made the party he had 'just wanted to get out somewhere and throw my hat sky-high'. He prepared for the summer like a boxer getting ready for a world championship contest. He played cricket at every opportunity, for the Trinidad Leaseholds company team as well as Shannon. He also took to playing football for Forest Reserve and earned a place on the company's athletics team as a sprinter, winning several major races and beating the island champion Ben Sealey over a hundred yards. Whenever he got the chance he was in the nets, sharpening his bowling. Connie had once simply relied on his natural athleticism for pace, but now he worked on his strength and stamina. He also decided that if he was to bowl at his sharpest he would have to abandon his position at cover point and field closer to the wicket. When it came to batting, he at last began to heed the advice of those around him. 'We used to beg him to settle down and bat,' C. L. R. James recalled. 'All of us were looking for him to do great things, but he simply wouldn't settle down.' Connie's long-time supporter Austin had also had a word with him about limiting his extravagance until he was set. The Trinidadian would never totally rein in his natural instincts and at times would vindicate the observers who felt his batting was genius misdirected, but from now on his periods of focus would be greater and his impact more telling, in first-class matches at least. 'When I landed in England I was as fit a man as I had ever been in my life,' Connie said. He was also more determined.

The tour began in April with a series of warm-up matches against Berkhamsted, Dulwich and a scratch XI assembled by the cricket patron Hubert Martineau and played on his private ground near Maidenhead.

The opening first-class match against Derbyshire was won by two wickets. Challenor batted well and Browne, using the in-dipper Root had taught him, bowled to great effect, taking eight wickets. Medium-pacer Archie Slater did the damage for Derbyshire, exposing a West Indian weakness against the swinging ball in bagging eight for 24 in the tourists' second innings. With the game looking likely to end in a draw it was Connie who turned it into a win, smashing seven fours as the winning runs were

knocked off in quick time. 'I ought to have been careful, but I did not feel careful,' Connie would say after it
emerged that his captain had instructed him to bat for a
draw. This vignette set the tone for the summer, giving
Connie a surge of confidence that seemed to last right
through until September.

The West Indians' next first-class match was against
Essex at Leyton. The weather was brutally cold. For the
home side Jack Russell scored 147, to which Connie provided the perfect riposte – a sparkling 130 not out in ninety
minutes including three sixes and fourteen fours. His first
94 runs came in just an hour.

At the Oval, Hobbs and Andy Sandham shared a stand
of 253 as Surrey chalked up a massive lead, but Connie
struck a half-century in the tourists' opening knock and
then walked out in the second with Harry Peach causing
mayhem with his swingers. Having learned more than
just bowling tricks from Alec Kennedy on the previous
tour, Connie passed by Peach on his way to the wicket and
remarked that he would need to do better 'if he wanted to
get me out'. Whether the comment caused Peach to try too
hard is difficult to say, but Connie backed his mouth up by
belting 60 not out and saving the tourists from defeat.

The sun shone at Fenners, where the tourists won by
nine wickets. Connie took ten wickets in the match and
Fernandes struck form with the bat. May ended with the
West Indians undefeated. It seemed like they might make a
success of things.

The first real setback came when the West Indians
travelled to Dublin to play Ireland. Left-hander Trevor
McVeagh made 102 in the home side's second innings and
the West Indians were set a target of 352 to win. Roach
and Fernandes put on 117 for the first wicket, but after they

were out the batting fell apart and Ireland took the game by 60 runs.

It was a humiliating defeat, and one that caused great anxiety amongst the West Indies management. The tour was being backed by a wealthy businessman from British Guiana named O'Dowd. He had advanced the money to cover the costs and expected to get it back through ticket revenues, but sales so far had been poor and seemed likely to get worse after the defeat in Dublin. There was little doubt in the mind of Harry Mallett, the team manager, that the West Indians needed a strong performance in their next game, against Middlesex at Lord's, not only to save this tour but to safeguard future tours too. Connie had been rested for the disastrous game against Ireland. He had torn fibres in a thigh muscle when fielding in the covers against Surrey and the injury had been made worse when he had been struck on the thigh when batting a fortnight later. The combination of pull and bruising led the doctor who examined him, a Barbadian former cricketer (Connie makes no mention of his name, though it seems possible it was John Cameron, who had toured England with Old Cons in 1909), to warn Connie against playing for two weeks.

It put the West Indian management in a difficult position. Connie was the team's star attraction. Mallett went to see the player on the eve of the Middlesex game. 'You are our draw card, if you drop out, we shan't do much business,' he said bluntly, adding, 'but you must decide for yourself. I don't want you to harm yourself.' Connie understood what was at stake, and perhaps he also saw the golden opportunity Lord's provided to showcase his talents. He announced that he would play.

The following morning Connie was given as much

treatment as was available in those days – he soaked in a hot bath, had a massage, and was then liberally coated in embrocation and wrapped in warm towels. Nunes was warned that if the West Indians found themselves in the field first thing, Connie should not be brought on to bowl and should field close to the wicket.

The mustachioed Old Malvernian Frank Mann won the toss for Middlesex and duly elected to bat on a slow wicket. Despite the warning, Nunes threw the new ball to Connie, who opened the bowling with Francis. Connie quickly got the wicket of Harry Lee for seven but that was the West Indians' last success for a while. On a lifeless pitch Middlesex batted all day. At the close they were 313 for six: the lanky all-rounder Nigel Haig and Jack Hearne (usually known as Young Jack to distinguish him from his distant cousin, the expert medium-pacer J. T. Hearne) had put on 153 for the second wicket, Haig making 119 and Hearne 75. Patsy Hendren, batting unusually sluggishly, was 65 not out overnight, having been dropped by Connie in the slips off Francis in the last over of the day.

Sunday was a rest day, which gave Connie more time for hot baths, massage and embrocation. By Monday morning the wicket was a fraction faster. Middlesex added 39 runs to their overnight total, Hendren – finding his form – striking 38 of them and reaching his sixth hundred of the season. It was the signal for the home side to declare on 352.

The confidence of the tourists was low after the Dublin debacle. Against an experienced attack they prodded and poked tentatively, like men searching in darkness for something they fear might bite. By lunch they were struggling at 79 for five. In light of his injuries, Connie had been held back. He came in at number seven, striding to the wicket with great purpose. Unlike the West Indian batsmen who had preceded him, Connie bristled with aggression. He had a feeling that this was his day, his summer. Facing Gubby Allen – bowling fast from the Pavilion End – he made not the vaguest pretence of playing himself in, driving his second ball for a couple of runs. The first ball of Allen's next over he bludgeoned for four. The following delivery he struck for three.

At the Nursery End Connie found himself facing leg-spinner James Powell. Powell was a professional who had distinguished himself in his debut season by taking eight for 72 in an innings against Gloucestershire. His first ball to Connie was a googly pitched on a good length. Connie came down the wicket as it left the bowler's hand. The field was spread for him, but it made no difference: Connie swatted the ball over mid-on. It flew over the old Nursery stand and landed on the pitch beyond. Powell came in again. This time a leg break. Connie was down the pitch quickly again, striking the ball to the boundary for four. Then a couple of twos off the last deliveries of the over.

Martin took a single off Allen's second ball. Connie eyed up the young fast bowler. The first delivery went for four, the next three brought six more runs, all driven or slapped with a cross bat in front of the wicket. The crowd was small, but Connie's hitting had roused them.

Allen was in his prime and quick, one of the fastest bowlers in England at that time, but Connie treated him like he was bowling a tennis ball on asphalt. The first delivery of his next over he took two, the second was clogged over midwicket for four, the third slogged straight back past the bowler with a cross bat. It smacked into the pavilion railings and bounced twenty yards back onto the field.

Allen decided that the best policy was to bowl full and outside off stump. The first ball he tried pitched on a good length and was angled towards first slip. Connie refused to be shackled. Planting his foot down the wicket he swung the bat in a great arc. The ball flew over cover point's head, continued to rise and landed in the seats high up in the new grandstand.

This astonishing shot – a six almost square of the wicket on the off side – brought Connie's score to 49. The import of the moment was not lost on him. Next ball he played a simple leg glance and ran his first single, much to the merriment of the crowd. His fifty had come in eighteen minutes off twenty-two deliveries. It remains one of the fastest in cricket history.

Mann turned to the niggardly leg-spinner Hearne in the hope of bottling up the West Indian. Hearne succeeded in reducing Connie's scoring rate to a run a minute, which was a triumph in the circumstances. Connie had been in the middle for a devastating fifty-five minutes when Mann threw the ball to his young leg-spinner Ian Peebles – then just twenty and on holiday from university. Peebles had never before bowled a googly, but he tried one now. It was overpitched, not what he intended, but it became a yorker, went straight under Connie's bat and bowled him. Connie shook his head and walked back to the pavilion and a standing ovation. While he had been at the wicket the West Indians had added 97 to their total – he had scored 86 of them.

Watching, Plum Warner declared it was the finest display of hitting he had seen since Gilbert Jessop, and that Connie had done it in more orthodox style. Sitting in the pavilion, Charlie Macartney, the great Australian batsman who was in England with his wife, shook his head in amazement and announced that Connie was the hardest striker of a cricket ball he had ever seen.

The West Indians had made 186 when Connie was out.
Nunes and Martin carried the tourists past the follow-on
mark, but wickets continued to fall regularly and they were
all out for 230, giving the home side a lead of 122.

Middlesex came in to bat again at six o'clock, the nightwatchman Allen opening with Lee. In the final half-hour
Connie and Francis bowled at their quickest. The experienced old pro Lee played back to Connie, but was beaten
for pace and bowled. Allen took a painful blow in the chest
from a Francis bumper and soon after spooned the ball
straight back to the bowler. The home side ended the day
182 ahead with eight wickets in hand.

The weather on the final day was sunny and hot. A
decent crowd of more than two thousand turned up to
watch what seemed likely to be a fascinating day. They
were in a for real treat. Connie opened the attack from
the Nursery End. His thigh still twinged occasionally but
he was determined to ignore it. He soon had Hendren in
trouble. One delivery beat the bat and whizzed a fraction of an inch past the stumps. Another rose sharply and
struck the batsman in the chest, sending him staggering
backwards. Hendren, who would take quite a battering
from the West Indians over the years, refused to be intimi-
dated. He began to unfurl his range of shots. At the other
end Hearne looked equally unruffled. The score gradually rose. After forty minutes Nunes removed Connie and
brought on Small. The medium-pacer made no impact
and the score mounted to 98 for two, with Middlesex 220
ahead. Just as it looked as if the only thing that would
bring the home side's innings to a close was a declaration, Small did enough off the seam to beat Hearne and
bowl him. Nunes immediately brought Connie back into
the fray, this time giving him the benefit of bowling from

the Pavilion End, traditionally the one favoured by the quicker bowlers. Connie galloped to the wicket. The strip had hardened in the sun, and with the help of the slope he seemed to be bowling half a yard faster. The fourth ball of his second over, delivered from wide of the stumps and angled into the batsman, hit the seam, jagged back even further and sent Haig's middle stump spinning. In his next over Connie bounced Edgar Killick. The Middlesex man held up his bat more in a protective gesture than as any kind of shot. The ball caught the edge and was taken by Francis in the slips. Mann came in and drove Small to the boundary. Hendren fell to the first ball of Connie's next over, the faintest edge to an express delivery flying low to Francis. The fifth ball of the over was a replica of the delivery that had done for Haig. It was far too good for Peebles and knocked his middle peg clean out of the ground. Later he'd tell people it was the quickest delivery he'd ever seen in his life. Not that he had seen it.

Price and Powell both stood rooted to the spot as lightning deliveries from Connie smashed their stumps. In the 6.3 overs he'd bowled since switching to the Pavilion End, Connie had taken six for 11 and the home side subsided from 100 for three to 136 all out. As the West Indians left the field Nunes held his players back to allow Connie to lead them off and enjoy the standing ovation from the members as he trotted up the pavilion steps, boot spikes clacking on the concrete. Looking back, he would recall how at that moment his head was filled with a vision of what might have been – a dusty young clerk busy amongst the files in the office of a Trinidad solicitor 'waiting for the newspapers with the cables of the Middlesex match'.

Despite the collapse, the West Indians still looked more likely to lose the game than win it. They needed to make

259 in the remaining 220 minutes of play. Middlesex had a good attack and the pitch had hardly got easier.

The watching Macartney spoke to Nunes. He advised the West Indian skipper to move Connie up the order, reasoning that if the hardest hitter in the team didn't come in until seven he might be too late to influence the result. Nunes rejected the idea. His team were susceptible to panic in the final innings of matches. He wanted a sound start, something that would calm any nerves. The fourth-innings collapse against Ireland was fresh in his mind.

Challenor and Roach opened. They established a good tempo, despatching the loose deliveries without trying to force things. Then as lunch approached Roach glided the ball down to third man, ran one and turned for the second. It was a mistake. The throw came in fast and flat and the opener was run out. The West Indians had made 28.

Connie's batting and bowling on the previous two days had attracted newspaper headlines, and as the day wore on more and more spectators turned up to watch the match. The pitch had quickened and now, on the final afternoon, the batsmen faced the additional problems of the occasional delivery keeping low. Allen had been injured by the blow from Francis the previous evening, but Haig, swinging the ball both ways, and the tall and much quicker Jack Durston – who had been the main destroyer in the first innings – both bowled probing spells. The spinners, extracting a little turn, bowled a tight line, keeping scoring opportunities to a minimum and hoping to provoke rashness. As the afternoon wore on the tourists fell further and further behind the clock. Challenor and Fernandes had raised the score to 63 when Challenor fell for 33, bowled pulling at a ball that failed to rise as much as he expected. Another wicket went down at 70, the elegant

St Hill – without cigarette, on this occasion – bowled by Durston with one that scuttled like a rat. Fernandes and Bartlett added 36 before the latter fell. Small came in at number six, ahead of the more solid Martin, and when the score had reached 121 struck a return catch to Peebles. The West Indians needed 138 in ninety minutes to win; the home side required five wickets. Connie walked out to tumultuous applause from a crowd that had swelled still further as people finished work. As he took his guard a hush settled on Lord's. This was the crucial moment; everyone sensed it. There was an expectation of something wonderful, miraculous. Such a mood has greeted all the world's most exciting batsmen as they arrive at the wicket. It is a testament to their greatness, but it brings with it formidable pressure. The situation was tailor-made for Connie, but could he match the anticipation? He had made 86 in the first innings and taken 7–57 in the second; was it too much to expect him to perform so brilliantly for a third time?

There was one ball to come in Peebles's over. The leg-spinner had clean-bowled him with his first ball last time. This time Connie did not stay in his crease. The moment the ball left the bowler's hand he was down the wicket, crashing a drive that flew to the boundary for four.

Planning for the assault that he knew must come, Mann spread his field for Connie and crowded the bat for Fernandes. His bowling attack was depleted – not only was Allen absent, but Durston had been forced to withdraw with an arm strain. Only Haig was left of the pacemen, but he had three top-class spinners in Hearne, Peebles and Powell. Lee could provide back-up with his medium-paced trundlers.

Hearne was bowling from the Pavilion End, Peebles from

the Nursery. Since he still had 130 runs to play with, Mann decided to keep them both on to buy Connie's wicket. It almost succeeded. An over-ambitious drive from the Trinidadian fell just short of extra cover. After that escape, Connie focused his mind. He scored off practically every ball he faced, but took singles, twos and threes. After that first blow from Peebles he waited ten minutes before striking another boundary – a remarkable display of restraint by his own standards. Yet with Fernandes doggedly holding out at the other end, Connie still managed to keep the scoring up to just over a run per minute.

When he had reached 24 in relatively sedate style, Connie faced another over from Hearne. The leg-spinner had tied him down, bowling accurately to his field. Early in the over Connie drove Hearne to the boundary for four, then off the final ball he produced another of those remarkable shots that people spoke of decades later. Hearne pitched short and the ball kept low. It was the sort of delivery that had done for Challenor. But Connie did not attempt to pull to leg; instead, he used a horizontal bat to blast the ball straight back at Hearne. It whizzed past the bowler's legs and carried on at incredible speed, hitting the top of the pavilion railing and ricocheted up the steps, sending the members diving for cover.

His appetite whetted, Connie had to wait five deliveries before a Fernandes single brought him on strike against Peebles. The first ball he received from the leg-spinner was swept into the grandstand for another six. Hearne slowed things down by bowling a maiden to Fernandes, but 53 runs had come in half an hour and now only 85 were needed for victory.

Peebles was removed from the attack. His replacement Haig's first over went for eight – seven of them to Connie.

Hearne produced another tight over that earned the tourists just a single, but in Haig's next Connie bludgeoned 8 runs, bringing up his fifty in the process. Hearne felt the pressure of the attack too, and Connie took nine off his next over.

With just 57 needed Mann opted for a double change. Powell came on for Haig and Lee for Hearne. In Powell's first over Connie took 6 runs, but played the spinner with such ease that Mann suspected he was nursing the bowler, planning to keep him on for a later assault. He brought Haig back on. Connie greeted the opening bowler's quick return by belting 13 off his first five balls, including a massive six that flew over long on. He was striking the ball with immense power – Hearne, fielding a ball from him, suffered an injury to his hand that prematurely ended his season.

In front of the Tavern, spectators were standing on their seats to get a better view of the action. People were still streaming through the turnstiles as word of Connie's outrageous batting filtered out across the capital.

The tourists now needed just 32 to win. Connie was 82 not out. Fernandes too continued to play his part. Lee did his best to keep Connie quiet, bowling an impeccable line and length, but he would not be subdued and belted two fours from his over. He faced just two balls of the next over from Haig – another four and a single taking his score to 96.

Lee ran in to bowl from the Pavilion End. Connie rapped the first delivery for a single. The field came in for Fernandes, but he placed his forward defensive shot carefully and took a run. Connie now faced Lee. The delivery was slightly overpitched. Connie drove hard, the ball evading long off and long on, and banging into the pavilion rails to bring him his hundred.

The applause had barely died down when Connie was out. The West Indians needed only five more to win. Connie had batted for just over an hour, hit two sixes and twelve fours and made 103 of the 133 he and Fernandes had added for the sixth wicket. For a second time in the day the members rose in cheering appreciation as he walked towards the pavilion steps, while the crowd, the ground staff and even the normally phlegmatic MCC gatemen rushed to the boundary edge to applaud him.

The game was not yet won or lost. With the first ball of the next over Haig had the diligent Fernandes caught by Allen for a priceless 54. It was the final excitement of the match. Martin and Browne quietly knocked off the five runs needed to secure the tourists a morale-boosting win. More than that, it announced the West Indians as a force in the game, a team with a personality and a style quite different from anything that had gone before.

A large crowd gathered in front of the pavilion, cheering for Connie. His innings had created such a sensation that when the teenage Denis Compton joined the Middlesex staff a few years later he found the old pros in the dressing room still talking about it in tones of wonder. Warner too would recall the innings vividly: 'Two of his strokes I shall remember to my dying day. The first was when he hit a good length ball of Allen's over extra cover's head far up into the grandstand; and the second when he played back to Hearne with such tremendous force that the ball, after striking the pavilion rails, ricocheted amongst the seats, scattering the members of the MCC and Middlesex and bringing destruction to wood-work and paint in its train.'

Connie's brilliant innings was indeed a thing of wonder. It was also a puzzle to C. L. R. James, reading about it in the newspaper back in Trinidad. Aside from the memorable flogging of George John, Connie had never batted with such violent certainty in the Caribbean. It was, James thought, as if his talent, freed from the shackles imposed on it by the racial attitudes of the Caribbean, had finally broken out and found its full expression. Perhaps that is true. What is inarguable is that during the tour something changed in Connie. All the potential for violent mayhem that lay within him was suddenly harnessed. He had gone from being a boy cricketer with impressive ancestry and a future to one of the best all-rounders in the game.

The match confirmed Connie as one of the world's most exciting cricketers. It was not just at Lord's that his feats had stirred people. Back home, the *Trinidad Guardian* published a special supplement to mark the performance, while up in a little-considered corner of East Lancashire they were also talking animatedly about it and making plans as to what to do next.

For the first Test at Lord's the West Indies omitted Bartlett, Neblett, Wight, Scott, Rae and Hoad. England fielded a full-strength team with the exception of the unfit Hobbs. Chapman won the toss and elected to bat. The morning began well for the tourists. Connie, Francis and Griffith all bowled fast and straight, digging in the occasionally bouncer and ruffling the feathers of openers Herbert Sutcliffe and Charles Hallows of Lancashire. The Roses pair were both struck several times by bumpers but stuck to their task in gritty fashion for eighty minutes, taking the shine off the ball and the wind out of the pacemen. With the score on 51 Hallows was caught for 26, the West Indies' first-ever Test wicket. It fell to Connie, of course. Tyldesley came to the wicket, was completely baffled by Connie's slower ball and narrowly avoided being clean-bowled. With Browne bowling well and apparently having the beating of Sutcliffe, the West Indies were in good shape when lunch came.

In the afternoon Sutcliffe fell to Francis for 48, Connie taking the catch. The arrival of Hammond saw a shift in the momentum of the game, however. The Gloucestershire batsman launched straight into the attack and struck 45 in fifty minutes before Connie returned and – still nursing his grievance – produced a lightning-quick delivery that sent his stumps sprawling. Jardine batted slowly, but when Chapman came to the wicket to join Tyldesley the pace picked up again. The captain, playing an unorthodox and at times slapdash innings, made a half-century and the Lancastrian a century as 96 runs were added in a little over an hour. England were all out for 401 early on the second morning. Connie was the pick of the bowlers with four wickets for 82. Francis, Griffith and Small picked up a brace apiece, while Browne had bowled well without any luck. Though the total effectively batted them out of what was only a three-day match, the tourists could be pleased with their work.

Challenor and Martin opened for the West Indies and survived until lunch with few scares. In the afternoon they took the total to 86 before Martin was lbw to Tate for a patient 44. Challenor was then out to Larwood for 29, a wicket that precipitated a dramatic collapse. While Nunes battled hard for 37 and Connie struck a few lusty blows late on, the tourists lost eight wickets in quick time and were all out for 177. Vallance Jupp, skipper of Northants, was the best of the English bowlers, taking four for 37 with his heavily tweaked off-breaks.

Larwood was injured and could not bowl, but Chapman still enforced the follow-on. Tate clean-bowled Challenor for a duck and as in the first innings the dismissal of the great man seemed to have a terrible psychological effect on those who followed. Wickets fell with rhythmic regularity and by the close West Indies were 55–6 and looking utterly rattled. The following day Small and Browne raised morale with some spirited hitting but the inevitable could not be staved off for ever and England won comfortably by an innings and 58 runs. The Kent leg-spinner Freeman took four for 37 and Jupp three for 66. The success of both spinners highlighted another weakness in the West Indies team – they struggled against slow bowling.

The tourists bounced back, beating Jupp's Northamptonshire side by an innings and 126 runs. Connie's brilliant streak in first-class matches continued as he hammered 107 in an hour and a half and took thirteen wickets for 112 including a hat-trick. The effort so exhausted him that he had to be carried back to the hotel by his team mates.

After a couple of rain-affected matches against Yorkshire and Nottinghamshire, the West Indians arrived in Stoke-on-Trent to play Staffordshire. This would be Connie's first encounter with S. F. Barnes. Barnes was one of the great professionals of League cricket, and in temperament he could not have been more different from Connie. He was as dour and laconic as he was brilliant. A master craftsman who could break the ball both ways off the wicket and swing it in and out through the air, he rarely bowled a loose delivery, and though merely medium pace had a top-spinner that leapt up off the wicket and bruised many a knuckle and wrist. He had taken 189 Test wickets at under 19 apiece while barely bothering to play county cricket at all.

In 1928 Barnes was playing as a professional for Castleton Moor and occasionally for Wales (for whom he was

qualified by residency – he had a business in Llandudno)
and Staffordshire in the Second-Class Championship,
which in those days included the minor counties and some
county second XIs. In the latter competition he had been
on devastating form, taking 15–67 in the match against
Cheshire and eight in an innings against Lancashire II. He
would finish the season with fifty-five wickets at 7.34 each.

The home side batted first and were skittled out for
99, Connie clean-bowling Barnes – a decent batsman at
League and minor counties level – for eight.

When the West Indians batted Challenor played with
refined calm to reach 71 before Barnes got the better of
him. Connie struck 38 before falling lbw to the unher-
alded Herbert Sedgwick and the tourists were shot out
for 159, Barnes taking four for 30. In the second innings
Staffordshire improved, scoring 181, but the West Indians
coasted to victory by eight wickets. Barnes, however,
claimed the consolation of Connie's scalp. The Trinidadian
had reached his thousand runs for the tour during the
match and was impressed by what he had seen of the great
man: 'he was well over fifty; but on a day's bowling he was
and is the finest bowler I have played in England'.

At Edgbaston Connie bowled extremely fast, knocking
Bates unconscious with a bouncer. The next batsman in
was Bob Wyatt. The first two balls from Connie both
struck him on the head and he went for four. 'Fortunately
they were glancing blows and did not knock me out,' Wyatt
recorded with typical restraint. Jack Parsons had won the
Military Cross in the First World War and was training
to become a clergyman. He stood his ground, striking
161, including four successive sixes off the slow bowler,
Scott, one of which flew over the sightscreen and into the

tea room, shattering cups and saucers. As if to show that anything Parsons could do he could do too, Connie played another whirlwind innings, belting 70 in just forty minutes. Despite his efforts, Warwickshire won the match by seven wickets, the aptly named Scottish pace bowler Andrew Speed taking nine wickets for 99.

Nunes won the toss in the second Test at Old Trafford and took first use of a wicket that had been heavily watered. The pitch was a pudding that offered little to the bowlers, but also made fast scoring difficult. The West Indians were bowled out for 206. Once again it was the spinners Freeman and Jupp who did the damage, with seven wickets between them. Hobbs, restored to the side, came in with Sutcliffe and the pair moved assuredly to a century stand, though the Surrey man would later say that the first few overs he received from Connie were some of the quickest he ever faced in his life. He also complained about the number of bouncers that were bowled at him, telling the press that he did not play cricket in order to get knocked about. According to Connie, Jardine also moaned about the bumpers – an irony indeed.

With 118 on the board Hobbs took an uncharacteristic swish at Browne and was well caught by St Hill in the deep for 53. Soon after Sutcliffe edged Griffith and was caught at the wicket. Tyldesley did not last long, and England found themselves three down for 131. The West Indians failed to press home their advantage and Jardine and Hammond gradually turned things around. Their partnership was worth 120 when Hammond fell to a brilliant catch by Roach off Connie, who took particular satisfaction in once again triumphing over his bitter foe. Chapman pulled a muscle and had to retire. Jardine had reached 83 and looked set for a maiden Test hundred when Connie ran him out with a brilliant piece of fielding. Prior to that the future England captain had incensed the West Indians when he hit his wicket but refused to walk, claiming that he had finished his shot and therefore the ball was dead. The umpire gave him the benefit of the doubt. Jardine was technically correct, but the haughty way he had behaved rankled with the West Indians. Most had been raised on the idea that the English were all terrifically sporting gentlemen who would rather stop a bullet than exploit a loophole or employ gamesmanship. To discover otherwise was a profound shock. Later, when C. L. R. James made some remark to Connie, comparing unfavourably the behaviour of West Indian club cricketers with that of those in the county game, his friend erupted in a rare fit of rage shouting, 'No, no, they are no better than we.' Perhaps it was the patrician Jardine he had in mind.

England posted a first-innings lead of 145 – not as many as it might have been, but given the brittleness of the tourists batting against Freeman and Jupp, surely more than enough.

So it proved. Challenor and Roach were both out for ducks. St Hill and Martin batted well to add 55, but then a couple of quick wickets fell just before close of play, leaving the tourists on 71 for four. The next day's play lasted less than an hour. Freeman took five for 39, backed up by the slow left-arm of Jack 'Farmer' White, captain of the side in Chapman's absence, who took three for 41.

This crushing defeat knocked the stuffing out of the West Indians. They travelled up to Llandudno to play Wales in a gloomy mood. It was to be their second encounter with Barnes. On a damp wicket and with a moist sea breeze blowing in from the bay, the master bowler was in his element. In the first innings he took seven for 51 and in the second five for 67 despite fielders dropping Challenor three times off his bowling. Wales won easily. Drawn matches followed against Leicestershire, Somerset, Glamorgan and Gloucestershire.

Before the final Test at the Oval, the West Indies resolved to do better on the famously excellent, fast wicket. Nunes won the toss and again chose to bat. Challenor and Roach got off to a flying start, adding 91 in just seventy minutes, and Connie made a belligerent 37, his highest score of the series, but the final total of 238 all out was a poor one. Tate had done most of the damage with his probing medium pace, backed up by the speed of Hammond and Larwood. The Sussex seamer seemed unconcerned, however. He regarded the games against the West Indies as a bit of a waste of time, devoting only a couple of paragraphs to them in his autobiography and concluding that they didn't really count as Test matches.

It certainly didn't seem much of a test for England's batsmen, who scored 438. Facing a monumental struggle, the West Indies again buckled. Martin scored a brave 41, but no other batsman made it to twenty. For the third time England had crushed the West Indies inside three days without having to bat twice. Tate's attitude may have seemed patronising, but perhaps he had a point.

In the penultimate game of the tour, against Sir Julian Cahn's XI at the Folkestone Festival, Connie delighted the crowd by striking 62 in forty-five minutes in a high-scoring draw. Leveson Gower again sent out a powerful side to play the West Indians in their final match at Scarborough. There was to be no repeat of the nail-biting excitement of 1923, however. Hobbs made 119 against a fierce barrage from Connie, who took seven for 68 in the first innings. He then enlivened proceedings with a rapid half-century.

Despite these performances the tour ended with an eight-wicket defeat.

Five wins and twelve defeats in their thirty first-class matches was a disappointment for the West Indians. The disastrous second Test seemed to shatter their self-confidence – certainly the tourists' record before that match was much better than after it. They won four games before Old Trafford and only one following it. Fatigue was also a factor. The West Indians were not used to playing cricket six days a week, nor over such a long period. Many of the players had struggled to adapt to local conditions. The ball turned and swung more than they were used to and came on to the bat far slower. The swinging ball in particular was something they struggled to deal with, especially when confronted by masters such as Tate and Barnes.

The West Indian fast bowling at least had left an impression. Herbert Sutcliffe told Warner during the Lord's Test that he had 'never faced finer fast bowling'. Even Tate had good words to say. He thought Connie, Francis and Grifith 'very good bowlers when the ball was lifting' and recalled a delivery at the Oval from Connie shortly after rain had fallen that jumped so alarmingly from a length that Hendren, who had played forward, found it flying 'far over his head'.

Wisden was sniffy about the West Indies' performance, wondering if the heavy defeats against England had not proved that the visitors had been given Test status too hastily. Wyatt's assessment was more charitable than most. He felt the tourists were an attractive and entertaining side who were always worth watching, but that they had a number of weaknesses, the chief of which was against slow bowling, 'which they never seemed to master'. While Warner, seeking reasons why the team might have underperformed, wondered if perhaps their 'somewhat mercurial temperament' had been affected by travails in the cold weather of May and had never recovered.

Connie's poor showing in the Tests was thought by some to have undermined his self-belief and he had struggled with injuries from June onwards. Despite his fitness regime he was also dog-tired. Across England people were eager to see him play. As Harry Mallett knew, Connie was box office, and so forced to play in practically every game to ensure the financial success of the tour. Connie was the only tourist who ended the trip as a player everyone could agree was of international calibre. He was, as Warner noted, 'the biggest personality in the side'. He finished second in the West Indians' batting averages with 1381 runs at 34.52 and topped the bowling with 107 wickets at 22.95, becoming one of the few cricketers to complete the double while touring.

Connie's figures in the Tests – five wickets at more than 50 apiece and 89 runs in six innings – were unimpressive, but he had still made a lasting impression. He was one of the quickest bowlers in the world and always ran to the wicket with a dynamic intensity that suggested excitement was imminent. Like many great bowlers – Shane Warne might be a good recent example – he always gave the impression that, even when he was swung away for six, it was all a part of his masterplan.

Like his bowling, Connie's batting tended to operate at only one speed – fast. He had a good eye, quick reflexes, nimble feet and supple wrists, which combined allowed him to play unorthodox shots – glancing, cutting, driving and pulling from outside off stump in a style that would later become familiar with great West Indian cricketers such as Viv Richards. He rarely bothered with defence and as a consequence no innings ever lasted long. But even his short assaults could be enough to turn a game on its head – as he showed against Middlesex at Lord's. It was just the sort of batting that would succeed in matches restricted to six or seven hours on a Saturday afternoon. Which was, of course, one of the reasons why Connie's plan to use the tour to secure a professional contract for himself had succeeded.

Chapter 5

Cricket for the Atomic Age

The men from Lancashire had been watching Connie during the summer tour. His performance at Lord's convinced them that he was their man. That season the club they represented, Nelson, had won the Lancashire League title, the Worsley Cup and the Junior League Championship. But the team's star and professional Jim Blanckenberg, a South African who had played thirteen times for his country, had announced his intention to leave for a more lucrative contract at East Lancashire, the league's wealthiest club.

Nelson were not wealthy. In fact, they were in deep financial trouble. Gates had been poor for many years and the club was three thousand pounds in the red. Many felt Nelson should go for a cheaper professional, someone local, until their economic situation had stabilised. Instead, the committee opted to gamble.

The three men who approached Connie after the Middlesex match offered him a three-year contract that – after some haggling involving the ever-helpful Charlie Macartney – bettered that of the highest-paid Lancashire

League professional. What's more, they promised him talent money (performance bonuses), passage from the Caribbean and leave to return every winter. Connie had become increasingly frustrated with life in Trinidad, a place where, like his father before him, he found himself, to paraphrase James, being treated as a first-class cricketer but a third-class citizen. Nelson was the opportunity he had craved, indeed financially it far exceeded anything he had hoped for, yet he did not bite right away.

Before he made any decision Connie did what he always did when faced with an important choice: he consulted his wife Norma. Connie had first met Norma Cox in Port of Spain in 1921. A pretty, intelligent girl, the daughter of a chemist who had died when she was young, she had lived all her life in the capital and exuded a certain big-city sophistication. Theirs was a long and often tricky court-ship. Between work, travel and cricket, the couple rarely found much time to spend together. Eventually Norma had become so frustrated that she had issued an ultimatum: cricket or me. She would recall with a fond smile Connie's heartbroken response, 'Please let it be cricket and you. I can't give up either.' Norma might have found Connie's frequent absences at matches, nets or on foreign tours irritating, but she stuck by him loyally. In response, Connie had focused more sharply on the game he was becoming increasingly certain would provide security for their future. They were eventually married on 25 July 1927. A daughter, Gloria, was born the following April, a few weeks before Connie had set off on that momentous tour to England. Norma would be the focal point of Connie's life, his 'comrade, adviser and inspiration'. When he explained Nelson's offer to her, she was in little doubt that they must take it. Connie was twenty-seven years old and at his peak as a player; such a chance might not come again. The upheaval in Norma's own life would be immense. While Connie had his work on the cricket field to occupy him, she was often left isolated at home in a foreign town far removed from anything she was used to. She remained calm and brave throughout, backing her husband all the way. Indeed, at times during their early days in Lancashire it would only be Norma's determination and cool head that prevented Connie throwing in the towel and returning home.

Nelson was a cotton town that specialised in high-quality textiles. When Connie and Norma arrived (Gloria was left with relatives in Trinidad for the first year they were in Lancashire) the town was relatively prosperous, with an unemployment rate much lower than the national average. The Wall Street Crash changed things dramatically. Textiles were particularly hard hit by the economic crisis: many smaller mills closed, others operated on much lower capacity with fewer workers, and wages were reduced. While the mills of Nelson were less vulnerable to cheaper foreign imports than those of Oldham, Burnley and Rochdale, which made lower-quality material, joblessness in the town still rose to 25 per cent in 1931. (In nearby Burnley, around a third of the workforce were unemployed.) Unemployment created not only poverty but also uncertainty. There were strikes in the mills and widespread disillusionment with mainstream political parties, while extremists on both the left and right gained ground. Gradually the situation stabilised, with unemployment dropping to 12 per cent by 1936, but with the rest of the Lancashire cotton belt struggling to survive, playing in the Lancashire League opened Connie's eyes to the reality of life for the English working class. He would write much later of his realisation that 'When I was a young boy in

Trinidad, going to school and picking fruit and vegetables from the garden, Hargreaves, the captain of Nelson, my exact contemporary, was working in a cotton mill.' It was not a distinction Connie envied.

Aside from the cinema, sport was the main recreational activity. As well as the cricket club, Nelson boasted a team that played in the Third Division (North) of the Football League and had, a few years earlier, defeated Real Madrid during a pre-season tour of Spain.

The streets of Nelson were hilly, cobbled and, or so it must have seemed to the new arrivals from Trinidad, perpetually rain-swept. Connie and Norma took up residence in a tiny terraced house in Howard Street with a grumpy landlady who made it plain they were there under sufferance. The house was just opposite Whitfield Elementary School. After the home-time bell the children would line up by the Constantines' front window and take it in turns to peep in, watching the strangers from the Caribbean going about their daily lives. It was like some early form of reality TV show, albeit one for which the participants had not volunteered. Connie found those first weeks taxing in the extreme. Nelson was a tight-knit community into which strangers rarely ventured. There was only one other black person in the town, a rag-and-bone man. Connie was pointed at in the street; children asked if his skin colour was the result of working down a mine, or if it would wash off with soap and water. Letters arrived daily, some offering welcome and support, others beginning 'Dear Nigger' and degenerating from there. The scrutiny was hard to bear, the questioning worse, but gradually, with Norma always a calming presence, Connie came to see that much of what he encountered was not racism, but curiosity born of ignorance. Nelson was a tough, working-class town whose inhabitants had grown up together. For an outsider, making a home in such a community would never be easy, but gradually Connie's charm and infectious laugh broke down barriers, and in an area steeped in the traditions of nonconformism – temperance hotels serving draught sarsaparilla were commonplace – the fact that Connie did not smoke or gamble, and rarely drank more than a half-pint of mild, stood him in good stead.

The change was gradual, and greatly helped by the arrival, in Connie's second season, of Gloria (as anyone who has lived in a small town will know, there is nothing like a child for helping you make friends). Eventually Connie was playing dominoes in the tap room of the Red Lion in Earby, and joining Nelson's most famous – and noisy – supporter Alwayn Nightingale in the Nelson Preparatory Workers Club. He came to appreciate the warmth and good humour of the Lancastrians, which seemed to chime with his own personality and those of his friends in Trinidad. 'For every one insult there were ten thousand human expressions of warmth and friendship towards me,' he would later remember.

And then, of course, there was the cricket. Nelson's Seedhill was an idyllic ground. C. L. R. James thought it 'as pretty a ground as you will see anywhere'. On the outskirts of town, bounded on three sides by open country, the view from the pavilion was not of the smoke-wreathed mills of popular conception (though they were there in the town below) but of hills, fields and woodland 'as beautiful as it seems only the English countryside can be'. Like all the Lancashire League grounds, Seedhill was spick and span, the pavilion freshly painted every year, the trophies and the brasses of the function and committee rooms polished until they glowed. Seedhill might not have been

Lord's, but it was a place of civic pride, both loved and respected.

Cricket had become popular in the area around Nelson during Victorian times. When the Ten Hours Act had been introduced in 1847, reducing the working week to fifty-five and a half hours, there had been fears that working men would use their increased leisure time for drinking and gambling. To prevent that happening, new cricket clubs were formed across Lancashire, often with the help of Methodist and other nonconformist organisations that were committed to clean living and self-improvement. Cricket was considered a wholesome activity – which, compared with many of the alternatives, it plainly was.

The Lancashire League grew out of the North West Cricket League that, inspired by the format of the Football League, had been founded in 1890. The Lancashire League that Connie entered had barely changed since 1899, when a rule that allowed two professionals per team was amended to permit just the one. The Lancashire League contained fourteen clubs, all within thirty miles of one another.* They played each other twice, home and away, each season in League matches, and also competed in a midweek knock-out competition, the Worsley Cup. Fierce rivalries built up. Haslingden and Bacup, Church and Accrington, Nelson and Colne were locked in parochial battles with long histories and perceived grievances on both sides. The animosity was so strong that, on occasion, the police had to be called after fights broke out.

The arrangement of League matches was sacrosanct. One innings per side, with no time or overs limit. Wickets

---

* By the time Connie joined the Lancashire League, one of the founder clubs, Bury, had quit and been replaced by Todmorden, just across the county line in Yorkshire.

were covered at both ends, so that rain did not interfere as much as it did in first-class cricket, where wickets were left uncovered. Games began on Saturday afternoon at two o'clock and ended at seven, with additional minutes added for lost time. The timing of matches was of the upmost importance, and the watches of the umpires, scorers and captains were synchronised before start of play. Clearly the timed finish lent itself to gamesmanship. In tightly contested matches the temptation to waste time with field placings and the like was plain, and a source of bitter contention. Burnley's Australian professional, Arthur Richardson, notoriously shifted the field continuously during a rancorous encounter at Rawtenstall that ended in a draw with the home side apparently poised for victory. Richardson was booed off the field by an angry crowd and the Burnley team required a police escort when they left the ground. The League wrote to Richardson, explaining that while his tactics were not illegal they considered them 'indiscreet'. Richardson responded in a robust letter which the League minutes described as 'the most impertinent ever addressed to the League'. He was fined, and the letter destroyed so that future generations would not be exposed to its indecency

In the inter-war years most people employed in manufacturing worked a half-shift on Saturday morning, leaving them free to watch sport in the afternoon. The ritual of finishing work, returning home for lunch and then heading off to football or cricket was one that persisted for well over half a century, and League cricket, with its post-lunch start, fitted in with it perfectly. In fine weather the Lancashire League guaranteed a full five hours of cricket for the entrance fee. Most working people had neither the time nor the money to travel miles for their sporting entertainment, so local clubs thrived. And why would you bother to take a train or a bus when the Lancashire League boasted cricketers such as Connie?

During Connie's heyday the clubs attracted large crowds, generally bringing in gate receipts of around three hundred pounds, with money also spent at the tea hutch and in the clubhouse. Admission prices ranged from threepence to one shilling, and membership levels were high. Those who wanted a seat were advised to arrive early. Others were happy to arrive at start of play and stand for five hours.

The Lancashire League operated in isolation: it was outside the control of the MCC – guardians of most cricket in England – and was much more egalitarian than the first-class game. There were no separate entrances to dressing rooms for amateurs and pros, nor any other distinction based on class or – as in the Caribbean – colour. It was a little world all to itself, drawing strength from its parochialism. Here, Connie noted approvingly, 'a cricketer is just a cricketer and nothing else'.

The Lancashire League clubs had hired professionals from the start. Initially these were journeymen cricketers whose main task was the upkeep of the ground, a tradition that would continue for decades – even big names like Hedley Verity and Bill Alley were expected to do their bit mowing the outfield and preparing the wicket. All that changed in 1897, when Yorkshire sacked the brilliant and often drunk all-rounder Bobby Peel and Accrington stepped in and hired him for the following season. Peel was a mercurial genius, one of the finest slow bowlers of his day, a forceful batsman and the sort of maverick personality that has always appealed to sports fans. Whatever Accrington paid Peel they easily recouped in increased gate receipts and memberships. Other clubs took note. The quality of the professionals rose. In 1901 Burnley's pro, S. F. Barnes – who'd previously been at Rishton – was picked to tour Australia with Archie MacLaren's England side. He took nineteen wickets in his first two Test matches. Cec Parkin, the chirpy and truculent England all-rounder who would incense the MCC by writing a newspaper article arguing that a professional should be made captain of England, played five seasons for Church, taking close to five hundred wickets for them and opening a tobacconist's in the town. In 1910 Bacup and Rawtenstall became the first Lancashire League clubs to hire overseas professionals – Alexander Kermode and Elicius Dwyer, both Australians who had played county cricket. Neither was of the highest class, but Dwyer holds the unique distinction of being the only man with seven initials ever to play first-class cricket (his full name was John Elicius Benedict Bernard Placid Quirk Carrington Dwyer).

Then Accrington took things up a notch and signed the Lancashire League's first overseas star. Charlie Llewellyn was – reputedly – the son of a white Englishman and a black woman from Saint Helena. Born in Pietermaritzburg and raised in poverty, he emerged as a hard-hitting left-hand bat and bowler of either medium pace or conventional slow left-arm spin into which he mixed a cunningly disguised googly. Llewellyn had first played for South Africa in 1896,* and by 1910 he was playing county cricket for Hampshire and doing it so well that he was named as one of *Wisden*'s Cricketers of the Year. Twelve months later he quit Hampshire to join Accrington – apparently telling the county that with a wife and three small children to support

---

* Llewellyn played fifteen Tests for South Africa between 1896 and 1912. The next non-white player selected for South Africa was Omar Henry in 1992.

he needed the extra money. Llewellyn was something different, his strokeplay devastatingly stylish, his bowling astute and clever, his cover fielding breath-taking. Massive crowds turned up to watch him. In his first season with the club, Accrington's gate receipts doubled. The South African stayed at Thorneyholme Road for ten seasons, taking close to a thousand wickets, nearly a hundred catches and making 6276 runs, including a League record knock of 188 not out against Bacup. It was a record Connie would eventually break.

Llewellyn had set new standards in terms of style and he had opened the eyes of the clubs to the benefits of signing foreign stars – something which in those days was largely missing from the county circuit.

In 1922 Nelson astounded the cricket world when they elected to replace their pro George Geary – an England Test player with thirteen thousand first-class runs and more than two thousand wickets to his name – with the great Australian fast bowler Ted McDonald, a year after he and his new-ball partner Jack Gregory had destroyed England in the Ashes. The signing of McDonald – allegedly paid sixteen pounds a week by the club – caused a huge furore, because while Lancashire League supporters were delighted at the chance of seeing the great paceman, the cricket establishment was not so positive. *Wisden* editor Sydney Pardon highlighted what he considered the absurdity of somebody playing in a Test at Lord's one day and then going off to play for a Pennine village team the next. It was a common refrain at the time, and would remain so for many decades.

When George Headley signed to play for Haslingden, Lionel Tennyson (by now the Third Baron Tennyson) felt moved to write, 'This trafficking in foreign players is unwholesome, if not positively offensive ... I make no mistake when I declare that every native boy with an aptitude for cricket dreams of the day when he will be "bought" by some English boss.' As Connie pointed out, his lordship was apparently unaware of the difference between slavery and free enterprise.

That the leagues were paying more than the counties added to the rage. Just as today some people are affronted by news of a footballer leaving the English Premier League to go and play in China, so the authorities now condemned McDonald for having the temerity to reject life as an amateur in the Sheffield Shield in favour of making a good living from the game in the 'lesser competition' of the Lancashire League. Unsurprisingly, it was men with large private incomes, such as Tennyson and Hawke, who were most affronted by the notion of cricketers earning money.

McDonald eventually left Seedhill after three seasons, during which he had exceeded all expectations (his greatest performance was taking ten Burnley wickets for 18 runs). He had qualified by residence to play for Lancashire, and now joined the county club. The thought that county cricket might soon be flooded by foreign professionals caused another pompous outcry. More revealing was the fact that, shortly before moving to Lancashire, the Australian signed a two-year extension to his Nelson contract. This little deal seems to have been beneficial for both player and club – the county reputedly bought out McDonald's contract for two hundred pounds and agreed that Lancashire would play a first-class fixture at Seedhill as a goodwill gesture. McDonald, meanwhile, had likely pushed up his wages at the county, who must at least have matched what his new contract at Nelson was offering. It was the sort of smart wheeler-dealing the League clubs specialised in, and something that Connie would come to exploit and enjoy. Indeed, Connie's sense of his own financial value would be sneered at by some, one of his amateur West Indian team mates intimating to a British journalist on the 1939 tour that the great all-rounder knew far more about money than cricket.

Connie's wages at Nelson were massive by the sporting standards of the day. His initial contract was worth six hundred pounds per season, plus bonuses of between two hundred and fifty and five hundred pounds, and travelling expenses from the Caribbean for his family. On top of that there would be collections – this was a league-cricket tradition that rewarded good performances by both the professional and his amateur team mates. When a batsman scored fifty, or a bowler took five wickets for less than a certain number of runs, a hat was passed around the crowd so they could express their approval in coppers and six-pences. A successful pro might reasonably expect to live on his collections money and bank his salary. When the future Yorkshire great Emmott Robinson played for Ramsbottom before the First World War, he brought a stout canvas bag with him to every game to carry the coins home in.

Even without the cash collections Connie's pay was more than most county cricketers earned in a long, hard six-days-a-week season. Surrey paid Jack Hobbs something in the region of £780 in the mid-twenties, but he was the biggest star in the English game. It was close to double the maximum wage of a professional footballer (England centre-forward Tommy Lawton played for Burnley Cricket Club during Connie's time, and once picked up a collection after scoring a half-century that was the size of his monthly wage packet at Everton). Whether Connie was the highest-paid sportsman in Britain at the time is hard to judge – boxers such as the world lightweight champion Jack 'Kid' Berg likely earned more – but what we can say is that his earnings were comparable to that of a doctor or solicitor, and six or seven times the annual wage of a mill worker or coal miner. Financially, at least, the Constantine family had joined the English middle class.

It was George Pope who told the Australian Cec Pepper – the only professional whose reputation would come close to matching Connie's – that, 'The important thing as a pro is that when you are on the field you project your personality.' This was something that came naturally to Connie, who had charmed and amazed crowds wherever he had played. His showmanship was natural. Some, however, felt that his time in League cricket had led him to overdo things. Jack Hobbs for one thought that Connie was too concerned with the reaction of the crowd and that at times his antics descended into pantomime, while the cricket writer Sir Home Gordon observed that Connie was 'a shrewd chap who felt that it paid to clown'. He claimed that in conversation Connie had suggested that he was aware of the situation, but, Gordon went on, 'Why should he be blamed, when it brought him annually sums of money larger than anyone else had obtained from actual matches?'

There was a feeling in traditional cricket circles that the style of Lancashire League cricket was generally designed to appeal to non-cricket fans – an accusation often levelled at limited-overs cricket in the seventies and latterly at T20. The notion that those watching league games were actually football fans who didn't appreciate the subtleties and style of 'proper cricket' was a comfort to purists, who were aware that annually Nelson attracted bigger crowds than many counties.

That there were theatrical incidents which would not have been condoned in first-class cricket is undeniable. Fred Root relates an episode involving Connie and the Todmorden wicketkeeper Tommy Carrick. Carrick was a vociferous appealer, yelling for anything that looked close. Against Nelson, with Connie batting, Carrick called out 'Owzat?' for an lbw. Connie turned swiftly 'leered at Carrick, and howled "Not out"' at ear-piercing volume. This incident startled the diminutive wicketkeeper, who confessed to Root at the end of the over that Connie had 'feared him', and that he didn't think he dared appeal any more. Root reassured him, and when the incident was repeated in the following over Carrick responded to Connie's performance by rising to his full height and shouting 'Thee shirrup. I'm not asking thee; I'm asking t'umpire.' It was not the sort of behaviour that Lord Hawke would have applauded.

Yet the notion that Lancashire League matches were not actually cricket, but some kind of showboating carnival should be dismissed. The former England, Derbyshire and Worcestershire medium-pacer Root was the professional at Todmorden. A tough and at times cynical man, whose experiences on the first-class circuit had left him with a bitter taste in his mouth, Root was unequivocal in his praise for the Lancashire League, which he felt was the home of 'cricket as I understand and appreciate the game'. It was cricket that 'is scrupulously fair, never sentimental, and is just what the public thrive on'. He noted that the first-class counties looked down their noses at the Lancashire League, likening it 'in their own minds to a circus or music hall version of the game', but considered this to be inaccurate and narrow-minded. He believed the League provided top-class cricket and praised those who organised it for 'disregarding any MCC rule which, in their opinion, would spoil the game ... They make their own local rules and make them extremely well ... Never have I played in any sort of cricket that provides greater thrills than the Lancashire League.'

As Root told it, Lancashire League crowds were exceptionally knowledgeable, the cricket extremely well organised and of a high standard, 'the amateurs comparing with many county players and the professionals among the best in the world'.

He did not give praise easily (his general view was that cricket had never recovered after the First World War, and that the standard in the inter-war years was poor, 'with many players winning caps who would not have got in a county second XI in 1914'), so his views carry weight. Other professionals who played league cricket in Lancashire tend to have formed similar opinions. The games were hard fought and competitive – as one later pro, Basil D'Oliveira commented, the crowd expected the team to 'shed blood for the cause'. Besides, it seems unlikely that a hard-bitten professional like S. F. Barnes would have involved himself in anything resembling a circus.

Whatever his style of play, for the star pro it was not merely a case of turning up. As Connie wrote: 'Any first-class cricketer ... whoever he may be or whatever he has done who believes that he can just walk into the League and proceed to be a success is making a great mistake.'

High-class professionals came and went during Connie's years in the Lancashire League. Accrington had the Australian Test all-rounder Alan Fairfax; another Australian test player, Arthur Richardson, was at Bacup for three seasons and was succeeded by Ted McDonald when the paceman had finished his time with Lancashire; Burnley signed Connie's West Indies team mate Manny Martindale; Church had Alby Roberts, a New Zealand Test player, and later the medium-pacer Lennox Brown of South Africa; Colne had the great Indian all-rounder Amar Singh; at East Lancashire Jim Blanckenberg was followed by two New Zealand Test cricketers, Ian Cromb and Bill Merritt; Jamaican batting genius George Headley spent four seasons at Haslingden, Trinidadian Edwin St Hill three at Lowerhouse; Ramsbottom had Australia's Sid Hird, who'd five first-class hundreds for New South Wales to his name; Rawtenstall had the South African off-spinner Jim McNally; Rishton also employed Bill Merritt, and he was succeeded by two Australians, Bill Hunt, a slow left-armer who'd played a single Test, and all-rounder Bert Tobin, who'd come close to playing for his country in the Bodyline series; Todmorden had tearaway England fast bowler Nobby Clark, then his England Test colleagues Fred Root and George Macaulay. Some of the pros were highly successful and massively popular, others were not.

Connie outlined the appetite for cricket in Nelson: 'On any fine afternoon in the week there are three nets going, the first division, the second division and the colts, it is nothing surprising to have thirty or forty people practising and hundreds of people looking on estimating the form for the coming matches.' In such an environment reputation counted for little, as the great Test player Hugh Tayfield of South Africa discovered during a difficult season with East Lancashire in 1956.

Seedhill might not have been as hot as the Port of Spain Savannah, but in the commitment and determination of his Nelson team mates Connie must have been reminded of his days playing for Shannon. The Lancashire League players took the game seriously; they were performing not just for themselves, but for the honour of the communities they represented. They worked for one another and gave everything they had. It was an attitude Connie shared. Often frustrated by the lack of team spirit in the West Indies Test side, he found it in abundance at Nelson and thrived as a result.

In Connie's nine seasons at Seedhill, Nelson would win the Lancashire League title seven times, finish runners-up twice and appear in three Worsley Cup finals, winning two of them. However brilliant his performances, it would be a mistake to think that Nelson's success was solely down to Connie. After all, during McDonald's time as pro they had failed to win a single title, missing out twice to Bacup, whose professional was the far less illustrious Archie Slater.

Connie found himself in a strong team – Root estimated it to be of Minor Counties strength – and opening the bowling for many years with Alf Pollard, a very capable amateur seamer of whom Connie said 'he never bowled a full toss or long hop in ten years at Seedhill'. During his nineteen years playing in the Lancashire League, Pollard took 1390 wickets by, in his own modest words, 'doing a bit either way off the pitch or in the air'. Clifford 'Chick' Hawkwood was one of the mainstays of Nelson's batting when Connie first arrived, and Connie thought very highly of him. He even persuaded his team mate to try to make a go of it with Lancashire. In his first Roses match Hawkwood hit a century. He would spend five seasons at Old Trafford without ever quite reaching those heights again. Johnny Greenwood was also a fine batsman. In 1935 he scored 721 runs at an average of 37.94. Sadly for Nelson, his performance was duly noted by Farnworth of the Bolton League, who persuaded him to join them as a professional. Alec Birtwell was another of Connie's team mates at Nelson. A gifted amateur sportsman, he had once played such a defensive innings for

Lancashire against Kent that Neville Cardus described him in the *Guardian* as 'a more or less agile sandbag'. The club captain, Harold Hargreaves, who had greeted Connie and Norma at Liverpool docks on the day they arrived, was a talented bowler and another mainstay of the side.

Connie began his career with Nelson in April 1929. However much he Norma were struggling to adjust to life off the field, on it the Trinidadian was an instant success. Nelson won the first six matches of the season convincingly. In his first home match, against Bacup, Connie hit 87, sharing a partnership of 102 for the third wicket with Chick Hawkwood. A month later, Connie hit a spectacular century and in company with Hawkwood broke the club record for a second-wicket stand. The first encounter with East Lancashire and Jim Blanckenberg drew a crowd of over ten thousand to Seedhill. It was to be a fearsome clash.

When the two men had bumped into each other in the street earlier in the season Blanckenberg had assured Connie that race was not an issue as far as he was concerned. That, at least, was how Connie interpreted things. In truth Blanckenberg's attitude to non-whites seems to have been consistent with that of South Africa's apartheid regime. In a notorious later incident at a testimonial match to raise money for Lancashire player Jack Iddon, Blanckenberg refused to have a drink with George Headley, saying, 'I'm a great admirer of your cricket, but where I come from we don't fraternise with you fellows.'

At Nelson, when Blanckenberg came out to bat Connie offered him his hand – a conciliatory gesture designed to placate a crowd whose passions could run high. Instead of taking it the South African simply turned his back. Connie felt insulted. Furious, he unleashed a string of bouncers, all aimed at Blanckenberg's head and chest.

However repugnant his views on race, Blanckenberg was certainly courageous. He took everything Connie dished out without flinching and scored 77 before the West Indian clean-bowled him. At the end of the match Blanckenberg walked into the Nelson dressing room wearing only a raincoat, opened it to reveal a body covered in livid bruises and shouted to Nelson's skipper, 'Look what that bloody pro of yours has done to me!' Connie offered no apology.*

Another fierce encounter was the clash with Nelson's deadliest local rivals, Colne. Connie would later recall that as an outsider he did not share the chronic rivalry that the amateur players had with one another. Nevertheless, he was quickly brought into the bitter spirit of the thing when several members of the Colne side sledged him in terms that were, he felt, 'meant to wound' – a phrase that suggests a racial element. Connie, it should be said, had been nursing a grievance against Colne pro Archie Slater since the West Indians' tour of 1928. Slater had been playing for Derbyshire at the time, and words were exchanged between the two after Slater had apparently stepped over the line with some of his comments.

Slater was a bowler good enough to have twice taken all ten wickets in a Lancashire League match (a feat matched only by Roy Gilchrist, Cec Pepper, Fred Hartley and Tom Lancaster), and when Connie batted against Slater he faced an added problem: the orchestrated appealing of the Colne side. Whenever Connie was struck on the pad or beaten by a delivery a huge chorus of 'Owzat!' went up from the fielders. Since some of the appeals began before the ball

* Blanckenberg retired from cricket after his time with Nelson. It has been suggested that he was a Nazi sympathiser and went to live in Hitler's Germany: he is thought to have died in West Berlin, though there is no formal record of his death. *Wisden* did not publish an obituary.

had even arrived at the wicket, Connie perceived it as premeditated cheating. A firm believer in fair play, he was furious. When Colne batted he unleashed a string of vicious bouncers and slammed the ribs of batsman after batsman. His message struck home. Shortly afterwards, a 'peace conference' was called at the Colne president's house; Connie, Slater and representatives of both clubs attended. Slater was ordered to behave himself in future and Connie to refrain from bowling so many bumpers. Hands were shaken. Games between Nelson and Colne would never again be 'like a bloody war'.

These controversies aside, Connie loved the cricket in the Lancashire League. On previous visits to England he had always got on well with professionals such as Patsy Hendren while struggling to find common ground with the gentlemen amateurs who ruled the roost. Connie put this down to his colour. That was certainly a factor, but class played its part too. As an aspiring professional cricketer, Connie was effectively a tradesperson, and no gentleman was going to spend his days drinking with plumbers. In the Lancashire League there was no class divide and the cricket was played in a manner that perfectly suited Connie's style. 'It may be "cricket" under certain circumstances for two batsmen to camp at the wicket and knock up double centuries apiece in the course of two or three days,' Connie wrote, 'but the average cricket lover would much rather put down his money to see a sparkling 50 knocked up in half an hour.' Playing for Nelson, he said, 'opened out and enriched my life, because for the first time I was doing what I enjoyed doing for a living'. His joy in playing the game transmitted itself to spectators. Connie took delight in entertaining. His fast, aggressive bowling and big hitting were crowd-pleasing in themselves, but it was once again his fielding that people remembered. Connie retained his speed across the ground and his bullet-like throw, while his catching was as athletic and agile as ever. To this he added a few mischievous tweaks, snatching a catch at slip and pocketing the ball, or getting under a skier in the covers and catching it one-handed behind his back. Watching cricket writer Roy Genders was suitably thrilled. 'This surely,' he wrote of Connie, 'was cricket that heralded the atomic age.'

With the nuclear Trinidadian Nelson retained their League title, Connie contributing 820 runs at an average of 34 and 88 wickets at 12 apiece as well as saving hundreds of runs with his brilliant fielding. The impact of Connie on the spectators who loved what Root called his thrilling and virile cricket was shown in the 1929 Seedhill gate receipts: £2112-6s-7d was taken through the turnstiles, almost double the revenue of the previous double-winning season. Crowds had risen from a high of eight thousand to four-teen thousand (quite a crowd in a town with a population of forty thousand). Nelson's gamble had paid off. In three seasons Connie's drawing power would wipe out the club's debt and leave them handsomely in profit. Memberships at Seedhill would rise until they outstripped even those at glamorous East Lancashire. Not only did Connie help Nelson, he also put around a hundred pounds on the gate at away fixtures too. Between 1929 and 1933 it is estimated that Connie boosted attendances at Lancashire League matches by around fifty thousand. Nelson broke box office records season after season. At East Lancashire in 1931 spectators paid £340-14s-0d to see Connie and his team mates in action; at Burnley the following year the take was £340-5s-10d. At Seedhill for the Worsley Cup clash with Colne in 1935 the crowd paid £367-13s-7d, a record that

would stand for nineteen years. The adult admission price
during this period was sixpence.

In his first season Connie's performances had been brilliant, but he had also forged strong bonds with his team
mates, creating the sense of kinship he had often found
missing on West Indies tours. He never lorded it over the
amateurs, treating them with respect as fellow cricketers,
and offering advice and encouragement. It is a measure
of his success that at the end of the season, when Nelson
went on a short tour of Scotland, they asked Connie to captain the side. He celebrated in the opening game against
Northern Counties at Inverness by smashing 175 not out
including four sixes and twenty-nine fours. One mighty hit
flew straight out of Northern Meetings Park and landed in
the garden of the Provost of the Cathedral. Nelson won by
271 runs. The rest of the tour saw Connie on fine form with
the ball, picking up seven wickets against Morayshire, six
in the match with Ayr and five in the fixture with West of
Scotland.

Gloria joined Connie and Norma in 1930. The family
moved to a new home in Buccleuch Street. By the end of the
summer, thanks to Connie's earnings, they'd move again to
a two-up, two-down stone-built terrace in Meredith Street,
overlooking a bowling green in a more middle-class part
of the town. Connie also acquired a car, an Austin 7 – still
quite a novelty in the cotton towns. He and his small family
would use it to drive out into the countryside for picnics, or
to visit the hothouses of Marsden Park, where the tropical
flowers and steamy warmth reminded them of Trinidad.
Sometimes they'd take friends. Gradually Nelson began to
feel like home.

Gloria's arrival was a great help to Norma, who had
spent a lonely first season in Nelson. Norma and Gloria

went to watch all of Connie's big matches, the little girl amusing herself by hopping up and down the pavilion steps. She'd have a happy time at Nelson Preparatory School, a sometimes more difficult one at secondary school in nearby Colne – where being the only black child in the school caused occasional problems – and go on to study at the University of St Andrews – a considerable achievement in the days when two-thirds of university places were reserved for men – before becoming a teacher.

The 1930 season was badly affected by rain: seven of Nelson's fixtures were abandoned. The championship hinged on the meeting with Bacup at Seedhill in the penultimate game of the season. Bacup, for whom Richardson was having a superb year, shaded a narrow victory and carried off the title by just two points. Connie accumulated 621 runs during the truncated season, the highlight coming in July when he blasted 106 not out against Todmorden. He was effective with the ball too, taking eight for 24 at Ramsbottom as the home side was dismissed for 67.

The season also saw another memorable encounter with S. F. Barnes, then the professional at Rawtenstall. Connie came in to bat against the man he considered the greatest bowler of all time with the score on 68 for three. Wickets fell steadily at the other end until nine were down for 118. Connie's contribution was 45, but it had been a struggle largely because Barnes cannily ensured he saw as little of the strike as possible. 'He set two men in the gully, very close in, and two silly mid-ons and neither I nor anyone else could shift them. His bowling was as good as that, and they never looked to be in any danger.' Connie eventually made 98 before falling caught and bowled to the master bowler. He would regard it as one of the best innings of his life.

In 1931 Nelson won seven of the first nine matches (the

other two were abandoned because of rain), and stayed at the top of the table all season, winning the championship by a clear eight points. Connie hit 801 runs and took ninety-one wickets. He was ably supported by Harry Armistead (508 runs), Billy Windle (411 runs) and Alf Pollard (47 wickets).

As well as winning the League, Connie also helped Nelson to victory in the Worsley Cup, played from three o'clock on weekday afternoons to an unusual format that saw the batting team suspending its innings at the end of the over if they had reached 130, and restarting if and when the opposition posted a similar score. Thanks to Connie's bowling, Nelson rarely had to bat twice.

During the course of that season Nelson offered Connie a new contract. It was worth £650 a year plus benefits. Given the boost Connie's electric brand of cricket had given to the club's finances, the pay rise was no more than he was due. As Root observed, 'Constantine deserves it, and he gets it,' before adding a cautionary note: 'but he would not be so fortunate with many county teams.'

Rain-affected wickets and overcast skies saw bowlers dominating the 1932 season. Connie failed to reach five hundred runs, but made up for it by taking ninety-one wickets at 8.15 a piece His best performance came when East Lancashire came to Seedhill. Connie took eight for 21 as the visitors were skittled out for 34. Three days later Connie came close to matching that performance, taking eight for 24 as Rawtenstall subsided to 59 all out.

Connie was the biggest star in the Lancashire League, and found 'the job of a professional to a League club a joyous one'. The game was played in the kind of uncomplicated hard-driving style he loved. Teams set out to win matches. Caution, a besetting vice of the county game, was absent. Batsmen were determined to strike the ball and bowlers to get the opposition out. There were good reasons for this. Playing just one or two days a week, the teams were fresh and able to give their best in every game. There was none of the drudgery, the 'hard yakka' that Root had endured during his days at Derbyshire and Worcestershire, that Barnes resented during his few seasons with Lancashire. As a result there was a bubbling enthusiasm to get on with the game. Cricket was played in all but the most inclement weather. Unlike in county cricket, the players were not 'always looking around the horizon for a drop of rain or a small cloud to obscure the light, and then running thankfully into the pavilion like gingerbread men afraid of melting'. Connie loved playing cricket and would always love it. To see men who were paid to play the game worn down to a point where they had little enthusiasm for it pained him.

A feature of many Lancashire cricket seasons was a game at Blackpool in which mainly Lancashire League pros would play for Sir Julien Cahn's XI or Sir Lindsay Parkinson's XI against Lancashire. Connie's first appearance in this fixture was in 1932, when he lined up alongside Alan Fairfax, Arthur Richardson, Bill Merritt and S. F. Barnes in a match that was part of Frank Watson's benefit year. It was here that Barnes paid what was, for him, a rare compliment. As Connie went out to bat on a rain-reduced day the master bowler called after him, 'Get some, Connie, and show 'em the sort of hitting we have to put up with in the League.' Honoured by Barnes's comment, Connie thrashed 106 not out in just forty-four minutes.

In 1933 Nelson lost the League title to Todmorden by a single point after a surprise defeat to second-bottom Enfield in the final match of the season. Connie scored one thousand runs exactly – a record for Nelson that would stand until another Trinidadian, Larry Gomes, surpassed it in 1977. He was never dismissed for a duck, hit three centuries and seven fifties. He also took ninety-six wickets to give him the best all-round figures ever produced by a Nelson professional. Had he played in all twenty-six League games – he missed two matches to play for the West Indies – then it seems certain he would have completed the double. Amongst Connie's best bowling were eight for 18 against Todmorden and a six for 36 against Rawtenstall. The pick of his batting was the 136 he struck against Rawtenstall; he got good support on a number of occasions from Harry Armistead, a gifted batsman who matched Connie for hundreds that season. Nelson also reached the final of the Worsley Cup, losing to East Lancashire to complete a season of near-misses.

In 1934, while cricket fans in the rest of England eagerly anticipated the county season and the arrival of the Australians, those in East Lancashire had something else on their minds: the forthcoming clash between 'The Nelson of Constantine and Headley's Haslingden'. Fortuitously for those eager to see the great men in combat, Haslingden's first fixture of the season was against Nelson. The West Indies team mates met up before the game which took place on a typically bleak Rossendale day. Nelson batted first and struggled to 170 for 8 before declaring. Constantine was out for a duck, while Headley, in his first League season, was surprised to find himself opening the bowling with his off-spinners (this in fact was standard practice – the pro always got first go with the new ball whatever his bowling style). In reply, Haslingden got off to a shaky start, Connie dismissing one of the openers in his second over. The dismissal brought Headley to the wicket. The Jamaican turned his first ball into the covers and set off for a run, only for Connie to swoop like lightning. Seeing the great man in full flight, Headley's batting partner panicked and turned back to his crease, leaving the Jamaican stranded mid-pitch. Run out first ball. Nelson and Connie triumphed by 60 runs.

After this inauspicious start Headley adapted to the new conditions with customary speed. He abandoned off-spin in favour of brisk medium pace and batted beautifully, setting a new Lancashire League record by scoring 1063 runs. In five seasons with Haslingden, Headley would score 4937 League runs, including nine centuries and thirty-three fifties, and take 264 wickets including five in an innings on sixteen occasions. In 1937 he scored 1360 runs, a Lancashire League record that was eventually broken by Everton Weekes in 1949.

For Connie, 1934 was a mixed bag. He missed five matches through problems with a knee cartilage that slowed up his bowling and made fielding painful. For the first time he felt retirement creeping towards him: 'I could not find my pace properly, I could not move quickly enough on my feet to deal with bowling as I wanted to when I was batting and I am afraid I missed a few catches that Nature firmly forbade me to jump to.' Yet he still managed to take ninety wickets at 8.28. Despite his creaking joints, he was at times devastating with the ball. In the second match of the season, on a chilly day, Bacup were 93 for six chasing Nelson's total of 95. Connie stepped in, picked up a hat-trick, and the match was won a by a single run. The following week, Accrington were the visitors to Seedhill. On a sunny May afternoon a crowd of eight thousand watched their idol take ten wickets for 10 runs in 6.1 overs. At the other end, Alf Pollard bowled six overs and gave away just one run. An extra boosted the Accrington total to 12.

Stories that some Nelson members complained that Connie
had been 'a bit expensive' are likely apocryphal. Connie's
figures were a League record, surpassing the feat of local
amateur left-arm spinner Fred Hartley of Bacup, who had
taken 10–16 against Ramsbottom ten years earlier.

Sixteen days later Connie took eight wickets for 7 runs
as Lowerhouse's batting was demolished for 27. In the
final fixture of the season, Rishton were bowled out for 25,
Connie taking seven wickets for 5 runs. He also made two
centuries that season, against Haslingden and Rishton, finishing with 657 runs. His performances helped Nelson win
the Worsley Cup. In the first round he struck 77 against
Burnley and followed it by taking four wickets for 32. In the
final against East Lancashire at Seedhill he bowled twenty
overs, taking six wickets for 31 as the visitors were bowled
out for 81. He then struck 47 not out as Nelson romped
home by eight wickets.

By the end of the season, however, Connie's knee was
worse than ever. He was sent to a Liverpool nursing home
to have the cartilage removed – a serious operation in those
days, and one that ended many sporting careers. It must
have been a time of worry for Connie and Norma, but the
operation proved a success and he was soon back to full
fitness.

During the course of the 1934 season Connie had been
contacted by Rochdale of the Central Lancashire League.
Arguably the wealthiest club in the North, Rochdale
offered Connie a four-figure salary plus benefits to play
for them. It was clear that even in their new, more stable
situation Nelson could not match such a salary, but in any
case Connie did not want to go – though he was flattered
that Rochdale's figure was even higher than the amount
Accrington had offered Don Bradman for his services

(Connie knew the size of the Australian's salary because it seems Accrington had entrusted him with making the opening approach. He would later recall long telephone conversations between Lancashire and Australia, 'costing pounds per minute'. Eventually Bradman decided to stay at home after he was offered a better job to keep him there) – yet such an increase in salary was hard to ignore, especially since he had now entered his fourth decade.

By now matches featuring Connie were accounting for just under half of the Lancashire League's total gate receipts. Losing the West Indian to a rival league would not only affect Nelson, but the other thirteen clubs too. In an extraordinary move, the Lancashire League committee agreed to subsidise Connie's pay with a benefit worth between two hundred and fifty and five hundred pounds.

Other clubs initially reacted badly to what was a clear breach of the League's own rules on impartiality. League secretary William Barlow responded by declaring that '£250 was not too great a sum to show that the other clubs in the League were grateful for the financial benefit conferred upon them by the remarkable drawing power of the most attractive professional the League has ever had'. Recognising when they were on to a good thing, the clubs fell into line. Connie stayed at Nelson.

In the autumn of 1934 Connie received an invitation from the Nawab of Moin-ud-Dowlah to coach in Hyderabad. Connie duly accepted, and after the long sea voyage via the Suez Canal arrived in India to find himself treated like royalty. He was driven around in a Rolls-Royce, saw the Taj Mahal by moonlight and was shown the Viceregal Lodge. He stayed in the Maharajah's palace, where 'I was given a suite of rooms, and to describe the place would be to recount the marvels of the Arabian

nights. Gold couches, gold chairs, gold implements of every
sort . . . '

Such treatment for an overseas professional in India
was not so unusual in the inter-war years. Long before the
Indian Premier League came to dominate world cricket,
highly paid professional cricketers from across the globe
had been imported to the subcontinent by wealthy men
eager to use the sport as a means of besting their rivals.

Rajinder Singh, the Maharajah of Patiala, educated
at Cambridge and said to be second only to Ranjitsinhji
amongst Indian cricketers, was the leader of the trend. A
crack shot, an expert at billiards and a fine polo player,
Rajinder Singh built a cricket ground and needed a team
to play on it. He secured the services of Middlesex's expert
medium-pacer Jack Hearne and Bill Brockwell, a useful
seamer from Surrey, and brought them over to his vast
estates surrounding the Moti Bagh Palace in the Punjab.

When Rajinder Singh died in a riding accident in 1900,
his son Bhupinder succeeded him. The new Maharajah
was even more extravagant than his father, and just as
committed to cricket. He brought over the great George
Hirst for nine consecutive winters and also hired eccentric wicketkeeping all-rounder George Brown, the luckless
Yorkshireman Roy Kilner, his county team mates Abe
Waddington, Maurice Leyland and Wilfred Rhodes, and
Harold Larwood.

The Maharajah's most successful import was Frank
Tarrant, an Australian who was Hearne's team mate at
Middlesex. Tarrant bowled quickish left-arm spinners
that were lethal on any sort of damp wicket. He was
particularly successful in India, his most notable performance coming in 1917 when he took 5–9 and 7–36 as
the Maharajah of Cooch Behar's XI defeated the Bengal

Governor's XI by an innings in front of packed stands at Eden Gardens. The Australian seems to have taken to life in India, and as well as playing and coaching also umpired matches and took his share of groundsman's duties, laying one of the country's first grass wickets at the Maharajah's ground at Amritsar.

Rajinder Singh's main rivals amongst the cricket-sponsoring Indian nobility were Sir Nripendra Narayan, the Maharajah of Cooch Behar, who imported two spinners, George Cox and Joe Vine, from Sussex to Bengal and – in an impudent piece of business – lured Tarrant away from Patiala; the Maharajkumar of Vizianagaram who, in a coup worthy of an IPL franchise, secured the services of Jack Hobbs and Herbert Sutcliffe; and the Nawab of Moin-ud-Dowlah, who had hired Connie.

The professionals lived in the cricket pavilions, shopped for food in the local bazaar and, in between playing and coaching, did the odd bit of tiger-shooting. For a man like George Hirst, who had grown up poor amongst the woollen mills of West Yorkshire, the opulence and splendour of life in the Patiala household was quite an eye-opener. It was for Connie too. In Lancashire he had discovered that white people could live in poverty; now he found that non-whites could be rich. While in Trinidad social and economic divisions were generally a matter of race, in the wider world things were not so clear-cut. Nonetheless, race, or at least skin tone, did play a part in Indian society. There was a campaign to have Connie play for the Europeans in the Bombay Quadrangular Competition, against teams representing the Hindus, Muslims and Parsis. In the end the idea foundered because the high-caste, pale-skinned Brahmins who played in the European team objected to the idea of playing alongside a black cricketer.

During his trip Connie received a last-minute invitation from the Maharajkumar of Vizianagaram asking him if he would play for his team, the Freelooters, in the Moin-ud-Dowlah Gold Cup. In return, Connie would be payed a certain amount of money per run and per wicket. Intrigued, he agreed, though the telegram had come so late he didn't get to the ground until shortly after the match had started.

The Moin-ud-Dowlah Gold Cup tournament had first been played during the 1930–1 season. As its name suggests, it was the brainchild of Connie's patron, the Nawab of Moin-ud-Dowlah, who donated the splendid trophy, and it was contested between various invitational teams featuring high-class imported pros and the best Indian cricketers. In the first final the Nawab's team had been defeated by the Maharajkumar of Vizianagaram's XI, Hobbs, Sutcliffe and all. In 1931–2 the Freelooters carried off the Gold Cup due to the brilliant batting of Vijay Merchant and the fast bowling of Amar Singh. They retained it the following year thanks once again to Amar Singh, who took seven wickets in the match.

With Connie added to the line-up, the Freelooters might have expected to complete a treble of victories. However, they had lost the services of Amar Singh and found themselves up against an excellent side sponsored by the Maharajah of Patiala. Retrievers were captained by the Yuvraj of Patiala, the Maharajah's son, and featured ten Indian Test cricketers, including Mushtaq Ali and C. K. Nayudu (a big hitter whose exploits almost matched Connie's own), supplemented by the Australian leg-spinner Frank Warne.

The match had drawn huge publicity and fifteen thousand spectators crowded in to the Gymkhana Ground at

Secunderabad in anticipation of an enthralling contest. They were not disappointed. The Freelooters' captain, the Maharajkumar of Alirajpur, won the toss and elected to bat on the matting wicket. It proved a mistake. Against tight seam bowling from Mohammad Nissar they fell apart – all out for 125, with Connie contributing 12 before being caught off the military medium of Nayudu.

When Retrievers batted Connie tore into them with the new ball, taking six wickets. His deliveries flew off the matting, sending many of the batsmen scuttling away to square leg, but the catching was poor and opener Nassir Ali's 91 prevented the Freelooters claiming an unlikely first-innings lead. Batting for a second time, facing a deficit of 63, the Freelooters appeared to be on the way to setting a big target when Merchant and Phiroze Palia put on 151 for the third wicket, but after they were out the innings fell to bits, Connie contributing just a single to the total of 233. 171 was still a fair number of runs to chase in the fourth innings and Connie soon had Retrievers in trouble when he picked up the quick wickets of Mushtaq Ali and C. S. Nayudu – C. K.'s less celebrated brother – but with the score at 67 for four, Lala Amarnath arrived at the wicket and slashed a blistering hundred to see his team home by three wickets.

A short while later the Maharajkumar of Vizianagaram organised a game in Delhi between the Cricket Club of India (which had been designed as the Indian equivalent of the MCC – a role it never quite assumed) and the University Occasionals. Connie was the star in a CCI team that also contained C. K. Nayudu.

Connie apparently did not recognise Nayudu from their previous encounter and when he was joined at the wicket by the great Indian batsman kindly reassured him not to worry about the fast bowling of Mohammad Nissar, as he

would take care of it. Nayudu plainly thought that was fine
and allowed Connie to farm the strike. After a while he
decided he had had enough of playing the fool, and when
he did face Nissar drove him for several sixes. Connie
looked on amazed.

Shortly afterwards Connie appeared in a friendly match
for the Maharajah of Patiala's XI against the Viceroy's XI at
New Delhi. The game was played in intense heat, and with
the Viceroy's team apparently cruising to victory, Connie,
who had been bowling in a fairly sedentary fashion up until
that point, was invited by his captain to spice things up with
a bit of short stuff. The Indian batsmen were soon hopping
around, wickets tumbled and the match was unexpect-
edly won by the Mahrajah's team. His work done, Connie
returned to Nelson via the Suez Canal. He anticipated a rest
from his exertions, but instead found a telegram from the
West Indies Cricket Board waiting for him.

In 1935 Silver Jubilee Day at Seedhill saw a famous
Worsley Cup tie that pitted two of the world's finest all-
rounders against one another. Amar Singh, turning out for
Colne, was stockily built, with broad shoulders. A superb
fast-medium bowler, he'd taken 111 first-class wickets on
his country's 1932 tour of the British Isles. He was also a
powerful striker of the ball, with a first-class hundred to
his name, and an excellent slip fielder. Singh was Colne's
first overseas professional and his arrival had doubled gate
receipts. The first meeting of the two men, when Colne
travelled to Seedhill, drew a crowd of fourteen thousand.
For this midweek cup match, twelve thousand spectators
each paid sixpence entrance money. Colne batted first and
scored 164 largely thanks to the diminutive Les Bulcock,
an all-rounder who had been offered professional terms by
Glamorgan, who made 46.

Amar Singh was particularly good with the new ball, mixing swing with a devastating break-back. Like S. F. Barnes he never bowled a negative line, preferring to attack the stumps. After playing against him in the 1932 Test series, Wally Hammond was so impressed by Singh's cleverness that he told the press he believed he was the best user of the new ball in the game. Plum Warner also thought Amar Singh uncommonly good, writing that 'he would be a strong candidate for a world XI', while young Len Hutton, who'd come up against him in a tour match in 1936, reckoned 'there is no better bowler in the world than Amar Singh'.

Now he took the new ball at Seedhill and showed that his high reputation was well deserved, producing one of the greatest spells of pace in Lancashire League history. Bowling with skill and speed, and making the ball rear alarmingly off a length, the Indian ripped through the home side's batting. Only Connie was able to play him, reaching a half-century. With Nelson requiring 12 to win, the last pair were at the wicket – Alf Pollard and the wicket-keeper Freddie Dowden. Amar Singh, who had taken eight wickets, rushed in to bowl. A big appeal for lbw was waved away, a sharp chance missed. The score crept upwards until they were level. Pollard faced Amar Singh. The Indian dug deep, producing a fast delivery that beat Pollard for pace and slammed into his pads. The umpire's finger went up. The match was a tie. Amar Singh had finished with 9–61.

'It was great bowling, really great,' Connie would later recall. The rematch was played at Colne's Horsfield ground. Nelson won in front of another huge crowd.

In 1936, Nelson won the title for a third successive time. Chick Hawkwood returned to Seedhill and eclipsed Connie's achievements with the bat, scoring 835 runs at an average of 52.18. Connie made 632 and was back on top form with the ball, taking eighty-six wickets, his best performance a brilliant nine for 41 against Bacup.

At around this time Connie was approached by representatives of Lancashire to find out if he would be willing to play for the county – he was now qualified by residency. Though county cricket was not as racially mixed as it would become from the sixties onwards, a number of foreign players had appeared in it, including Indians and West Indians. Duleepsinhji was by that time captain of Sussex, but things had not always run smoothly. It was alleged, for instance, that during his time at Hampshire Charlie Llewellyn had been racially abused by some of his own team, while the aristocratic Duleep had initially been passed over for selection for the Gentlemen's team for their annual match with the Players at Lord's on grounds of race. On this occasion, however, things would not get even this far. Though Connie's appointment was supported by his friend the Lancashire chairman Thomas Higson, the proposal was rejected before it got to the full committee because, Connie wrote, 'certain members on the Lancashire Board would not tolerate my colour'.

When it was later proposed that Connie be approached again, the Lancashire professionals objected. One of them – Len Hopwood, an all-rounder who played a couple of Tests for England – recalled that the prevailing feeling in the dressing room was that the thought of 'a coloured chap playing for Lancashire was ludicrous'. Hopwood claimed that the Lancashire pros were so opposed to sharing a dressing room with Connie that they threatened strike action if he was given a contract. This, he stressed, was not through any particular animus to Connie, who they all liked, but because 'the thought of a black man taking the place of a white man in our side was anathema'. The English pros might not always be happy in their lot, but they were damned if they were going to let foreigners take a share of it.

Connie was ambivalent about county cricket and had landed himself in hot water with both Lancashire and Yorkshire after giving a newspaper interview in which he characterised the Roses Match as cautious, dreary and dull. There is no doubt, however, that he would have welcomed the chance to test himself in the County Championship. Whether it would have suited him is another matter. The daily drudgery of the circuit, with its endless travelling on trains and buses, second-rate hotels and sharp class divisions, was too much for men like Barnes and Parkin, and rankled with Fred Root. The Todmorden pro also had wise words on money, as he found dealing with the Lancashire League clubs much simpler than dealing with many counties, commenting: 'Promises are always fulfilled, and I find that when money is due it is paid.' Performance bonuses were paid on the day they were accomplished. This was 'vastly different from some of my experiences in county cricket', where money was sometimes paid 'seven months afterwards'.

In the Lancashire League, professionals were treated with respect, not as second-class citizens. Root noted how 'if a player's services are not to be retained he has to be informed of the fact before June 20th, allowing him time to find another engagement for the following season'. No such system existed in first-class cricket and professionals' services were dispensed with at a moment's notice. Even loyal county servants such as Maurice Tate found themselves treated with a harshness that bordered on cruelty. All in all, the prejudices at Old Trafford probably did Connie a favour in the long run.

Unfortunately, there would remain a feeling amongst some cricket followers that Connie had frittered away his talents far from the main arenas of the game; that he had chosen the soft option. Connie himself was aware of it: 'Many times I have been criticized, more in sorrow than in anger, for going into league cricket at all. I'll have read that I threw away my abilities and elected to join a game with technical inferiors in cricket skill. I only wish my critics had to face the batsmen and bowlers I met there, and to try and retrieve some of the situations with which I was faced. I resent the implication that I was taking things easy. To anyone who has watched a Lancashire League needle game the innuendo is ludicrous enough. Never in my life have I played harder than in Lancashire.'

Connie had decided that 1937 would be his last season at Seedhill. He had stayed far longer than was normal for a professional to remain at a single club. Though he loved Nelson and had liked 'each season better than the last', he needed a change. His time at Nelson had been such a success that he wanted to finish it at the top. He also wanted more time to study, for by now he was starting to think about life when cricket was over and was determined to finish what he had started over a decade before at John Ryan in Trinidad and become a lawyer. To that end he had begun working at a family law practice in Nelson run by his team mate Alec Birtwell. Connie's body was showing the wear and tear of a long career, but he also had an eye on the West Indies tour of the British Isles in 1939. He did not want to miss that due to League commitments and had decided that wherever he went it would be for just one season. Rochdale had persisted in their interest, and after extensive negotiations Connie agreed a deal with them for the 1938 season. Nelson quickly moved to dispel any rumour that Connie was leaving simply for more money, the club chairman issuing a statement that read: 'Constantine is not leaving the Nelson club on any question of terms. We are sorry to lose him ... There is no other cricketer in the world who combines all the qualities that Constantine possesses.' When he heard the news the Mayor of Nelson made a personal appeal to Connie to stay at Seedhill, but the deal had been struck and Connie was adamant. At the first home match after the decision was announced the Nelson Old Prize Band played 'Abide with Me' during the tea interval. Connie was touched, as he was by the response of the Nelson public. 'I could not walk a mile through the streets without being stopped literally hundreds of times by all sorts of people I didn't know from Adam: men, women and even youngsters begging me to stay.' They were, as he said, 'grand folk'. They loved him. The feeling was mutual.

Connie's replacement at Nelson would be the future India Test captain Lala Amarnath, the man who had hooked and pulled Connie so brilliantly in the Gold Cup game. A highly capable all-rounder, Amarnath holds the unique distinction of being the only bowler to induce Don Bradman to strike his own wicket. He would remain at Seedhill until the start of the Second World War.

Fittingly, in their greatest player's final season Nelson gained their fourth successive championship – a feat that has never been equalled. Connie was superb throughout the summer. Amongst the highlights was his 192 not out in 116 minutes against East Lancashire, which surpassed Charlie Llewellyn's record Lancashire League score. Connie – who was dropped when he was on one – hit twenty-seven fours and five sixes in the innings and gave the East Lancashire professional, Kiwi Test all-rounder Bill Merritt, a real mauling, crashing 26 off a single over from the leg-spinner. He also shared a remarkable ninth-wicket stand with Harold Hargreaves. The pair came together when Nelson were 141–8, and were finally parted by Merritt forty-four minutes later when the score was 262. Hargreaves had made 10. Merritt finished with nine wickets, though his rough handling by Connie meant they cost him 136 runs. Both men received crowd collections of eleven pounds, though as Connie remarked, Merritt had worked far harder for his.

Connie also hammered 110 against Church and produced a number of devastating bowling displays, taking seven for 11 as Bacup were bowled out for 39 and eight for 44 in Nelson's victory over Ramsbottom.

It was a magnificent last hurrah. In nine seasons at the club he scored 6363 runs at an average of 37.65 and took 776 wickets at 9.50. More than that, he had become the idol of the town and given it an international profile. Connie's success was not just down to his considerable prowess as a cricketer, but to his personality and his qualities as a man. Off the field he was a model professional, coaching the youngsters at nets, visiting sick fans at their homes, handing out prizes at Sunday schools, entertaining crowds at charity matches to raise money for good causes. Nelson's chairman, Tom Morgan, commented that Connie 'never gave the club a moment's trouble during the whole of his association with us'. John Kay, a journalist whose family had a long association with League cricket in Lancashire, said simply that Connie was the 'perfect citizen of Nelson . . . in every sense of the word a gentleman'.

Connie was proud of his connection with the town, and would continue to live in Nelson for another eleven years.

Nor did he underestimate the part Nelson had played in his development as a man: 'I am a better person for coming; I am better materially, I am better socially. I have grown more tolerant. I have grown less selfish. I am a better citizen for the time I have spent in Nelson.'

In 1963 he was given the Freedom of the Borough of Nelson in recognition of the part he had played in the history of the town. In 2011 a blue plaque was unveiled on the wall of the house in Meredith Street where he, Norma and Gloria had lived.

Chapter 6

Bubbles with a Dash of Brandy

The West Indian tour party returned home in September 1928. Connie now knew that his future lay in England. This would be his final Caribbean season as an amateur, the last chance he would have to play in the Inter-Colonial Tournament, which continued with its policy of outlawing professionalism. He had been exhausted at the end of the tour but now, refreshed by the voyage home, he produced some of his best form in the tournament played on the matting at Port of Spain.

Trinidad's first match was against British Guiana. Connie was the shining star of the victory, taking nine for 96 in the match and striking a quick fifty. In the final against Barbados he hit 133, the highest score by a Trinidadian in the tournament, beating the record set by his father in 1910. It was also the highest score of Connie's first-class career. Trinidad finished on 380. When Barbados batted they found Connie in irresistible mood. He clean-bowled Walcott for a duck, pouched a neat catch to dismiss Clifford Inniss and then dismissed Birkett and Kidney. Two more Connie catches saw the backs of Ward and Griffith as Barbados subsided to 108 all out. Following on, they fell apart again, Connie taking four wickets as they were dismissed for 109. It was a fitting end to Connie's career in the Inter-Colonial Tournament, and in recognition of his contribution the Queen's Park committee agreed to award him 25 per cent of the gate receipts from the final match. To some, it appeared a rather late acknowledgement of Connie's gifts.

In February Sir Julien Cahn's side toured Jamaica. It was a decent squad of cricketers that included regular Caribbean visitor Lord Tennyson alongside county veterans Andy Sandham and Ewart Astill. Also in the party were Nottinghamshire's Dodger Whysall (a *Wisden* Cricketer of the Year who would die a year later from septicaemia after injuring his elbow while dancing), Essex and England all-rounder Stan Nichols (who would play a bit part in Connie's Test career a few years later), tall paceman Jack Durston – the only Middlesex bowler Connie hadn't flogged during his two memorable innings at Lord's the previous summer – and Glamorgan's medium-paced swing bowler Jack Mercer, who would take more than fifteen hundred first-class wickets in his career.

At Sabina Park in early March Cahn's team took on a West Indies XI made up of the best Jamaican players reinforced by a few stars from elsewhere in the Caribbean, Connie and Small prominent amongst them. In a match scheduled for five days, John Holt batted brilliantly, scoring 128 and 56, while George Headley showed growing maturity in making a superb 143, though Connie watching from the pavilion felt that the young batsman's strokes lacked polish. Connie bowled well, but really caught the eye with his fielding, pocketing six catches in the match. Small was the outstanding performer with the ball, taking seven for

77 in the tourists' first innings. Sandham scored heavily for
the visitors, but could not prevent a comprehensive 144-run
defeat. Shortly afterwards Connie and Norma sailed off to
England to begin a new life in Lancashire.

In Connie's absence Trinidad lost the colony title to
British Guiana in September 1929. The island's great star
returned to Trinidad shortly after the tournament was concluded in preparation for the arrival of the MCC touring
party. He travelled via New York, where he and Norma
were the guests of the local West Indian community.
Despite the fact it was November, a match was arranged
and Connie's arrival trumpeted in the local press. He
had been billed as the world's fastest bowler and the most
prodigious hitter since Jessop, and justified the former tag
by taking seven wickets and laying out one of the local
amateurs with a nasty bumper. His fielding drew gasps
from spectators, and one catch he took was considered so
spectacular there was a pitch invasion of fans eager to press
money into Connie's hands. 'There was nothing else to do
but accept what the Gods had provided, and a few minutes
later I was bowling my fastest with my pockets bulging.'

The MCC party that arrived in the Caribbean after
Christmas was decidedly understrength – England were
also playing a Test series in New Zealand. Tate, Larwood
and Hammond, meanwhile, had all opted to stay at home
for the winter. The tourists were captained by thirty-seven-
year-old Freddie Calthorpe of Warwickshire (who was yet
to play a Test), and had a notably wrinkled look – Andy
Sandham would later write that this was at the request
of the West Indian cricket authorities, though that seems
highly unlikely. Yorkshire all-rounder Wilfred Rhodes was
fifty-two, and had played his first Test in 1899. George
Gunn, recently turned fifty, hadn't won an England cap

since 1912, while forty-two-year-old Nigel Haig had been absent from Test cricket for eight years. Ewart Astill was forty-one, Sandham thirty-nine, Ronald Stanyforth thirty-eight. Forty-year-old Patsy Hendren was at least still an England regular. He had played in all five Tests in England's 4–1 Ashes triumph the previous winter. Jack O'Connor was thirty-two. The players under thirty were Greville Stevens, who had barely played for two years due to business commitments, Bob Wyatt and Leslie Townsend. Wicketkeeper Les Ames, who had one Test cap, was twenty-four. The one real nod to potential was the uncapped Bill Voce, who had turned twenty that summer. Had it not been for the youthful Nottinghamshire pitman, the average age of the side would have been nudging forty. No one could doubt the side's experience, however.

For the West Indians, the Test failures of 1928 tour had prompted debate about the captaincy. Each of the four colonies put forward a candidate, but such was the rivalry between them that no one name could be agreed upon. As a compromise, or perhaps a fudge, it was decided that each of the proposed should take charge on his home turf. One matter that was not open to discussion was the race of the captain – all four were white.

The tour opened in Barbados with two games against the colony. Both were drawn. Barbados had not lost to an English touring party since 1905. In the first of the games a seventeen-year-old schoolboy, Derek Sealy, stole the headlines with a century. For the MCC Hendren struck a double hundred and Sandham made 103. Challenor, making his final appearance in first-class cricket, scored 51. In the second match Tim Tarilton also bowed out of the first-class game, scoring 105 in an opening stand of 261 with Teddy Hoad, who made 147. Voce, meanwhile, announced his arrival on the international scene by knocking young Inniss unconscious with a bouncer.

Hoad, Barbados's nomination for the West Indies captaincy, took charge for the first Test in Bridgetown. Sealy was chosen to make his debut alongside two other local cricketers, paceman Griffith and off-spinning all-rounder Leslie Walcott. From Trinidad came Connie, St Hill, Roach and the wicketkeeper Errol Hunte, a man who for a couple of decades was listed in *Wisden* as not one but two Test cricketers, E. A. C. Hunte and R. L. Hunte. British Guiana was represented by debutant Frank de Caires and Browne, while Headley of Jamaica won his first Test cap; Connie offered the twenty-year-old debutant the sound advice, 'Play within your limitations. It's just another game.'

The West Indies won the toss and batted on what Sandham considered the fastest pitch he had ever come across. Hoad opened with Roach. The captain fell quickly and Headley – who walked out to booing from Barbadian fans incensed that the teenager had taken a berth that might have gone to a local – also failed. Roach, however, batted brilliantly for 122 and got good support from de Caires, who made 80. Sealy, at seventeen years and 122 days, was then the youngest man ever to play in a Test (he remains the youngest West Indian). One of the umpires at the Kensington Oval was the senior Joe Hardstaff, who extended his duties to offering helpful batting tips to the nervous youngster. It clearly worked: Sealy made a half century and the West Indies closed on 369, Connie blasting a six on his way to 13. Stevens was the pick of the bowlers, taking five for 105 with his slow leg-breaks.

When England batted Connie, according to Wyatt, 'bowled at lightning pace, and from the start of the innings he bowled bouncer after bouncer at the batsman's head

with only two men fielding on the offside'. Wyatt would
later claim that this was the first instance of a Bodyline
attack being used in Test cricket, and 'in view of what happened later in Australia it was interesting that no one made
any public protest at the methods adopted by Constantine'.
Sandham backs up Wyatt's assertion about the frequency
of the bouncers, though without the complaint. Connie's
friend the British journalist Denzil Batchelor would
describe Connie as a 'Champagne cocktail' cricketer –
effervescent but with a kick. Here was the brandy.

Wyatt's theme was taken up by Calthorpe at the post-
Test gala dinner. In his speech to the assembled teams and
officials the MCC captain claimed that a draw was inevitable since Connie bowled on or outside leg stump with
'four short legs and two deep'. In Calthorpe's view, a more
conventional field and line of attack might have resulted
in victory for the home side. Neither Wyatt nor Calthorpe
made mention of Voce's braining of Inniss. Connie was
perplexed by the fuss. As far as he was concerned, bouncers
were a legitimate part of the fast bowler's arsenal. He had
first been instructed to bowl them by Bertie Harragin in
match against Barbados, and on the 1923 tour of England
had noticed how Warwickshire paceman Edward Hewetson
bowled a series of short balls aimed at the body of Tim
Tarilton that caused the Barbadian opener to 'edge out
of his wicket' and led to him being clean-bowled shortly
afterwards. Reviewing the incident, Connie realised that
George John had deployed the tactic in club matches on
Trinidad and he had determined on the same approach.
Not everyone complained. When he had bowled a series
of bouncers at Hammond in a match against the MCC in
1926 the batsman had objected, only to be told by the non-
striker, Lionel Tennyson, to 'shut up and bat'. And that was

what Connie expected batsmen to do. In his entire career he never once complained when short-pitched bowling was directed at him. After all, he had a bat.

Whatever style of attack Connie was employing, England opener George Gunn certainly played it in a singular and unorthodox manner, walking down the wicket before the ball had even left the bowler's hand, holding the blade high in the air and playing dead-bat defensive shots off the back foot once the ball had been delivered. Connie attempted to use Gunn's advance to his advantage, by continuing his follow through in an attempt to get him out caught and bowled. Gunn continued on his merry way, however, dropping the ball down at his feet then blowing a raspberry at Connie before scuttling back into his crease to avoid a run-out.

Connie – who Wyatt thought never bowled faster than in this series – continued digging the ball in short. He hit the ageing Gunn several times. One blow under the armpit caused the Nottinghamshire veteran to throw his bat in the air in agony. But no matter what he tried, Connie could not get Gunn out; he eventually fell to St Hill for a bruising 35. England made 467, Sandham continuing his good form with a big hundred and Hendren – who had become a firm favourite with the locals thanks to his genial clowning in the outfield during breaks in play – galloping to 80. West Indies had picked only four bowlers and paid the penalty as the innings wore on and fatigue set in. Connie finished with figures of 3–121 achieved in an exhausting thirty-nine overs. He had also made three stunning catches close to the wicket to get rid of Hendren, Haig and O'Connor.

A drained West Indies went in to bat for the second time 98 runs in arrears. It was the sort of situation from which they had struggled to recover in England. In the Barbados sun, however, they rallied brilliantly thanks in the main to Headley, who struck 176, dancing down the wicket to Rhodes in a style that made Connie 'laugh with delight'. Roach got 77 and de Caires 70 as England were set 287 to win in 165 minutes. The visitors contented themselves with a draw. Following the game Harold Austin presented Connie with a bat for giving the best all-round performance in the West Indies side. The man whom many considered to be the father of West Indian cricket then gave a touching tribute to the two Constantines he had captained: 'There is no more charming and keen cricketer than Mr Constantine senior, and as, ladies and gentlemen, the son has inherited the father's manners and keenness for the game. We enjoy watching you, Mr Constantine, as much as you enjoy your cricket.'

In Trinidad the MCC got a rude shock when a combination of St Hill's batting and the left-arm wrist spin of Ellis Achong – who took seven wickets – sent them to a 102-run defeat in the first colony match.

In the return match, in which Connie was unable to bowl due to severe cramp, the MCC gained their first victory of the tour, but only by the narrow margin of 22 runs. Voce bowled several long and hostile spells and took 12–110 as the Trinidadian batsmen failed to get to grips with the angle of his attack and the pace and bounce he generated off the coconut matting. Top scorer was Mervyn Grell, the captain, and he only made 34 not out. Connie did little with the bat, but by his own estimation fielded at the top of his abilities to take nine catches in the two games. He fielded close in, fearlessly so, for 'it was obvious the English captain had advised them to move me, for presently one or two batsmen took a steady look my way and, as the occasion arose, attempted to lay me out cold, as of course they had every right to do'. Connie would later point out that the tactic of batsmen deliberately hitting the ball at close fieldsmen was far more dangerous than short-pitched bowling, yet nobody seemed to complain about it, nor in his view ought they to.

One incident in the match involving Connie caused some merriment. Voce bowled a bouncer to the Trinidadian, who struck it high into the air and into the outfield. George Gunn was under it. The Nottinghamshire man was wearing a big sola topi to protect him from the sun, but rather than simply throwing his hat to one side to get a better sight of the ball, he took it off gracefully and held it in his left hand while catching the ball with his right. The crowd were rapturous in their appreciation of this bit of eccentricity. Connie himself could not have done it better.

The bizarre system of rotating skippers saw Grell take charge of the West Indies team in the second Test. His qualifications for his role were limited and his career record – 487 runs at 28.76 and three wickets at 34.40 – hardly suggests he was worth a place in the team. On top of that, the selection committee also made a mess of picking the remaining ten. Despite the good showing at Bridgetown only Roach, Headley, de Caires, Connie, Griffith and Hunte were retained from that side. In came Trinidadians St Hill, Small, Achong and wicketkeeper Nelson Betancourt. These wholesale changes ultimately benefited nobody but England.

The visitors won the toss and batted. Connie and Griffith opened the attack. Both bowled with controlled hostility and Gunn, Sandham and Stevens were all back in the pavilion with just 12 on the board. Hendren and Ames batted cautiously and well, but despite their efforts England were all out for 208, Griffith taking five for 63 and Connie two for 42. Achong also picked up a couple of wickets. The West Indies' chances of taking a big lead on first innings looked slim as Voce tore into the home side, bowling as many bouncers as Connie had in Bridgetown. Roach went for a duck and Headley, de Caires, Small and Grell all fell cheaply. With his side 168 for seven Connie came to the wicket. He turned the situation around in less than an hour, hammering out 52 – including two mighty sixes – in just fifty minutes. Voce bounced him repeatedly but Connie stayed true to his father's maxim and used the bat to hit the ball. He received solid support from Betancourt, who made 33 on his debut. Voce finished with four for 79 and Astill picked up four for 58.

Thanks in the main to Connie, the West Indies led by 46. It was not enough. Hendren and Ames again batted well, the Middlesex player striking 205 – though Connie, of all people, dropped him early on – and the Kent wicketkeeper 105. Achong was injured and could not bowl, leaving Connie and Griffith toiling in the hot sun. Between them the pair bowled seventy-eight overs as England cruised to 425–8 declared. Winning the match seemed out of the question and even saving it was rapidly in doubt as Roach bagged a pair. St Hill, Hunte, Headley and de Caires all passed 30 only to get out when apparently well set, and with nobody anchoring the innings the West Indies were gradually picked apart by the pace of Voce, who took seven for 70 to help England win by 167 runs.

After the match the MCC team manager, Harry Mallett – well known, of course to the West Indians – approached Connie and asked if he might agree to bowl fewer bouncers in future. According to Mallett, the English batsmen were fearful of being injured. Connie assented, and was then surprised in the next Test when Voce sent

down a barrage of them. It seemed the truce only applied
to one team.

In Georgetown, Inter-Colonial champions British
Guiana were twice thrashed by the MCC. Hendren hit
254 not out in the first match and 171 in the second. Ames
and Sandham also made centuries while Rhodes took eight
for 103. For Guiana, the only bright spot was the batting
of Wishart, a young left-hander who made a couple of
half-centuries.

The West Indies selectors appeared to take this poor
showing to heart, and instead of loading the side up with
local players as they had done in Trinidad picked only
Fernandes – the skipper for this match – Vibart Wight,
Browne and Charles Jones from British Guiana. De Caires
and the now fully fit Achong were omitted despite playing decently in the Tests. Roach, Headley, Sealy, St Hill,
Francis, Hunte and Connie made up the rest of the team.
Hunte would keep wicket and also open with Roach, who
must by now have been getting used to the promiscuous
swapping of partners. The hosts provided poor accommodation for the West Indian team, and Connie and George
Headley were forced to share a bed. To Connie it must have
seemed yet another example of how little the Caribbean
cricket authorities valued their cricketers.

Fernandes won the toss and elected to bat on a perfect
strip. The West Indies raced to 144 without loss, helped
by appalling English fielding that saw Hunte dropped four
times. Finally Wyatt clung on to one to send the wicketkeeper back to the pavilion for 53. Roach was unperturbed
and went on batting exuberantly. He struck three sixes
and twenty-two fours before being out for 209 – the first
West Indian to score a double hundred in a Test as well as
the first Trinidadian ever to accomplish the feat. Headley

proved an able partner, scoring 114. The second wicket did not fall until the home side had reached 340. Sadly that precipitated a major collapse and the West Indies were all out for 471, far short of the sort of mammoth total their excellent start had promised.

England started badly and deteriorated from there to be all out for 145; Hendren top-scored again with 56. Connie did the damage, taking four for 35, though Wyatt characterised England's batting as lamentable. With his team 326 ahead, Fernandes seemed bound to enforce the follow-on, but possibly feeling that his bowlers were tired and fearing final use of a wicket likely to aid the English spinners, elected instead to bat again. His thinking was proved correct, as Rhodes and Astill exploited the rough outside off stump that had been created by Bill Voce to excellent effect. Headley batted brilliantly in difficult conditions and reached his hundred – the first West Indian to hit a century in both innings of a Test, and only the fifth man to do so in Test history. Sensing that a draw was their only hope, the English bowlers began to bowl wide of off stump, the sort of negative tactic Connie deplored. It mattered little. England needed 617 to win – clearly an impossible target. The visitors set out to bat for a draw. The remarkable Hendren played an heroic rearguard action in scoring 123, while Gunn and Calthorpe also contributed with solid batting, but Connie, ably supported by Francis, was in irrepressible form, claiming five for 87 in a marathon forty overs, and the last England wicket fell with a quarter of an hour remaining. The West Indies had secured their first Test win by the handsome margin of 289 runs. They were, Wyatt concluded, 'simply far too good for us'. After the disappointments of 1928, the victory was greeted with jubilation across the Caribbean. Roach and Headley had both made magnificent contributions, but most West Indians recognised that Connie was the man who had driven his side to victory. He was the most popular player in the region and the force of his personality inspired the team. With Connie around, anything seemed possible.

On home territory Nunes returned to captaining the side which was stuffed with Jamaicans: Headley, Martin, Barrow, Passailaigue, Scott, Da Costa and Gladstone. The remaining places went to Roach, de Caires and Griffith. Francis, who had taken six wickets in Georgetown, was dropped and Connie was also absent. Reports claimed he was nursing an injury, but his omission seems to have owed more to the now traditional inter-colony squabbling, the need to secure good crowds by selecting local favourites and the saving of money on travel expenses.

Since the series was tied it was agreed that the final Test in Jamaica should be played to a finish: a 'timeless Test'. Wyatt described what followed as 'some of the most extraordinary Test cricket in which I've ever played'. England batted first and piled up a mighty total of 849. George Gunn, playing in his last-ever Test, made 85, Sandham a triple hundred, Ames 149, Hendren 61 and Wyatt 58. The West Indies were bowled out for 286, giving England a massive first-innings lead of 563. Because the Test was timeless, Calthorpe declined to make them follow on even though his team had a ship to catch. England batted in cavalier fashion and the innings was declared at 272–9, setting the West Indies a meagre 836 to win.

Headley made 223 before he was stumped off Wyatt's military medium pace. The match had now been going on for seven days and the home side stood on 408 for five. On days eight and nine rain fell heavily. Since the MCC boat was due to leave on day ten it was decided that the match would have to be declared a draw. By then Connie and his family had already sailed for England.

Calthorpe was heavily criticised for his decision to bat again, but Wyatt who as he would show during his own time as captain in the Caribbean, tended to be cautious, felt the skipper had made the right call – to avoid batting last on a wicket that might have deteriorated or been affected by rain was the sensible thing to do.

In England, the feeling was that by coming away without a series win the tour party had comprehensively failed. Wyatt believed this to be unfair. As far as he was concerned, the English had a tendency to underestimate the quality of the West Indians, particularly on home soil: 'They are fine natural players and take a tremendous amount of beating.'

The batting in the series had been dominated by two men: Patsy Hendren and George Headley. Hendren was master of the hook and the pull, which helped him greatly in the West Indies. Short and thick-set, with a large behind and a generally ungainly look, he had a powerful sense of fun and general good humour that endeared him to team mates, opponents and spectators alike. He scored 1766 runs on the tour at an average of 126.14, and made six centuries, four of them doubles. Headley equalled the world record by hitting four centuries in the Test series and his 703 runs in a four-Test series has never been surpassed by a West Indian. He was an excellent player on bad wickets, kept his head perfectly still and played the ball very late, watching until the last moment before committing himself to the shot. His footwork was nimble and, like many West Indians who would follow him, he had an unorthodox streak that often saw him square-cutting off the front foot. The only other West Indian batsman who impressed was Roach. He scored 467 runs at 58.37, but he was remarkably inconsistent, switching apparently randomly from the sublime to the stupid. For West Indian supporters, watching him was a nerve-racking experience. He was a batsman, some observers noted, who never seemed to be 'in'.

For the home side, Connie had been the pick of the bowlers. Wyatt thought Connie one of the fastest he had ever faced: while not tall he had 'very long arms', took a long run up and leapt into the air before his delivery stride. Even for the brave and pugilistic Wyatt it formed a 'terrifying picture'.

Connie had been ably supported by the pacey Griffith, while Francis did well in the one game he was picked to play in. Had the fast-bowling trio who only the year before had been heralded by one Caribbean newspaper as 'the finest in the British Empire' played in all four matches, a series victory might have been the result.

That they didn't said something about the West Indies' shambolic selection process. Twenty-nine cricketers had been fielded in four games, with Passailaigue, Gladstone, Grell and Betancourt all making what would prove to be their sole Test appearance. A lack of consistency and a failure to keep faith in players, even when they had been successful, could only have undermined confidence and prevented any kind of bond between team mates. As Connie noted, 'The West Indies' weakness has always been organizing its strength to the best possible result.'

It must be conceded, however, that such selectorial tinkering was not confined to the Caribbean, as anyone who lived through England's 'season of four captains' would testify.

Chapter 7

A Mob Down Under

The party to tour Australia assembled in October 1930 in Panama, where the local West Indian community were happy to welcome them and an exhibition match was staged. Connie arrived from Lancashire via Trinidad. He knew some of the squad from previous tours, while others were unfamiliar to him. One man who was a stranger not only to Connie but to almost all the other members of the group was the new captain.

After the unhappy compromise of the England series it was clear something needed to be done. Grell was the only captain who had won a Test, but that was evidently put down more to fortune than good judgement as his claim, along with those of the other captains who had served during the series, was disregarded. Resolute in the idea that the captain must be white and therefore – inevitably – privately educated, the selectors opted to give the job to George Grant, the Trinidadian universally known as Jackie. Grant was not in the country when the decision was made. He had gone up to Cambridge in 1927, and in 1929 gained his Blue as well as scoring 691 runs in first-class matches at an average of 31.40. In the 1930 season he had done marginally better, hitting 716 runs at 44.75 and scoring his maiden first-class hundred in the match with Sussex. Grant was a decent batsman, then, but the decision to hand the captaincy to a young man who had never taken charge of a side in a first-class match was a mark of either boldness or desperation. Grant was just twenty-three years old. He had never played Test cricket or indeed first-class cricket for Trinidad. In fact, he had barely played a match in the months leading up to the tour. Though Grant would, over the next few years, prove himself to be a tenacious batsman, a tidy fielder and a leader of some tactical shrewdness and imagination, there is little doubt he owed his captaincy to just one thing – the colour of his skin.

Scepticism about Grant's appointment ran through the squad, in particular amongst the senior players. As Connie summarised somewhat bitterly, 'Whatever they taught him at Cambridge it could not have been our respective merits as part of the team.'

Grant's vice-captain was another white Trinidadian with no Test experience, Lionel Birkett, though the tall right-hander had at least earned his place, compiling a double century against British Guiana in the 1929–30 Inter-Colonial Tournament.

Oscar Wight, the other novice in the party, was also white. The twenty-three-year-old from British Guiana was reputedly a hard-hitting batsman with a reputation for flogging the bad ball, but had an abysmal tour, batting just three times and scoring a total of 45 runs.

All the rest had played international cricket. Griffith, Francis and Connie formed the nucleus of the attack, with St Hill as medium-pace back-up and Scott the spinner. Roach, Barrow, Martin and Hunte could all play as openers; Headley would bat at number three. De Caires, Bartlett and Derek Sealy made up the rest of the middle order. Barrow was wicketkeeper, with Sealy his deputy. The players were paid three hundred pounds each for the tour.

Connie, normally so positive in his attitude, saw the task ahead as an almost impossible one. The West Indies were setting out to take on 'the most solidly welded and hard-tested team in the world on their own grounds in a continent that was strange to us', with a squad 'hastily gathered up from various places and . . . more or less unfamiliar with one another's play'. Their captain, meanwhile, 'had seen none of us in action'.

The journey across the Pacific to Australia took a month. The team used the time to improve their fitness – engaging in daily workouts, swimming before breakfast and playing deck cricket with improvised nets. The wooden deck made for a fast, lively track, which sharpened up the batsmen's reflexes against the pacemen. Headley later said he thought this was good preparation for Australian conditions, though as we shall see the wickets did not prove to be quite the hard bouncy pitches the West Indians were expecting.

The ship called in at Wellington, where the West Indians played a two-day match against a New Zealand XI in damp and blustery conditions. The pitch at the Basin Reserve was lively, the sky was overcast and the ball moved around in the air more than most of the West Indian batters were used to. Rain played havoc with the second day's play and brought the match to a premature and frustrating end. Connie showed that the sea voyage had not dulled his edge and took six wickets for 24 as Wellington struggled to 195 all out.

The tour party arrived in Sydney. Connie and some other black West Indian players had been unsure what

kind of reception they would receive in Australia. It has
been suggested that part of the reason Grant was chosen as
leader was that as a public schoolboy and Cambridge grad-
uate he would soothe any concerns the locals had about
the visitors. At that time Australia had a far from liberal
policy on immigration; black people were generally denied
entry. However, once customs had been cleared and forms
filled out declaring their race (many of the team described
themselves as European – which, as British subjects, they
were) the West Indies were touched by the warmth of
their welcome. Such cordiality and human decency would
mark the coming months. As Connie noted, 'Throughout
that tour there was never the slightest hint of discrimination against us, either by onlookers or players or officials.
We were treated as cricketers, given a magnificent time and
made to feel friendliness wherever we went.'

The possibility of the West Indies visiting Australia
had been discussed by Charlie Macartney and George
Challenor as far back as 1926. However, at that time the
Australian board of control refused to sanction a tour, fearing the disruption it would cause to the domestic season and
concerned about losing money. Macartney's enthusiasm
had eventually won the Australian Cricket Board over and
they had arranged a schedule for the visitors that included
five Test matches – each of which would be played to a conclusion – as well as seven games against the state sides that
played in the Sheffield Shield. On top of that there would
be a couple of games against country district XIs and a trip
to Tasmania. It was a gruelling itinerary, with thousands
of miles of travelling between games in conditions none of
the players had ever experienced before. For men used to
playing weekend matches for local club sides, it was sure to
strain both stamina and morale.

The Australian cricketing public were excited at the prospect of seeing the West Indians. Headley and Connie in particular were sources of fascination. While Headley was described as being like 'a young Bradman', Connie was compared to a panther, the *Australian Cricketer* noting that he was 'a brilliant player capable of doing anything in any department ... He appears to be a law unto himself in the field.' The magazine concluded that Connie had 'the strongest field personality of any cricketer that has ever visited Australia'. Given that previous visitors included Ranjitsinhji, Gilbert Jessop, C. B. Fry and W. G. Grace it was quite an accolade.

Aside from Headley and Connie, the Australian cricket writers also praised Martin and St Hill, who was compared to the wiry off-spinner Don Blackie of Victoria – a player perhaps best remembered nowadays as the oldest debutant in Test history.

Attention was also drawn to the temperament of the West Indians, who were – or so it was claimed – mercurial and light-hearted, always willing to attempt the impossible. This prevailing view among those outside the Caribbean would persist for decades – until Clive Lloyd decided to lay it to rest for good.

One problem that couldn't be denied, and of which Connie himself was keenly aware, was the lack of team spirit in the side. The West Indies is not, of course, an actual country, but a construct made up of islands and a section of South America. Though the independent colonies had much in common, they also had plenty of differences, which were intensified by questions of class and race. The Jamaicans mocked the apparent pretentiousness of the Trinidadians, who in turn looked down on the backwardness of the men from British Guiana, and so forth. Rivalries built up over the years in the inter-colonial tournaments were hard to put to one side in the interests of this aggregate body of a 'country' that did not, never had and never would exist. In Australia, the situation was exacerbated by the choice of captain. 'We were more like a mob,' Connie said. 'Grant did his best, but he did not know us well enough.'

A two-day net session was arranged in preparation for the meeting with New South Wales and the new batting sensation, Donald Bradman, who had made a world-record Test score of 334 against England a few months earlier. The watching press men singled out Connie when writing their first pieces on the tourists. The power of his strokeplay and his brilliance during the fielding drills had caught their eye.

At nets, the West Indians found themselves facing Arthur Mailey. He had retired from first-class cricket the previous year, but the Australian remained a leg-spinner of the highest quality. He baffled Connie with his googly and amazed him with his ability to make the ball rip off the surface. The Trinidadian was in good company. In a charity match a few weeks earlier Mailey had clean-bowled Bradman with a viciously spinning wrong 'un. The problems Mailey posed the tourists were a hint of what was to come.

After the second day of nets a gala dinner was held, at which the West Indians were fêted by an assortment of cricketers and cricket officials and fed on fillet of veal and baked Alaska. The following day the hard reality of touring Australia began.

New South Wales were the Sheffield Shield champions. The state's batting line-up included Bradman, Stan McCabe, Alan Kippax – considered the best batsman in the country at that point – and the brilliant Archie Jackson. Bertie Oldfield was behind the stumps.

The West Indians left out Griffith, along with Hunte, de Caires, Sealy and Wight. Grant won the toss and elected to bat. The crowd was better than anticipated, with many Australians eager to get a first glimpse of the exotic visitors. For Connie, the sight of the New South Wales team created a sense of both awe and envy. Here were men who were 'hard-boiled, tough, grimly confident ... who asked and gave no quarter'.

Much these days is made of how certain touring players will be 'targeted' before Test matches. It is no modern innovation. Facing New South Wales Connie knew to expect a 'needle game', because 'it is well known that advice is often given from "headquarters" ... that the confidence is to be knocked out of some particular visiting bowler or batsman so that he shall be dropped ... or lose faith in himself'. Connie had seen England doing it with his fellow Trinidadian Puss Achong and would later learn that on the 1930 tour of England the Australians had set out to smash Voce around when they played Nottinghamshire so the home selectors would ignore a player whose pace and lift they feared. Connie played cricket in an exuberant manner, but he was as tough a professional as any. Winning mattered to him. That the West Indians were not tightly knit enough as a team to act like the Australians disappointed him greatly.

To the surprise of the spectators, the West Indians batted studiously and cautiously. It did them little good. When Connie – last man out – fell to a spectacular catch by Wendell Bill the score was a paltry 188. When the state side batted Connie bowled at a furious pace and in the field amused spectators during dull moments in play by catching flies that were buzzing round his head, or turning cartwheels. Later it would be claimed that he took a catch while turning a somersault, an apocryphal story that gave some indication of the way Connie's acrobatic fielding fired the public's imagination.

Twenty-nine thousand people, the largest crowd Connie had ever played in front of, turned up at the SCG for the second day, largely to see Don Bradman bat. His sensational performances in England in 1930 had made the boy from Bowral a hero, but by his own admission his form that season had been patchy. He had played cricket more or less continually for eighteen months and was feeling jaded. There was also an unsettling dispute with the Australian Cricket Board, who believed that the serialisation of his autobiography in a British newspaper was a breach of his contract. A third of his £150 good-conduct bonus from the 1930 tour had been withheld as a fine. Rumours in the press said Bradman was unpopular with his team mates, who thought him an aloof glory-seeker. None of that could detract from the cricket supporters' fascination with a man who accumulated runs in a manner the game had never before seen.

Inspired by the crowd and the challenge of bowling to Bradman, Connie bowled at his quickest, troubling all the batsmen with his extra lift and bounce. Even Bradman looked uncomfortable against him – an impression that was to have consequences in the future. With Francis also bowling fast, the West Indians had the best of the day, restricting New South Wales to a small lead. Connie took 6–45 and 'felt very pleased'.

The tourists' second innings was notable for one of Connie's trademark displays of hitting. Coming in with his side in trouble he unleashed a series of searing drives and pulls – some orthodox, others the extraordinary product of his unique imagination – that confirmed all the hyperbole that had surrounded him on arrival. Against Chilvers he produced an extraordinary shot, a cross-batted swipe that carried the ball over point and on to the Hill for six. Another huge blow off the bowling of Hunt bounced on the Hill Stand roof and landed in the Showground next door. For good measure, Connie also smacked another six on to the top of the Sheridan Stand. In thirty-five minutes he blazed 59 runs, finally falling to a caught and bowled that astounded even him, a straight drive intended 'to make a hole in the bowling screen' juggled and held. Connie left to a standing ovation. He had whacked four sixes and four fours in his innings. A watching Monty Noble, the former Australia Test skipper, called it one of the most sensational innings he had ever witnessed, and claimed that he had not seen hitting like it since before the First World War, concluding that Connie was 'certainly unique in everything'. Others compared the Trinidadian to Australia's greatest all-rounder, Jack Gregory. Few doubted that they had seen a genius in action.

But it was not enough, and though the West Indians fought hard when the state side batted for a second time needing 223 to win, Fairfax and McCabe saw them home by four wickets.

Defeat by such a narrow margin after only a couple of days' net practice was considered a decent performance by the tourists. Moreover the West Indians' attractive style of play had brought in the crowds. Australian newspapermen praised Connie's all-round brilliance and had kind words to say about Headley. Doubts were expressed, however, about the cohesion of the team and Connie noted that a number of journalists agreed with him that the side's lack of knowledge of their opponents, something that might easily have been rectified by a couple of days' study, was another problem.

The Australians made no such mistake. Already they had prepared scoring charts on George Headley and the rest of the West Indian batsmen. Such science was new to the visitors, and rarely used in England either, where such advanced preparation was considered somehow ungentlemanly. The Australians had no such compunction. Connie was impressed: 'Everything is tabulated and indexed, so that, before a Test, the Australian captain has only to consult the records to find every detail of weakness and strength in every opposing player ... Every detail of the game is prepared with as much thoroughness as a General would prepare a major offensive in a world war.' If such calculation seemed at odds with Connie's apparent attitude to the game as an entertainment, then it should be remembered that he was also a professional. The fact that the Australians made a science of cricket might be deplored by some purists, but in Connie's view 'no real cricketer agrees with them'.

In the next tour match, the West Indians were easily beaten by Victoria in a game that exposed their weakness to slow bowling, Australia's greatest strength at the time. That most of the damage had been done by Bert Ironmonger at least added an eccentric touch. At that point in his career the slow left-armer was claiming to be forty-three, when he was in fact closer to fifty. A hopelessly uncoordinated fielder, his team mates nicknamed him 'Dainty', while his batting was so inept it was said that his natural position in the order was number twelve. Yet he could bowl long spells without losing accuracy and extract turn from even the most benign surface. Given any help by conditions, he was lethal. He took eight wickets for 31 in the tourists' second innings and finished with thirteen in the match.

Connie's main recollection of the game was meeting

The West Indian cricket team in England, summer 1906. Back row (*left to right*) Richard Ollivierre, Charles Morrison, Lebrun Constantine, George Challenor, John Parker, Tommie Burton, Oliver Layne, Archie Cumberbatch. Middle: Bertie Harragin, Harold Austin, Percy Goodman, George Learmond. Front: Keith Bancroft, Sydney Smith

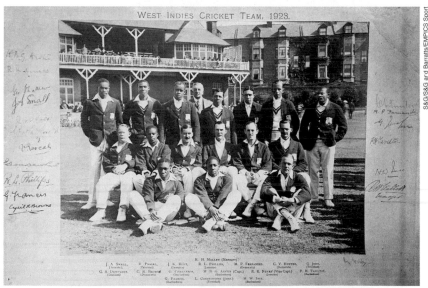

The West Indians in England, May 1923. Back row (*left to right*) Joe Small, Victor Pascall, Joseph Holt, manager Harry Mallett, Raymond Phillips, Maurice Fernandes, Clarence Hunter, George John; middle row: George Dewhurst, Snuffy Browne, George Challenor, Harold Austin, Karl Nunes, Percy Tarilton; front: George Francis, Connie, Harry Ince

Connie in London,
September 1929

Connie, Joe Small and
Barto Bartlett looking
chilly at Burbage Road,
Dulwich

Connie with Shannon,
Trinidad and West Indies
team mate Wilton St Hill,
1928

The 1928 West Indians posing for a Jaeger clothing advertisement; they may have been glad of the extra jumpers

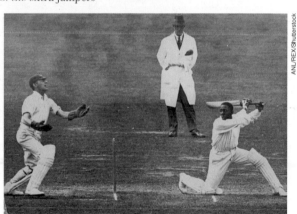

Connie in action against Middlesex at Lord's – the game that would change his life

During the game against Nottinghamshire at Trent Bridge, Connie and his team mates are presented to King George V

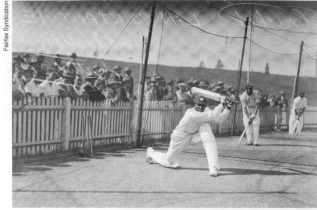

Crowds gather to
watch Connie in the
nets in Sydney at the
start of the 1930–1
tour

Even at practice
Connie never
failed to entertain
spectators

Connie posing in
his delivery stride
for the benefit
of Australian
photographers

A pensive-looking
trio: Connie, Herman
Griffith and George
Francis during the
1930–1 Australia tour

Connie looking
suitably glum in
Sydney

Connie walks out
on to the field past
excited children, circa
1932

The 1939 West Indian tour party. Standing (*left to* right) Gomez, Clark, Stollmeyer, Johnson, Bayley, Weekes, Williams, Hilton and Cameron; sitting: Martindale, Headley, Kidney, Grant, Connie, Barrow, Sealey

On his final tour Connie's bowling was slower but had more guile. In action versus Essex

Despite the years, Connie remained as expansive a batsman as ever, as he demonstrates against Middlesex

First-class cricketers at Lords's 1944, including Connie, Gubby Allen (standing, third right) and Len Hutton (standing, far right)

Connie and Wally Hammond, now firm friends, at Lord's in 1944

1944: Connie leads out the West Indies XI at Lord's for a game against Hammond's England XI

Connie in conversation with two West Indians who followed him into the Lancashire League, fast bowlers Charlie Griffith and Wes Hall

Connie, Norma and Gloria arriving at Westminster Abbey for a service of thanksgiving to mark the independence of Trinidad and Tobago

It took Connie a long time to earn the right to wear the barrister's wig and gown; his pride in them is undisguised

a black man named Sam Morris. Connie thought him a Barbadian. In fact, Morris had been born in Tasmania of Jamaican parents. He had played first-class cricket for Victoria and won a single cap for Australia, turning out in the second Test of the 1884–5 Ashes series after most of the original side went on strike over pay. Morris was the first black cricketer to play at the highest level.

The trip to play South Australia in Adelaide brought the visitors face to face with Clarrie Grimmett, one of the greatest slow bowlers in history and a man so dedicated to leg spin he trained his dog to retrieve the ball so he could bowl long spells on his own. On a placid wicket that offered him little help Grimmett took nine for 114 as South Australia cruised to a ten-wicket win.

Using the scoring charts and by shrewd observation Grimmett had discovered a fault in Headley's otherwise immaculate play: his over-reliance on the cover drive. By bowling on leg stump he could frustrate the young Jamaican and tempt him into rashness. He adopted a similar approach with Connie. Connie's response was to try to flog Grimmett out of the attack. It was a policy that failed dismally. The Trinidadian would later write that he would rather have 'batted all day against Grimmett than face Mailey for three overs'. The fact was, though, that he never did bat against Grimmett all day, or even for a session. The leg-spinner exposed a weakness in Connie's approach to batting. Too often he seemed intent on play-ing his own game rather than the situation. Some blamed this on the crash-bang style of the Lancashire League, as failures of later batsmen would be blamed on limited-overs cricket. Perhaps playing in the League exacerbated the problem, but Connie always had a desire to dominate when batting, to show the bowlers who was boss. Against the best, particularly spinners, he often came a cropper as a result.

After two heavy defeats the West Indies eyed the coming Test match at Adelaide with some trepidation. Bill Woodfull's team was a powerful one: Bradman, Kippax, McCabe, Jackson, Ponsford and Fairfax was one of the most prolific batting line-ups in Test history. The bowling was weaker, with only Grimmett truly outstanding, though Tim Wall could bowl at a lively pace. Behind the stumps the nimble Oldfield was arguably the best wicketkeeper on the planet.

The West Indies had the edge when it came to a pace attack – Connie, Griffith and Francis had all performed well enough, but the spin bowling was average at best and, though Bradman and the rest of the Australian team would later deny it, the pitch had not been prepared to favour fast bowlers.

The Australians fielded ten of the team who had appeared in the final Test against England at the Oval four months earlier. The only change was Alex Hurwood, an all-rounder who came into the side at the expense of Percy Hornibrook. Hurwood was making his Test debut. For the West Indies, the Test debutants were the captain and vice-captain, Grant and Birkett.

Grant elected to leave out Wight, de Caires, Hunte, St Hill and Sealy, surprising many people by designating Birkett to open the innings alongside the erratic Roach.

For Australia, Tim Wall and Alan Fairfax took the new ball. It was hardly an awe-inspiring opening attack and Roach and Birkett played with confidence. Grimmett was soon brought on. On a slow wicket even the appearance of the great wrist spinner did little to alter the momentum of the West Indies openers and the fifty partnership came up in just thirty-six minutes.

Getting little help from the wicket, Grimmett was rely-
ing on subtle variations in flight and eventually made the
breakthrough when he looped a ball a little higher, tempted
Birkett into an injudicious drive and took the resultant
catch himself. Headley came to the wicket only to depart in
the same over, a Grimmett googly biting and kicking, Wall
snapping up the chance at short leg. Martin batted stoutly
and struck anything short or overpitched to the boundary,
while Roach carried on in his usual hit-and-miss manner
at the other end. At lunch the tourists were 96 for two.
Roach reached his fifty after the resumption but was out
shortly afterwards, stumped by Oldfield off the bowling of
Hurwood.

Roach's dismissal brought Connie to the wicket. After ten
runs had been added, the Trinidadian decided to strike a
blow against Grimmett. The canny little spinner was not so
easily dealt with, however. With only a single to his name,
Connie hit against the spin in an attempt to swing a leg-
break to the on-side boundary, but succeeded only in skying
the ball to Tim Wall at square leg.

The West Indies were eventually dismissed for 296, with
Grant undefeated on 53. He had been at the crease for over
three hours. Doubts may have been cast on his right to
be captain, but his grit and application was indisputable.
Connie thought it a fine innings. Grimmett ended with
seven for 84 off forty-eight overs.

Ponsford and Jackson opened for Australia. Connie
bowled with typical aggression despite the burning heat,
banging the ball in short and fizzing it around the batsmen's ears. But the wicket was painfully slow and the home
side passed fifty shortly before lunch. In the afternoon
things swung the tourists' way. Francis took the edge of
Jackson's bat with his second delivery, to have him caught

at the wicket for 31. Francis then did Bradman for pace with his first two deliveries without finding the stumps and in the nervous moments that followed Ponsford was run out thanks to a Constantine-esque piece of fielding by Birkett.

Despite his success, Francis was taken out of the attack by Grant and replaced with Griffith. What might have looked like a blunder by the young captain was quickly revealed as a stroke of genius when Bradman cut the new bowler straight to the skipper at second slip and returned to the pavilion for four.

Griffith came close to bowling McCabe first ball, and had a big shout for leg before against Kippax turned down by the umpire. Either might have made the situation irreparable for the home side. As it was, the middle-order pair gradually pulled things around despite tight bowling from Martin, carrying the total to 200, the pace of the scoring accelerating as the West Indians tired in the brutal heat.

Grant took the new ball. McCabe slashed Griffith's second delivery with it straight to Grant at second slip, but the normally reliable skipper dropped it. Fortunately for Grant, when he had added just sixteen more runs McCabe mistimed a hook shot off a Connie bouncer, sending it steepling almost straight up into the air. Taking no chances, the all-rounder ran down the pitch to pouch it himself.

With the score on 190 for four Bill Woodfull came to the wicket to a standing ovation in recognition of his Ashes-winning captaincy of the summer. Kippax was on 99 when the two batsmen got in a complete muddle over a quick single and both finished at the same end. Woodfull unselfishly left his ground – run out for six. Kippax duly made the most of the captain's sacrifice and completed his century. By the close Australia were 297 for five, leading by one run with the elegant Kippax 118 not out.

The following morning the Australians raced away. Connie's first two overs cost 19 runs. Kippax seemed set for a massive score when, on 146, he edged a delivery from Griffith and was caught by wicketkeeper Barrow. Scott, the West Indian leg-spinner, then ran through the home side's batting, taking four wickets in nine deliveries. Australia were all out for 376, a lead of 80 runs. In the circumstances, Grant and his men could feel reasonably pleased with themselves.

Unfortunately, the weakness against slow bowling highlighted in the state games had not been rectified. As expected, Grimmett was soon bowling. He adopted his leg-side mode of attack against Headley with a view to frustrating the number three. It worked. With his score on 11 and the leg-spinner nagging away at him, the West Indian jumped down the wicket to drive, was utterly deceived by the flight and comfortably stumped by Oldfield.

On his slow walk back to the pavilion Headley thought back to the advice Connie had given him before his Test debut: 'play within your limitations'. For the rest of the tour he would do just that, making the Australian spinners work to get him out.

Martin dealt with Grimmett more patiently, but was then run out by Bradman. Connie came in and, as usual, went immediately on the attack, clubbing 12 runs off the first six deliveries he received from Hurwood. Against Grimmett Connie moved across to the off, thinking to slam him through midwicket, only to misjudge the spinner's loop and end up bowled around the legs for 14. If his advice to Headley had been sound, he seemed reluctant to follow it himself. At 74 for four, still six runs adrift, the tourists were in major trouble.

Birkett and Grant both batted resolutely and Barrow

produced a few decent shots, but the tourists were all out
for 249, Grant again undefeated – this time with 74 to his
name. He was the first player in history to make two undefeated half-centuries in a Test match. Grimmett had bowled
tirelessly to take another four wickets, finishing on eleven
for the match.

Needing 170 to win on a wicket that had livened up a
touch, Australia got off to a good start. After lunch Connie
opted to bowl spinners in the hope of taking advantage
of the bowlers' footmarks, but he could not unsettle the
Australian openers, who both reached half-centuries. The
tourists fielded brilliantly but little could be done to halt the
home side's progress and at tea they were 160 without loss.
The winning hit was made by Jackson five minutes after the
resumption. The match ball was grabbed by a small boy
on the boundary who later presented it to the West Indies'
twelfth man, young Derek Sealy, as a souvenir. It was the
only gift the Australians had offered.

From Adelaide, the tourists took the train to Melbourne
and from there the boat to Tasmania. The climate on the
southern island was much colder than on the mainland. It
was here that many of the West Indians saw snow for the
first time.

Despite the temperature, the visitors enjoyed themselves. A good crowd turned up to watch the first match at
Launceston. At lunch, with the home side 119–2, Connie
and his team mates were introduced to future Australian
prime minister Joseph Lyons. The meeting with the
politician seemed to inspire the West Indians, and in the
afternoon session St Hill took four for 57 as Tasmania
crumbled to 184 all out.

The following day was a rest day. The team were taken
to a local cherry orchard where Connie amused his hosts

by climbing up one of the trees to get at the best fruit. The next day when Connie came to the crease he performed a much more impressive feat. Joining his captain with the West Indians struggling at 122–4 he immediately began crashing the ball around the ground with such ferocity his bat cracked and had to be replaced. Connie broke in the new willow by blazing a couple more boundaries to reach 24 in just five minutes. James was brought back into the attack to try to stem the flow of runs. Connie cuffed his first delivery over cover and into the open pavilion for six. Off the next ball Des Brain dropped a towering hit and Connie responded to his escape by driving the following delivery to the cover boundary to reach his fifty. He had been at the crease for twenty minutes.

In the afternoon Connie was not quite so explosive, but still scored at a rate better than a run a minute. His century was reached with a pull for four off Nash that slapped into the fence at square leg with a noise like a rifle shot. The hundred had taken fifty-two minutes and included ten fours, a six and a five. But there were to be no more fireworks. Nash clean-bowled him next ball. Connie's whirlwind century is still the fastest ever scored at the North Tasmania Cricket Association Ground. Nash later commented that it was the greatest innings he ever saw, while Green could recall only one delivery Connie did not score off, a bouncer that sailed over his head and these days would have been called as a wide.

After Connie departed there was an inevitable feeling of anticlimax and the innings closed on 353, a big lead for the visitors. In their second knock Tasmania subsided to 119 all out. The West Indians had won by an innings and 50 runs. It was their first victory of the tour, and while Tasmania were not of the same standard as the other Australian state sides (they would not be admitted to the Sheffield Shield until 1977), after so many crushing defeats it was a welcome boost to team morale.

Shortly after close of play the team were travelling again, this time by train to Hobart for their second match on the island. The game at the Tasmania Cricket Association Ground began on Christmas Eve and continued through Christmas Day, the first Connie had spent outside Trinidad. He took six wickets for 25 runs in Tasmania's first innings and produced a memorably acrobatic catch at short leg to send Brain back to the pavilion. Rain ended the game early and the visitors sailed directly to Sydney for the second Test. The tour was barely a third of the way through and already the West Indians had travelled many thousands of miles by train and ship. If at times they appeared unfocused, perhaps that was unsurprising. Connie, the draw card, had so far played in every game. Grant had often nursed him in the field, bowling him only sparingly, but there is little doubt that tiredness had crept in.

Australia made a single change to their winning team, the veteran Bert Ironmonger coming in for Tim Wall. The fact that the home team had replaced their one genuine quickie with a left-arm spinner was a clear indication not only of their opinion of the West Indians' abilities against slow bowling, but also of the type of wicket that had been prepared at the SCG. The tourists fielded the same XI as they had at Melbourne.

Woodfull won the toss and elected to bat. The innings got off to a bad start when Jackson waved his bat outside off stump to Griffith and was well caught by Francis, one-handed at first slip, for eight. Bradman then came to the wicket for his first-ever Test innings on his home ground. He walked out to a huge roar from the twenty-two

thousand-strong crowd and was soon into his stride, pulling Connie to the boundary – the first four of the day.
Bradman appeared in invincible form, glancing and cutting
with his characteristically metronomic precision. So it was
a surprise to everyone when he was caught at the wicket off
Griffith for 25.

Kippax then survived an appeal for caught and bowled
by Francis, who swooped across the pitch to knock up a
drive with his right hand before catching it with his left.
The West Indian fielders all believed it was out, but umpire
George Borwick ruled it a bump ball. Unimpressed by the
decision and Kippax's refusal to take Francis's word, the
tourists simmered throughout the rest of a long day.

Kippax departed soon after lunch, caught by Bartlett at
mid-on off Griffith for 10. Unfortunately, in tumbling forward to take the catch the fielder jammed one of his fingers
into the turf, fracturing a bone. He would take no further
part in the match.

Undeterred by the placid wicket, Connie bowled really
fast, digging the ball in short and sending bumpers whis-
tling round the batsmen's ears. He found the edge of
Ponsford's bat with one fearsome delivery that kicked up
from a length, but the pace carried the ball high over the
slip cordon and racing to the boundary.

The hundred came up in 132 minutes with Ponsford,
tenacious as ever, on 37. McCabe batted in more cavalier
fashion, hammering the ball to the boundary with drives,
cuts and pulls before he fell lbw to Scott.

With the score on 140 for four the day was still evenly
poised when Woodfull arrived at the wicket. The two
Victorians took the score to 187 at tea without undue
alarm, though the crowd were unimpressed with Ponsford –
who had reached 87 – and barracked him for slow scoring.

After the interval Ponsford made his century and the score passed 200. Grant took the new ball but, as is so often the case, this served only to increase the scoring rate. Ponsford in particular began, by his own lights at least, galloping along to 174. At stumps Australia were 323 for four, the stand between Woodfull and Ponsford worth 154.

The West Indies had stuck to their task for most of the day, but in the final hour, as they tired, their outfielding became ragged and – some judged – noticeably less enthusiastic. The latter, at least, seems heavily influenced by popular racial preconceptions. When Tony Greig made his notorious 'When they are down, they grovel' comment on the eve of the 1977 England–West Indies series he was expressing a view with long historical roots. That his team were subsequently thrashed by Clive Lloyd's men is surely the final word on its veracity.

Heavy downpours washed out the whole of the second day. Most observers seemed to feel that the rain had little effect on what was still a perfect strip for batting. Despite that view, twenty wickets would fall on the third day for just 220 runs.

Australia had not added a run to their overnight total when Woodfull nicked Connie to Barrow. Fairfax began with three boundaries, but was then superlatively caught by Connie diving forward from backward point to grab the ball inches from the turf off the bowling of Francis. Oldfield arrived at the wicket and soon left again, run out by Headley for a duck. Scott then did what he had shown himself to be good at – mopping up the tail. He got Ponsford for 183, bowled Grimmett for 12 and had Hurwood caught for five. The spinner finished with four for 66, his final spell bringing him three wickets for just 9 runs.

Australia's last six wickets had fallen for 46 runs and Grant and his men were pleased at restricting the home side to a manageable total of 344. 'The game did not look so bad for us,' Connie noted, before adding 'but alas . . .'

Birkett fell before lunch for three and after that the wickets tumbled. Headley edged a ball into his stumps off Fairfax and was out for 14, Martin went to the crafty Grimmett for 10 and Roach was stupidly run out to reduce the tourists to 36 for four with Bartlett unable to bat.

Connie and Grant were now at the wicket. They were the West Indies' last hope for making a recovery, but when Connie had reached 12 he again attempted to paste Grimmett for six. His high, looping sweep shot failed to clear the boundary and Bradman took the catch at deep square leg a couple of yards in from the rope. Grant adopted a more pragmatic approach, but after taking half an hour to reach six he was caught in the slips off Ironmonger. At tea the visitors were seven down for 80.

After tea Barrow fell to Fairfax. Scott made a steady 15 not out, but when Griffith fell to Grimmett the innings was over with the total just 107.

Little Clarrie Grimmett was once again the main tormentor, with four for 54. His mastery, like that of Shane Warne, was as much psychological as it was physical. The pitch offered little, the ball barely turned, yet the visitors were utterly bewitched by Grimmett, frozen like field mice before a swaying cobra.

Trailing by 262, the West Indies were asked to follow on. The tumble of wickets continued unabated and by the close they were 67 for five. This time the damage was done by the medium-paced swingers of Hurwood, who dismissed Birkett for eight, Headley for two and Martin without scoring. Roach and Grant batted determinedly, but as the safety

of the close approached Fairfax pulled off a brilliant catch
to dismiss Roach off the bowling of McCabe.

Connie came to the wicket and took guard in an apparently nonchalant fashion. The impression was confirmed
when Hurwood promptly bowled him around his legs. The
look of surprise on Connie's face as he heard the sound of
the ball rattling his stumps seemed to watchers to indicate
that he was unsure of where his feet were planted. Like his
wild swish at Grimmett, it spoke of a man whose mind was
elsewhere.

Grant and Barrow held on until the close, but only
bad weather could now save the tourists from crushing
defeat. Sadly for the West Indians, nature offered them
no help and on Monday morning the Australians took just
twenty-four minutes to secure a massive win. The match
had lasted less than ten sessions, three of which had been
lost to rain. The margin of the defeat – an innings and
172 runs – was so great that there were mutterings in the
Australian press about curtailing the series, an idea some
West Indies cricket officials seemed to be toying with too.
Certainly there seemed little to be gained from watching
their team go from one catastrophic defeat to another. And
then there was the inevitable question of crowds. In those
pre-television days, gate receipts paid for the tour, and how
many Australians would part with their cash to see such
one-sided matches?

Connie seemed fatalistic about the debacle, noting
that 'We could not get together in that tour; whereas the
Australians played up to that invariable formula of theirs:
"If one man can't do it, we've always got another."'

The next stop for Grant's battered team was Brisbane,
for a match with Queensland. It was yet another long train
ride for the tourists, though on this occasion sunshine

and the familiar tropical fruit on offer during the journey offered some compensation. Queensland were the weakest of the Sheffield Shield sides, but they still had good players, including the country's latest fast-bowling sensation, aboriginal Eddie Gilbert. Connie relished the prospect of facing the tearaway: 'The man was said to have bowled hundreds of overs with his arm in splints, to teach himself not to throw the ball. He is the only very fast bowler I have known who begins the over at a clinking good speed and gets faster every ball!'

The match was played at the Woolloongabba Ground, the first time this now-famous arena had hosted a major match. Despite the fears that the paying public would stay away, 4800 spectators turned up on the first morning. Grant won the toss and elected to bat. Roach and Martin did their bit, putting on 75 for the first wicket, though both were troubled by the extreme pace of Gilbert, who bowled off a short run-up and with his sleeves rolled down – two facts that led to continual suspicions about his action, arm splints or not.

Roach was first to go, but Headley saw the tourists safely through to lunch. In the afternoon the Jamaican fell to a delivery from Gilbert that trickled onto his stumps from an inside edge. The Aboriginal then had Martin 'strangled' down the leg side. Soon afterwards Grant slashed at a short, wide delivery from the paceman and was caught in the slips. Enter Connie. The Trinidadian took his guard, surveyed the field and launched into the attack. When Gilbert dropped one short outside leg stump, Connie crashed it over the pickets for a huge six. It was the first time the bowler had ever suffered such ignominy and so impressed was he by Connie's feat that he walked down the wicket and shook his hand.

Connie continued to flog the bowling until, when he had reached 75 in just fifty minutes, he jumped down the wicket to Mick Brew, missed the ball and was stumped. He had struck eight boundaries and left the field to a standing ovation. The fearsome Gilbert was one of those applauding him most loudly.

The remaining wickets fell cheaply as the tourists totalled 309. Gilbert returned figures of five for 65, which might have been even better had a number of catches off his bowling not been spilled.

Queensland made a terrible start – Connie took Gough's wicket with his first delivery, caught by Francis in the slips – and continued in the same vein, all out for 167. Connie took four for 43. As on so many occasions in his career, a good time with the bat seemed to have inspired him with the ball.

The West Indians had a big lead, but when they batted a second time they were soon in trouble, five wickets down for 80 and in danger of undoing all their good work. The third day again saw Connie at his brilliant best. He rattled along at a run a minute, smashing thirteen boundaries and taking seventeen off one Goodwin over. Gilbert continued to bowl at ferocious pace, and though Connie dealt with him in extravagant style, Sealy did not handle him nearly so well. Having already been struck one painful blow on the back, he failed to avoid another bouncer and was knocked out by a sickening blow on the temple. He regained consciousness and was led groggily back to the pavilion.

If he was shaken by Sealy's injury, Connie gave no indication of it as he continued in the same belligerent manner. He was eventually dismissed in the most bizarre fashion when he had reached 97. Connie had apparently decided to get the last three runs in singles but, frustrated by his partner Birkett's unwillingness to sprint, eventually elected to hit a six instead. Straight-driving a Bensted delivery uppishly but with lashing power a few yards to the bowler's right, Connie must have anticipated just that outcome; instead, he could only look on in horror as the ball struck the top corner of Birkett's bat. The deflection flew to mid-on at such speed the fielder could only palm it away – straight into the hands of a team mate running in from midwicket. 'I went indoors a sadly injured man,' Connie commented.

The West Indians' innings closed on 265, Birkett batting soundly for 41. Queensland needed an improbable 408 to win and lost by 219 runs. Connie finished with three for 23 to add to his wickets in the first innings. The exhilarating all-round performance of the Trinidadian and the ease of the victory gave the West Indians the lift they needed before what would be only the second Test match ever to be played in Brisbane. The venue, Exhibition Park, was hosting its last major game before it was replaced by the Gabba.

Hurwood was unavailable for Australia because of work commitments. In his first two Tests he had taken eleven wickets at 15.45 each, yet he would never be picked to play for his country again. His replacement, Ron Oxenham, was winning his first Test cap since 1929. The West Indies were forced into one change. Bartlett was out because of his broken finger. Young Sealy – fully recovered from his blow to the head – replaced him.

Woodfull won the toss. Australia batted. Jackson was out to the third ball of the match, trapped in front of his wicket by Francis for a golden duck. Bradman arrived to a huge ovation from the ten thousand or so spectators. Connie and the West Indians were determined that Bradman would fail in the series, and so far they had done well enough against him. Connie felt that Bradman was vulnerable outside off

peg early in the innings. 'It was obvious he did not care
much for speed bowling when there were good fielders in
the slip.' With the great man at the wicket Connie carefully
arranged his field. 'I bowled carefully, to lull him into security without ever showing what was coming. Then, when
we had more or less let him get four runs, I gave him one
or two balls as bait, and then shot down my fastest on his
off stump breaking away.' The delivery found Bradman's
outside edge. Alas for the tourists, Birkett at first slip could
not hold on to the chance. It was a crucial error. Connie
had proved his point, but the Don was not a man to make
the same mistake twice. Now he gave the fast bowler a
look 'as much as to say that he saw it all, and then settled
down grimly'. It was certainly grim for the tourists. After
his lapse, Bradman went on to dismantle the West Indies
attack with clinical precision. With Ponsford in support, the
first fifty came up in just forty-one minutes. Bradman's footwork was immaculate and he sprayed his shots all around
the field. He and Ponsford ran brilliantly between the wickets, forcing quick singles at every opportunity. The West
Indies fielders became increasingly jittery, throws became
wilder, simple stops were fumbled. Bradman and Ponsford
both reached their fifties before lunch, by which time their
partnership was worth 126.

After the break Connie resorted to a short-pitched attack,
which succeeded in slowing the run rate and discomfited
Ponsford. As Connie tired however the batsmen went back
on the attack. The 200 was rattled up in 138 minutes and
a few balls later Ponsford took a couple of runs off Griffith
to reach his century. Griffith's next over saw Bradman join
his team mate on three figures. When he had reached 103,
Ponsford edged Connie to Grant in the slips, but the skipper spilled the chance. Infuriated, Connie dug one in and

watched as it struck the opener a painful blow square in the chest. Plainly shaken, Ponsford scored just six more before he waved his bat indecisively and edged Francis. This time Birkett made no mistake.

By tea Australia were 262 for two, with Bradman on 129 and the elegant Kippax – who had almost been run out when in single figures – on 15.

Bradman moved on to 150 after the interval and the run rate accelerated. Kippax posted his half-century in seventy-five minutes while Bradman galloped to 200. The 400 arrived in double-quick time, the last hundred runs scored in forty-six minutes against the flagging West Indies bowlers.

Connie laboured to stem the flow of runs, but remained luckless; Kippax was dropped by Scott off his bowling. When Kippax fell just short of his century, McCabe joined Bradman and the pair took the Australians through to the close without alarm. Bradman walked back to the pavilion on 223 – the highest score by any Australian in a home Test.

On the second day a crowd of close to twenty thousand turned up in the hope of seeing Bradman beat R. E. Foster's record Test score of 287. Sadly for them, Connie had other ideas. The fourth ball of his opening over was short of a length, Bradman went on to the back foot to pull, but it was on him too quickly and his shot sailed straight into the hands of Grant at deepish square leg. Much to everyone's relief, he held on to it.

Next Connie produced a brilliant piece of fielding, flying through the air to catch McCabe left-handed at third slip off the bowling of Griffith. The same bowler dismissed Woodfull not long afterwards, the Australian captain caught at the wicket for 17. Bowling tightly and fielding superbly, the West Indians tied down Fairfax and Oxenham. In an attempt to break the stranglehold the former attempted to slog Scott over cow corner and was caught at deep midwicket by Sealy. Again the tourists were unable to sustain the pressure. Oxenham and Oldfield batted at first steadily and then with increasing pugnacity, Oxenham striking sixteen from one Scott over. The pair had added 75 for the eighth wicket when Oxenham fell lbw to Francis for 48. Grimmett did not last long, the victim of another wonderful catch by Connie, this time at point off the bowling of Francis. Griffith quickly got rid of the rabbit Ironmonger, leaving Oldfield not out on 38 and the Australian total at 558.

It was a score that put victory beyond the West Indies' reach, but Grant's men took satisfaction from the fact they had picked up the last seven wickets for just 130 runs. Connie came in for particular praise from the local press – his catching had been magical in its brilliance and his throws from the deep had whistled into the wicketkeeper's gloves so fast and accurately they drew spontaneous rounds of applause from the spectators.

One aspect of the long hours of toil in the field that had appealed to Connie was the interaction with the Australian crowd. Connie always enjoyed the wit and wisdom of cricket fans, whether that was his friend Alwyn at Nelson, bellowing 'You've got him in two minds now bowler – he doesn't know whether to hit you for four or six,' or the West Indian 'mascot' fans such as Trinidad's Taffy or Flanagin of Barbados whose insults were generally couched in florid language and filled with biblical allusions. Once he had taunted Connie and the visiting Trinidadians with a shout that, when it came to batting, Barbados were the 'Alpha and Omega, the Beginning and the End, the First and the

Last'. Nothing that came from the stands in Brisbane quite matched that, but Connie enjoyed the barracking – much of it admittedly directed at the sluggish Ponsford – nevertheless: 'Some very bitter things have been said about barrackers, but I fail to see why a cricketer need worry about them – most of it is in good fun, and even if it is not, we cricketers are not delicate young ladies.'

With nothing to play for but a draw and a long time to bat to get it, Grant and his men were in an almost impossible situation. They began the task with a stolidity that was counter to their reputation. In the 115 minutes before the close of play they scored just 51 runs. Sadly, slowness did not mean stability. Three batsmen were dismissed by the home side for whom Ironmonger bowled a spell so tight that he conceded a mere 8 runs in 128 deliveries.

The next morning Headley and Grant walked out to the wicket. The pair had defended dourly but efficiently in fading light the night before, with Headley taking 104 minutes over his 19 and Grant taking a couple of singles in his thirty-five minutes at the crease. The crowd was a poor one, only two thousand spectators turning up for the start of what seemed likely to be a day in which the tourists either defended stubbornly or were brushed aside. Ironmonger and Grimmett began the attack. Grant got off to an aggressive start but the leg-spinner soon ensnared him – caught in the slips by McCabe for eight.

Connie now came out to join Headley – the two greatest West Indian cricketers of the era together at the crease. The Jamaican had been struggling against the spinners all tour, but had now adapted his stance in a bid to combat them, and he at last started to find some form. He began to move his feet more fluidly, stepping down the wicket and launching into a series of drives off Grimmett that stung the fingers of the Australian fielders. Anticipating a front-foot attack the crafty little spinner shortened his length, only to see Headley rock back and effortlessly cut him for four. Having savaged Grimmett, Headley next set about Ironmonger, hammering him to the boundary three times in a single over.

Connie had been relatively quiet at the other end. Sadly for the tourists, he was not to get into his stride, caught at point by Fairfax off the bowling of Ironmonger for nine. It was another Test failure, his downfall once again an attempt to force the pace against the Australian slows.

Birkett almost suffered the indignity of being caught by one of his own team mates, Vibart Wight having come on to the field to help the Australians after Ponsford and Jackson were forced off through injury and illness and no other twelfth man was available. Luckily his checked drive fell just short of the West Indian. Headley continued to bat brilliantly, reaching his fifty and then unleashing a series of powerful drives and cuts that took the West Indies past the hundred mark. Birkett did not last long, falling to Oxenham. After the interval, Grimmett was back to his old tricks, luring Barrow down the wicket with a well-flighted slower ball that deceived the batsman and left him well out of his ground as Oldfield whipped off the bails. Scott did not last long – bowled by Oxenham for a duck hitting across the line. Headley had reached 88 and was running out of partners. Francis, however, did not let his team mate down. Headley farmed the strike – often coming close to being run out in his eagerness – and eventually reached a well-deserved hundred – the first by a West Indian against Australia in a Test. Francis went soon afterwards to Oxenham and then Griffith was utterly bamboozled by Grimmett and trapped lbw, leaving Headley high and dry

on 102, more than half of his team's total of 193. Only two
other batsmen had made double figures.

The Australian lead was 365 and it was no surprise
when Woodfull enforced the follow-on for the second time
in the series. The West Indies' second innings began in
overpowering heat, caused at least in part by the eruption
of a volcano in New Zealand. It was not long before the
visitors were deep in trouble. They had made just 13 when
McCabe bowled Roach, bringing the heroic Headley to
the wicket. He quickly lost his first partner, Martin, to the
bowling of Oxenham and was joined by Grant with the
score on 29. Headley continued to bat as beautifully as he
had in the first innings, but when he had reached 28 he
played a fine leg glance off Ironmonger and was caught by
Oldfield.

Connie came to the wicket amidst the traditional
excitement that greeted his arrival. Once again he disappointed the crowd, playing round a straight delivery from
Oxenham and departing for 7. Grant clung on grimly,
taking twenty minutes to get off the mark and scoring at
barely a run every ten minutes. Birkett survived one chance
off Ironmonger but was then bowled by Grimmett for 13.
Grant's dour occupation ended when he was run out after
a foolish mix-up with Barrow and the wicketkeeper failed
to make much of an amends with the bat, stumped by
Oldfield after dancing down the wicket and missing one
from Grimmett. The leg-spinner then had Scott trapped
lbw. Sealy and Francis negotiated the last few overs of the
day, but with the West Indies on 115 for eight they had only
delayed the inevitable.

The end came swiftly enough the following morning, the
last two West Indies wickets falling for 33 runs inside half
an hour. The victory margin of an innings and 217 was the

most crushing so far. Utterly outclassed, the West Indies had already lost the five-match series.

There was little time for Connie and his team mates to brood as they immediately travelled south to Newcastle and Geelong to play two-day matches against the country XIs of New South Wales and Victoria. Two state matches, against Victoria and South Australia, were to follow, before the West Indies faced Australia again.

In Newcastle, the home side won the toss and elected to bat. They were quickly in trouble against the pace of Connie and Griffith, and the first six wickets went down in a tumble, the great all-rounder grabbing four of them. As was so often the case during the tour, the West Indians then let the opposition off the hook and NSW Country Districts effected an extraordinary recovery to finish all out for 251. A large crowd turned up the next day to watch the West Indians bat. They were initially disappointed as Headley fell early for 65. That brought Connie to the wicket. He may have been struggling with the bat in Tests, but here, far from his nemesis Grimmett, he was at his extraordinary best, belting six sixes and fourteen fours while making 147 in just ninety-three minutes. He was out shortly before lunch, by which time the visitors had shot into the lead – all out for 399.

Chasing a deficit of 148, the locals were again undone by the pace of Griffith and Connie, and were dismissed one short of making the tourists bat again. Connie took another five wickets for 24 runs, giving him match figures of nine for 77. It was an all-round display that would live long in local memory.

The big win in Newcastle must have given the belea-guered West Indians a boost, but if they travelled to Geelong for the next match at the Corio Oval expecting another comfortable win they were in for a rude shock. A seventeen-year-old student from Geelong College named Lindsay Hassett raced to 147 not out and the tourists were humiliatingly forced to follow on. The second innings began just after tea with Connie promoted to opener. As usual he adopted an aggressive approach and blasted twenty off the first over he faced from Freeman. De Caires soon departed for 17 but Connie continued in rip-roaring fashion, treating Freeman particularly harshly, and reached his fifty in thirty-two minutes. The West Indians' total reached three figures ten minutes later, with Connie on 74 and Martin on six. Connie had reached 80 when he skied one into the outfield and was well caught. The West Indians struggled on and the match closed with them 216 for nine, 119 runs ahead. The West Indies had got a draw, but the honours belonged to the part-timers. Without Connie's heroics in the second innings the game might well have been lost.

For their second meeting with the West Indians Victoria fielded what was really a second-string side – their best cricketers were involved in a Sheffield Shield match. Connie was rested, much to the disappointment of the first-day crowd of more than seven thousand, many of whom had come specifically to see if he could repeat his up-country heroics. They did get to see Headley, at least. The Jamaican batted fluently for 77 and 113, Roach made his first century of the tour and Grant also got a decent score in the first innings. With Francis and Griffiths in compelling form the West Indians came close to forcing a victory, the makeshift Victoria side holding out for a creditable draw with just one wicket remaining.

The tour moved on to Adelaide, where South Australia and their grand inquisitor Clarrie Grimmett lay in wait.

Grant won the toss and chose to bat. Headley demonstrated the good footwork that had contributed to his success in the previous Test, dealing with Grimmett with relative ease. The leg-spinner eventually had him caught, but by then he had made 75. When Connie arrived at the wicket to join Grant the pair launched into a controlled attack and plundered 97 runs in little more than an hour. Connie's contribution to the partnership was 63 scored at a run a minute. Had he at last got the measure of Grimmett? After Connie was caught and bowled by Lee, Grant continued and the innings closed on 383. Grimmett finished with five for 144 off a marathon forty-two overs.

Connie had batted with controlled power, and now he matched that with a superb spell of fierce, accurate pace bowling that utterly destroyed any hopes South Australia might have had of matching the tourist's score. In his opening spell of seven overs he took three wickets for 16.

In the hope of engineering a result the West Indians began their second innings in a hurry. The quest for quick runs meant that wickets fell regularly, especially to Grimmett, whose mastery of line and length made any attempt to force the pace against him dangerous. Grant made 42 and Connie bludgeoned his way into the thirties before an attempt to hammer the naggingly accurate Lee out of the ground saw him caught on the boundary at point. A second innings total of 208 left the home side needing 314 runs to win, and a day and part of the final session in which to get them. It was a tough target, but South Australia managed it, squeaking home by a single wicket. Connie had strained a leg muscle the previous evening and was unable to bowl.

For the West Indians, it was another case of letting a win slip through their fingers. Australian observers saw their failure to capitalise as a further sign of their inability to hold their nerve under pressure. Looking back, Connie would note disapprovingly that 'our fielding was terrible, and our raggedness as a team became more pronounced with every game we played'.

For the fourth Test in Melbourne West Indies brought back Bartlett – now recovered from his broken finger – in place of Sealy. Australia were unchanged from Brisbane.

Grant won the toss and elected to bat in torrid heat that seemed certain to make things tough for the fielding side. On what was the quickest strip of the tour so far, Roach and Martin saw off the opening bowlers with relative ease, but that was a minor task compared to dealing with Ironmonger and Grimmett. The slow bowlers were brought into the attack. Grimmett started off with three maidens then induced Roach to sky the ball to Kippax at deep point – unbeknownst to the West Indians, the modest opening stand of 32 was to prove their highest partnership of the entire match.

Headley began well, straight-driving Grimmett to bring up the 50. One run later Martin was so discombobulated by Ironmonger's flight he missed a full toss and was out lbw. With the score on 53 Birkett edged Ironmonger into the slips. McCabe grabbed the chance. By lunch the tourists were 60 for three, their only consolation the fact that Headley had progressed to 20 and looked in fine fettle.

The Jamaican continued impressively after the interval, but when he had reached 33 he lofted a drive straight to Jackson at mid-off. Grant was caught by Oldfield for a duck and Connie arrived at the wicket with the innings approaching crisis. He began with his usual devilish swagger, stealing a quick single, then slapping Grimmett square to the boundary. But when the score had reached

88 disaster struck. Bartlett was stumped by Oldfield when Ironmonger's loop lured him down the track, then Barrow's innings lasted just one ball, edged to Fairfax in the slips. The hat-trick delivery was delayed by fifteen minutes of rain. Scott survived, but in the next over Connie once again gambled on his ability to flog Grimmett over the pickets and lost, caught by Jackson on the square-leg boundary. The West Indies had plummeted from 51 for one to 88 for eight. Scott managed two boundaries off Grimmett to reach double figures, but was then idiotically run out by Francis. Ironmonger completed the rout by dismissing Griffith for a duck. The eccentric veteran had taken seven wickets for 23 runs in twenty overs. The pitch and conditions offered him no assistance whatsoever – against West Indian batting that was on the nervous side of suicidal, he hardly needed any.

The Australians came out to open their innings at a quarter to four. By the time bad light stopped play they were already more than a hundred ahead with just one wicket down, Bradman poised menacingly on 92 and Woodfull solid yet destructive on 75. The pair had struck a century partnership in an hour. The tourists' only success was the lucky dismissal of Ponsford, stumped when the ball cannoned back off Barrow's pads.

During the day talks were held between the Australian Cricket Board, the Victorian Cricket Association and the West Indies management about reducing ticket prices for the remainder of the Test. Only 3969 spectators had paid to watch the first day, and with the West Indies so thoroughly outclassed some inducement was clearly needed. As it was, any decision would prove irrelevant.

Overnight rain left the pitch soft, particularly at the Richmond End. From being the perfect batting track, it had now become a bowlers' paradise. Bradman struggled from the outset and was dropped before he had added to his overnight score. In his distress – the Don was never comfortable on difficult pitches – he lost concentration and failed to answer his captain's call for a quick single. Woodfull was stranded in mid-pitch and run out for 80.

Using his feet splendidly, Bradman gradually eased into gear and reached his century in 102 minutes. Jackson kept him company before he top-edged a ball from Connie high into the air over wicketkeeper Barrow's head. Birkett in the slips was quick off the mark and sprinted round to take a stunning catch. Another running mix-up accounted for McCabe. Bradman was then well caught at long off by Roach off the bowling of Martin. He had made 152, including two fives as well as thirteen fours. Kippax made 24. Connie pulled off a trademark gymnastic catch at short leg to dismiss Oxenham for nought. When Fairfax was out for 15 Woodfull declared with the score on 328 for eight.

Some in the crowd believed Woodfull had declared at just the right time to take advantage of the last bit of devil in the wicket. Others were convinced that the Australian skipper had left it too late and that the pitch was now fine for batting. The West Indies' haphazard approach would make it impossible to judge which interpretation was the correct one.

Grant chose to shuffle his batting order for reasons not altogether apparent, though in the age of uncovered wickets such changes were more common than they are today. Roach walked out to bat in the unfamiliar company of Connie. The traditional opener was soon out lbw to Fairfax. Connie, oddly subdued, had made just 10 out of a total of 32 when he became Fairfax's second victim, snicking to Kippax in the slips. Ironmonger then dismissed Headley for 11, superbly caught by the diving Fairfax,

and with him went any chance of the West Indies making
Australia bat for a second time. After that it was a proces-
sion, the biggest partnership of the innings the 23 Barrow
and Scott added for the eighth wicket. The final wicket,
that of Francis caught by Jackson off Grimmett, fell with
the score on 107. Australia had won by an innings and 122
runs in a match that had occupied less than two days. If
Brisbane had been a disaster for the West Indians, this was
a total catastrophe.

As if the hammering they had taken on the field was
not bad enough, it had by now become clear that the tour
was a financial mess and losing more money by the day.
In a bid to staunch the losses the Australian Cricket Board
informed the West Indies that they would no longer pay for
the players' taxis to and from venues. From now on the visitors would have to use public transport to get to matches.
Though the tourists accepted this announcement with
good grace it must have come as a further blow to their
self-esteem.

The next match for the cash-strapped and demoralised
team was the return against New South Wales in Sydney.
The state side were without Fairfax and Oldfield, while
Archie Jackson was forced to withdraw with illness – the
first signs of the tuberculosis that would prematurely end
his life two years later. His replacement was a youngster
named Jack Fingleton.

Desperate for some sort of uplift in fortunes, the West
Indians picked their Test top order, replacing only the
struggling Bartlett with the lively Sealy. Grant won the toss
and chose to bat on another easy-paced wicket. His side
responded as if it was the first day of the tour, putting all
the negativity of the past weeks behind them and batting
wonderfully. Headley posted his thousandth run of the tour

and Connie played cautiously, making an uncharacteristi-
cally orthodox 41 during which he made no attempt at the
outlandish or the astounding. In the eyes of many observers he looked all the better for it. The West Indians were
bowled out shortly before the close for 339.

The following morning Connie produced a superb,
sustained spell of pace bowling. He was brought on first
change. His time in the field had allowed him to observe
the way the ball was moving in the air and off the pitch.
Using a combination of away swing and off-cutters he
took six wickets for 24. Remarkably, all of them were
clean-bowled. He started as he meant to continue, rattling
Davidson's timbers with his first delivery – a fast ball that
broke back into the batsman – and pegging back Bradman's
off stump with a slower version of the delivery that had
done for Davidson in his next over. Bill batted solidly but
was run out by Grant after a mix-up for 41. Griffith then
trapped Kippax in front of his stumps. Connie returned to
the attack to clip McCabe off-stump via an inside edge with
another ball that darted in off the pitch and followed that
by knocking over Hunt and Theak. Finally, with McGurk
and Fingleton putting up stubborn resistance, Grant
recalled Connie to the attack for a third time and he duly
finished off the innings by sending McGurk's bails flying
with his third delivery. The home side were all out for 190,
Connie having shattered their resistance with short bursts
of controlled aggression on a flat wicket.

The West Indians came in to bat with a lead of 149.
They were quickly reduced to 37 for three, but then Sealy
and Martin came together and posted a fifty partnership
that took their team safely through to close of play. When
Martin fell lbw to Chilvers for 56 next morning, Connie
came to the wicket. In the next hundred minutes he flayed

the New South Wales attack in a calculated display of
power hitting that, remarkably, did not contain a single six.
(Arthur Mailey had bet Connie sixpence that he could not
score fifty without once lifting the ball over the boundary
rope; the Australian had lost his wager.) An innings that
Connie would consider his finest in first-class cricket was
ended just seven short of a century thanks to a brilliant
piece of fielding by wicketkeeper Davidson, who chased
over to square leg to retrieve the ball and scored a direct hit
with only one stump to aim at. Grant was able to declare at
tea with the total on 403 for nine, setting the home side 553
to win in four sessions.

On the final day a decent crowd was present to see if New
South Wales could pull off an unlikely win. After his heroics with the ball in the first innings Connie was relatively
subdued in this one. Hampered by an injured shoulder, he
bowled just eight overs, dismissing Fingleton. Francis and
Griffith did the damage and once McCabe had gone for
exactly 100 wickets fell regularly, Francis clean-bowling the
last three batsmen to end the home side's resistance. They
had made 466, giving the West Indians victory by 86 runs.

The win was popular with the crowd, who had come
to regard the tourists as plucky underdogs, and they were
warmly applauded off the field. It was easily the West
Indians' best and most consistent performance of the tour
so far. They had suffered a series of reverses but refused to
buckle. The win was a decisive riposte to those who thought
they lacked backbone or fighting spirit. To Connie's mind
the transformation came from simply trying 'to play cricket,
without regard to the waves of contradictory advice that we
had paid far too much attention to hitherto'.

Buoyed up by their victory in New South Wales and
with nothing to lose, the West Indies came into the final

Test in a positive frame of mind and determined to play attacking cricket. With that in mind the exuberant Sealy replaced Birkett in the middle order. Jackson was missing for Australia, replaced by Keith Rigg.

The Australians badly mismanaged their travel arrangements and five players, including Ironmonger and Grimmett, arrived in Sydney only ninety minutes before the start of play, having spent close to thirty-six hours on trains. Grant took full advantage of any tiredness the spinners might have been feeling, winning the toss and electing to bat on a faster surface than any the tourists had encountered so far. It was rumoured that this was a result of an appeal for a quicker strip that had been made by senior West Indians to a member of the ACB a week earlier. Bradman and others would later dismiss claims that the pitches had been doctored to suit the spinners as nonsense. But then they would.

Connie was pleased to be back at the SCG, which he regarded as the finest cricket ground in the world, though his contribution to the West Indies' first innings was a duck that earned him a good deal of scorn from the Hill. As it was, Connie's failure hardly mattered. Martin and Roach rattled up an opening stand of 70 before Grimmett struck, trapping Roach lbw for 31. Headley arrived at the wicket and after lunch began to carry the attack to Australia. His fifty came up in sixty-three minutes and he had soon over-hauled opener Martin, who had been at the wicket for an hour longer. At tea Headley had 84, Martin 70.

Headley reached his hundred after batting for 133 minutes and striking thirteen fours. He was out soon afterwards, lbw to McCabe. His standing ovation was well merited, for an innings considered by many observers to have been one of the finest ever seen at Sydney, a wonderful mix of powerful drives off the front and back foot and wristy cuts and glances. Grimmett was so impressed he later commented that Headley was the best on-side batsmen he had come across, superior even to Hobbs and Bradman.

Martin had played the anchor role and eventually completed his own century after 273 minutes at the crease. The light deteriorated shortly afterwards and the teams came off the field with the West Indies on 298 for two, Grant having made an enterprising 48.

Rain fell overnight and continued on Saturday morning, delaying the start until a quarter past two. The moisture had transformed the uncovered wicket from benign to spiteful. From the restart even Australia's medium pacers were getting the ball to lift alarmingly from a length, particularly from the southern end of the ground.

The West Indies continued batting for an hour and a quarter, during which time they added 52 runs and lost four wickets. The dogged Martin remained unbeaten on 123 when, with his side 350 for six, Grant decided to take advantage of the conditions and declared. Connie thought it a good decision, a sign that the young skipper had learned from previous errors. Whatever he might have thought of Grant's appointment, Connie always gave praise where it was due.

Tea was taken in the interval between innings and Woodfull asked for the heavy roller in an attempt to mollify the wicket. The Australian captain opened the innings in the company of Ponsford. They found the going tough from the outset. Francis bowled superbly, trapping Ponsford by first baiting his trap with a slower bouncer then following it with a much quicker one. The first was hooked easily for a couple of runs, the second flicked straight into the hands of Bartlett at short fine leg.

Bradman arrived at the wicket. He went on the attack almost immediately, forcing Grant to remove fielders from close to the wicket with a series of drives, pulls and cuts. With Woodfull giving a defensive masterclass at the other end Bradman scored 43 out of a total of 59 before falling to a splendid diving catch by Francis off the bowling of Martin. Kippax came in, scored 3 runs and was then caught by Sealy at slip to give Connie his first wicket of the match.

The light was beginning to fail again, but the umpire turned down Woodfull's appeal to leave the field and a few moments later Francis dismissed Rigg. Another appeal against the light was turned down and in the next over Woodfull was brilliantly caught by Connie flinging himself full-length at second slip off Martin's bowling. He had taken a hundred minutes to make 22. His departure and the arrival of Fairfax saw a further deterioration of the light and the players left the field with the home side on 89 for five.

Connie, at least, was surprised by the interruption: 'We suffered badly from umpiring during that tour ... Our appeals against the light were disregarded, but once or twice, when things were running our way on a wet wicket, play ended rather suddenly before time. There were some queer decisions about catches; when we got them something was wrong with them, but it was not so the other way round.' The last England team to tour Australia had made similar complaints. Until the introduction of neutral umpires it would be a familiar refrain from all tourists in all nations.

McCabe and Fairfax renewed the innings after the Sunday rest day. The pitch was much improved and the sixth-wicket pair quickly added 41. Then McCabe

misjudged one of Francis's bouncers – this one of the slower
variety – and pulled the ball straight to Headley. In his next
over Francis dismissed Oxenham, caught at the wicket for
a duck off one that lifted. The follow-on was averted thanks
to stout batting by Fairfax and Oldfield, who added 62 for
the eighth wicket. The pair were separated straight after
lunch when the wicketkeeper was run out attempting to go
for a second run. Fairfax was then stumped off Scott for 54.
The Australian innings was finished off by Griffith, who
clean-bowled Ironmonger. Francis had taken four wickets
for 48. Connie, still feeling the effects of his shoulder strain,
was used sparingly, sending down just ten overs.

West Indies had a lead of 126. Roach and Martin set
about adding to that, putting on 46 runs before Martin
chopped at one from Grimmett and sent the ball flying into
the hands of McCabe at slip. After tea Archie Jackson came
on as substitute fielder for Fairfax, who had a damaged
heel.* Headley and Roach both scored briskly after the
break. Roach struck a couple of boundaries off Ironmonger,
but was then caught at the wicket off the same bowler.
Grant arrived. He and Headley took the West Indies' total
into three figures, but then Headley moved too far across
his stumps trying to work Oxenham to the onside and
was bowled round his legs. Sealy fell for seven, run out by
a direct hit from McCabe. The light was poor but Grant
was too eager to get on with things to appeal against it. He
pulled Ironmonger twice to the boundary, but Connie was
less fortunate with his own attempts to swing the left-armer
into the stands and was caught in the deep by Bradman.

If some thought Grant had been reckless to bat on in bad

---

* This would be Jackson's final appearance on a first-class cricket field. He died,
aged twenty-three, on 16 February 1933.

light his decision was vindicated when a deluge washed out play for the whole of Tuesday, the fourth day of the match. The 4 p.m. inspection of the wicket saw Grant eagerly pressing for the chance to play, while Woodfull argued against it.

The tourists were scheduled to leave for home on the Thursday, so though the match was 'timeless' there was some doubt over whether it could be completed before the tourists set sail.

On Wednesday morning the two teams awoke to fine weather. The pitch was still damp, and after inspecting the wicket Grant elected to gamble again and declare – and in so doing became the first captain in the history of Test cricket to declare twice in the same match. The tourists' advantage was just 250. It was another commendably bold decision.

Woodfull and Ponsford opened the innings against Francis and Connie. The crowd was lively: 'You could hear their voices booming all together like the waves of the sea.' Just as in the Caribbean, wild wagers were being made and cynical catcalls directed at the players. It was just the sort of atmosphere the West Indians relished. The wisdom of Grant's decision soon became evident as the ball fizzed and kicked alarmingly from both ends. The two opening batsmen both gave sharp chances, but they were put down by fieldsmen 'who were horribly nervous and strung up'. In one incident that had a whiff of comedy about it a lifter from Connie found Ponsford's edge, only for the ball to fly straight through Barrow's gloves, rebound off his forehead and narrowly evade the grasping hands of Francis at first slip.

After the opening fusillade Grant brought on his spinners. Martin was easily dealt with by Ponsford, who struck him to the boundary three times in an over. With the score on 49 without loss it seemed Australia might be on the verge of a series whitewash.

But then came joy for the visitors. Woodfull top-edged a ball from Griffith high and almost straight up into the air. Barrow the wicketkeeper was nearest the ball, but Grant called on his best fielder to take the catch. Connie accepted the responsibility, running in from gully, eyes fixed on the ball, which seemed to have disappeared into the sun. It fell for what seemed like an eternity. 'Never before have I been frightened at a catch,' Connie would write. 'I went stone cold and my heart began to throb.' He had no need to fear: the ball landed safely in his hands. He held on to it. Woodfull was gone.

A few overs later Ponsford joined him – another fine catch by Connie, waist-high at deep mid-off, Martin the bowler. Kippax joined the grim-faced Bradman and brought up the fifty with a square cut for four. In the next over the incredible happened: Griffith clean-bowled Bradman for a duck, his first in Test cricket and only his second in first-class matches.

With only a few minutes of the morning remaining, Woodfull sent in Oldfield to shore things up. It proved an error, the wicketkeeper out for nought trapped lbw by Griffith. Connie then got Kippax, caught by Roach at square leg off a mishit pull. Half the Australian wickets had now fallen with just 65 on the board.

Debutant Rigg had struggled through until lunch, but was out shortly after the resumption hooking at a Connie bouncer and top-edging it to Barrow. Fairfax and McCabe were now together – the last two recognised batsmen. The score of 76 for six wickets represented the first crisis of the series for Australia.

Connie, fired up by the possibility of victory, bowled at express pace, at one point knocking the bat clean out of Kippax's grip. McCabe batted brilliantly against the quicks – as he would against Larwood and Voce a few years later – daringly pulling and hooking the shorter deliveries. With Kippax batting grittily the pair posted a fifty partnership in forty-one minutes.

Grant brought on his spinners but the runs continued to accumulate rapidly. Soon Australia had passed the 150 mark, the target for victory dwindling from treble to double figures. The pitch had begun to ease. It seemed that, once again, the West Indies might be about to let a potential victory squirm from their grip.

Then, when he had reached 44, McCabe pushed forward to a ball from Martin. It lifted off a length, struck the bat high and spooned up to Grant at mid-off. The 79-run partnership was ended. Australia required 96 to win with just three wickets remaining.

Oxenham came to the wicket and Connie returned to the attack, peppering the new batsman with bouncers. Despite the danger, Oxenham resisted. He had scored 14 and the total advanced to 180 when, in the final over before tea, Scott got one of his leg-spinners to bite. It beat Oxenham's bat and struck his pads. The umpire's finger rose.

Grimmett joined Fairfax after tea. The ninth-wicket pair took the score past 200. Grant called for the new ball. Francis and Griffith tore in, but to no effect. Grimmett flicked at a wide short ball from Griffith and Connie took off at backward point: 'I scratch it down with the tips of my fingers, and hold it; and he goes.'

With 37 needed to win, Ironmonger came to the crease. He was a batsman of proverbial ineptitude, with a first-class average a little over five and a Test average that was twice as bad. Fairfax was still there on 60, however, and as long as he could farm the bowling victory was possible. Fairfax did his best. Ironmonger did his bit. The scoreboard clicked. At 31 runs needed to win, with the end of another over approaching, Fairfax nudged the ball into the outfield and called for the single. The problem was that not only was Ironmonger not much good with the bat, he was also very slow between the wickets. In response to his partner's call, Ironmonger set off at a hobbling jog. The return from Martin flew in over the stumps at the bowler's end where Grant was on hand to break the wicket with the veteran spinner well out of his ground.

Australia all out for 220. The West Indies had won by 30 runs. 'There are moments a man will never forget!' Connie would later write of the victory. The tour had been arduous, and at times seemed perilously close to collapse, but he felt that the West Indians had learned much from it. Not least was the need to practise together more as a team. 'We lacked cohesion. We lacked assurance and strategy.' With the most experienced, battle-hardened, players in the team – Headley, Francis and Connie (all top League pros in England) – marginalised because of their race, that seemed unlikely to change.

Asked about the tour by the pressmen, Bradman commented that he was 'sure that not only the cricket of the West Indian team but also that of Australia has been improved by this visit'. He was full of praise for Headley, and had nice things to say about Griffith and Francis too, though he felt that all the West Indians ran poorly between the wickets. Bradman was also fulsome in his praise of Connie, whom he thought the best of all the West Indies fast bowlers, and 'without hesitation I rank him the greatest fieldsman I have ever seen'.

In private, however, he seems to have expressed some misgivings about Connie's attitude to the game, his unwillingness to adapt his batting to the playing conditions or the state of the game, his belief in constant attack. Bradman, like most Australian cricketers, was a pragmatist. Connie's ideas about entertainment and improvisation stood in marked contrast to his own more calculated approach. Indeed, it seems he found some of Connie's comments on cricket rather foolish. Jeff Stollmeyer said, years later, 'As young players we used, at first, to hang on to Learie's every word, but as time went on we found many of his theories foreign to our thinking. When in later years we were discussing Learie with Don Bradman, the latter made the rather caustic assessment: "It was a different game when he talked about it." Fair comment. It was.'

Whatever Bradman's opinion, the fact was that a tour that had looked like descending into shambles ended on a high note. The West Indies had won their first overseas Test match. The tourists were given an enthusiastic send-off when they boarded the boat for New Zealand.* The team changed ship in Wellington and sailed back to Colón on the SS *Mataroa*. In Panama, after a champagne reception, the cricketers bade farewell to one another and went their separate ways. Most returned to their homes in the Caribbean; Connie went back to his in Lancashire.

---

* Jackie Grant, who had topped the West Indian batting averages, was not among them. He had already left, bound for Rhodesia, where he was starting missionary work.

Chapter 8

The Whiff of Gunpowder

For Connie, the family cricket matches in Maraval would always be a warm and sustaining memory, while the games he played alongside his father and uncle for Trinidad were highlights of his professional career. The Constantines were a cricket family, part of the backbone of Caribbean cricket. Connie had hoped one day to have a son who might carry on the tradition, who he could teach the game as his father had taught him. It was not to be. Gloria would be Connie and Norma's only child. It was therefore with great pleasure that he followed his younger brother Elias's emergence as a first-class cricketer in the 1932 Inter-Colonial Tournament. The competition was held in Barbados. Trinidad met British Guiana in the final, with Elias helping secure victory by hitting 90 not out in Trinidad's second innings. The thought that he and his brother might one day play together for the West Indies was a notion Connie would cherish throughout the coming decade.

Two trial matches were held in Port of Spain to help selection for the forthcoming tour to the British Isles. Scoring on the matting wicket was remarkably low, considering the best batsmen in the Caribbean were all present. In the first match Jackie Grant – back from Africa – led a team against a side captained by 'Bunny' Edwards, a useful Barbadian batsman who, being white and privately educated, was a rival to Grant for the captaincy. The game was drawn, the outstanding batting display coming from Alma Hunt of Bermuda. His feats on that distant island had attracted attention and he justified the decision to invite him to the Port of Spain trials by making 50 and 36. He would later follow Connie's example and become a professional in Britain, playing for Aberdeenshire. No one else reached a half-century. Les Hylton, Vince Valentine – a stock bowler who could swing the ball both ways – and Ben Sealey all bowled well, but the first angrily disputed an lbw decision and would miss out on the tour as a result. In the second match a dashing right-handed batsman from Tobago, Cyril Merry, took over the skipper's role from Edwards. His team won by 102 runs. Wiles and Derek Sealy batted tidily for the winners.

The process of selection, always complex for the West Indians, was made more difficult by the presence in England of several West Indian cricketers it was hoped might provide occasional help. One of them was Connie, whose contract with Nelson precluded him from playing the entire tour but would free him for certain matches. George Francis was also playing as a professional with Radcliffe in Lancashire, having recently moved across the Pennines after a couple of seasons with Seaham Harbour in the Durham League, where he terrified batsmen with his pace and attracted huge crowds wherever he played – over three thousand paid to watch his debut. Rolph Grant, the captain's younger brother, was at Cambridge and Clifford Inniss of Barbados, apparently suffering no lasting damage from the blow on the head he had taken against the MCC, was studying at Oxford.

With this in mind, a fifteen-man squad was picked. Grant, who was considered by most Australian observers to have done a decent job on that arduous tour, continued as captain. He was joined by fellow Trinidadians Sealey, Roach, Achong and Wiles. Barbados supplied Hoad, Griffith and Manny Martindale, who had only just appeared on the scene. Headley, Martin, Da Costa, Barrow and Valentine came from Jamaica. The sole player from British Guiana was Cyril Christiani, a teenage wicketkeeper-batsman of great promise who would die of malaria aged twenty-four, while Merry became the first player from Tobago to be selected to tour. Strangely, no place could be found for Headley's friend Charles Passailaigue, who had scored a double century for Jamaica against Lord Tennyson's touring XI the previous winter, while the selection of Trinidad's Charles Wiles raised a few eyebrows – he was yet to play a Test, despite having turned forty.

By this time Headley was as big a star in the West Indies as Connie. He had bat sponsorship from William Sykes Ltd, had been used in the publicity of Nestlé and was supported financially by a triumvirate of successful local businessmen who didn't want to see him move to England and League cricket. The funds they could offer would eventually fail to match those available in Lancashire, however.

Having defeated England in the Caribbean and secured a rousing victory in the final Test against Australia, the West Indians travelled to England in good spirits. Their mood was lifted further by the news that Harold Larwood would be absent. The great Nottinghamshire paceman had sustained a stress fracture of the spine during the controversial MCC tour of Australia the previous winter, in which captain Douglas Jardine's ruthless employment of fast leg theory at times had seemed likely to end either with a death on the field or the collapse of the British Empire, and quite possibly both. Bill Voce was also struggling to recover from his exertions, while a third member of the pace attack, the amateur Gubby Allen (who had refused to bowl Bodyline on a point of principle and been indulged), seemed unlikely to be available due to business commitments.

Even allowing for the absence of so many first-choice fast bowlers, England were a very good side, strong in every department. The batting line-up – including Sutcliffe, Hammond, Leyland, Ames and Jardine – was both obdurate and stylish. Spin options included Verity, Farmer White and James Langridge, while Clark, Bowes and Macaulay were all fine performers with the new ball, especially in damp English conditions.

There were problems, however. Not least with morale. The bitter repercussions of what was surely the most acrimonious Test series in history would growl on throughout the summer. Jardine in particular would receive a mixed reception wherever he went – sometimes vociferously cheered, at others entering and leaving the field to disapproving silence. Divisions within the squad between those who supported the use of Bodyline and those who didn't ran parallel to a divide within the ranks of the MCC. As Plum Warner, a vocal opponent of leg theory, noted sadly, '1933 was not a happy season ... a certain section of the Press seemed determined to make trouble ... Nerves were frayed ... The cricket world turned upside down.'

In light of their poor performances on the Australia tour, the West Indies were granted just three Test matches, which would be played over three days instead of five. That had been quite sufficient last time. The MCC saw no need to waste two days of ticket sales.

Connie had read reports of the Bodyline series in the press with some interest. Four years earlier the MCC captain had accused him of bowling too many bouncers and endangering the safety of the English batsmen. Now the MCC was ordering its pace bowlers to deliver bumper after bumper; skulls had been fractured and ribs broken. In Lancashire it was commonly said that a man who couldn't take it shouldn't give it – an attitude Connie shared. The Bodyline tour highlighted the hypocrisy of the rulers of the English game.

For most of the West Indians the events in Australia the previous winter must have seemed an irrelevance as they arrived in Southampton in mid-April and promptly headed to London to buy overcoats. Practice soon got under way with a series of twelve-a-side, one-innings games in Gravesend, Reigate, Godalming and Peasmarsh. The tour proper kicked off with a two-day match against the Club Cricket Conference in the unlikely surrounds of Catford. Headley starred with the bat and Martindale took five wickets in the CCC's first innings as the tourists collected a comfortable innings victory.

The opening first-class match of the tour was against Northamptonshire. The West Indians were served notice of what was to come, as they were crushed by an innings and 62 runs. Only Headley looked capable of mastering the fearsome left-armer Clark, who had been bowling his own version of leg theory for some years. Clark ripped through the batting, finishing the match with ten wickets for just 61 runs.

Oxford University were held to a draw and against Essex

there were signs of improvement. Da Costa had amused his colleagues by having a rubber stamp of his signature made, claiming that it would save him from getting writer's cramp when he was – he jokingly predicted – besieged by autograph hunters. Now he scored his maiden first-class hundred, the first of the tour, and with Martindale bowling with real pace to finish with twelve for 105 the West Indians ran out comfortable winners. A Cambridge University side featuring Ken Farnes and Jahangir Khan was beaten by ten wickets.

Connie joined the team for the high-profile match against the MCC at Lord's. The home side was a strong one: captained by Jardine, it featured two other men who had or would captain England, Percy Chapman and Freddie Brown, as well as Patsy Hendren, Farmer White and Bill Bowes, the Yorkshire paceman who'd had a bit part on the Bodyline tour, inducing a plainly nervous Bradman to duck under a ball that clean-bowled him.

The tourists batted first and with Headley, who made 129, in commanding form posted a total of 309. Headley's innings was temporarily halted when he was struck a nasty blow in the ribs by a Bowes bumper and had to receive treatment. More violence followed when the MCC innings began towards the end of the first day. With only a few overs left before the close, Jardine sent out a nightwatchman, Walter Franklin, to open with Joe Hulme, who played his cricket for Middlesex. Connie tore to the wicket in ferocious fashion, four bumpers on the trot striking Hulme on the thighs and ribs. The batsman was clearly distressed, hopping about and rubbing at his bruises. He swished wildly at the fifth delivery, made contact and set off for a run only to be turned back by his opening partner with the words 'I know where I'm well off.' Martindale then launched an equally fierce assault on Franklin, dismissing him for a duck.

Connie and Martindale continued to test the courage of the MCC batsmen the following morning. Hendren had been a fine player of fast bowling, but now he decided to take precautions against possible injury, coming to the wicket in what is widely thought to be cricket's first helmet – a cap onto which his wife, Minnie, had sewn two extra peaks lined with foam rubber that folded down and protected his ears in the fashion of a deerstalker. Minnie told the press that her husband needed to protect himself against the new style of short-pitched bowling, drawing attention to the fact that he was now forty-four years old and two seasons earlier had been hospitalised by a bouncer.

Hendren was hugely popular, yet most reporters were scornful of his cautious approach. The *Daily Mail* remarked that 'Hendren's three-peak cap has cracked another glorious cricket tradition. No more excited babble of comment was ever caused by novel headgears as began at the Lord's when a strangely head-muzzled figure, suggesting baseball or fencing and at some angles reminiscent of a bout wrestler, walked in to the wicket.'

The *Daily Sketch*, meanwhile, called the cap 'ridiculous', saying it was 'a cross between an airman's helmet and an Eskimo's headgear'. 'Patsy would be well advised to leave this ridiculous contraption in the pavilion, or better still, send it to Australia.'

Hendren was unrepentant: 'The people can say what they like. I have been hit on the head four times, once by a Larwood bouncer in 1931 which caused a wound in which six stitches were inserted. I am still suffering recurrent headaches due to that bashing. Believe me, I'm taking no more risks.

'One of Constantine's deliveries was like a bullet, and if it had hit me I would have gone to kingdom come. I don't mind my face getting altered or my teeth knocked out if my head is protected. I don't think other players will get similar caps. They wear pads and abdominal and chest protectors, but have not the courage to wear a head protector.'

Whatever the efficacy or otherwise of his headgear, it was hot. When at the non-striker's end he handed it to the umpire. Nor did it benefit him much – he was caught by Roach off Connie for just seven.

Percy Chapman showed how to bat against the barrage, scoring 94, but with Connie taking four wickets the MCC were all out for 246. While Hendren's efforts to protect his head had been roundly mocked in the press, that did not mean the West Indians' tactics avoided scrutiny. With the Bodyline controversy rumbling on, watching reporters – eager no doubt to deflect blame away from Jardine and his team – accused the tourists of deploying the same tactics that England had used Down Under. It was conceded that Connie deployed fewer men on the onside – in fact, just three: fine leg, short leg and mid-on – than Larwood and Voce, but the short ball had been used frequently and batsmen had been struck. The *Manchester Guardian* took a slightly different line, commenting 'no leg trap was used by Constantine, but we could realize how helpless Hendren and Hulme would have been if Grant had emulated the Jardinian Theory'.

Connie was unrepentant. His intention was not to strangle scoring – the purpose of leg theory as deployed by medium-pacers such as Root – or to get batsmen caught at short leg fending away deliveries aimed at their throats. When he bowled bouncers he was testing his opponent's nerve. Any fast bowler who can force a batsman to hesitate before making the required back-and-across movement, or better yet make him step away from his wicket, is more than halfway to dismissing him.

Connie would always defend Bodyline as a legitimate tactic, partly because, like many fast bowlers, he felt that the laws of the game and the increasingly easy-paced pitches on which cricket was being played had slanted things too much in the batsman's favour (Root would make a similar point), but also because, having been maligned for using too many bouncers, he must have felt compelled to do so. That leg theory was stultifying dull to watch, more or less the epitome of the sort of negative tactics Connie deplored, seems to have passed him by. He was a man who liked to 'play' cricket, who wanted the game to be thrilling – Bodyline was anything but.

On this occasion, Connie denied using leg theory, feeling that his critics were getting in a stew over nothing. 'Bodyline was gunpowder in those days and the trained nose smelled it everywhere,' Connie noted. His own view was that, now over thirty years of age, he was no longer the speed merchant of his youth and that 'batsmen who got hit did so because they ran blindly into the ball pitched outside off stump and breaking'.

If the tone of the newspaper reports suggested indignation on behalf of the MCC's batsmen, it was clearly not the attitude of the club's hierarchy, who shared Connie's view. On the issue of short-pitched bowling the MCC remained intractable and – on 12 June – cabled the Australian Cricket Board to inform them that the short ball bowled to a packed leg-side field was entirely legitimate. The message caused such a furore there was talk of the 1934 Ashes series being cancelled.

When the West Indians batted for a second time they

were quickly in trouble, at 100 for six. Instructed by Grant to go in and grab back the initiative, Connie went to the wicket and struck two fours and a six in the first over he faced, cracked three fours to the leg-side boundary in a Bill Bowes over and raced to a half-century in twenty-seven minutes, much to the delight of spectators in the Mound Stand, who greeted each boundary with a great roar of approval. He received good support from Merry, who made 47. A total of 268 left the MCC needing to make the highest score of the match to win. On a crumbling pitch they did not even come close. Hendren top-scored with 61, but with Achong's spinners bouncing and turning the home side were dismissed for 179 to lose by a massive 152 runs.

Connie returned to Lancashire. In his absence a fourth consecutive victory followed against Hampshire, who were defeated by six wickets. Against Surrey at the Oval Roach played the innings of his life, plundering a century before lunch and finally falling for 170 compiled in three hours. Hobbs, in the late autumn of his career, stole the headlines with a flawless double century and the game ended in a draw. A narrow defeat to Worcestershire and draws against Glamorgan and Somerset, the latter featuring a Headley double hundred – the highest score ever made by a West Indian in England – followed. A drawn match against Middlesex proved costly, with Martin, a steady batsman often compared to Bill Woodfull, treading on a ball in the outfield and sustaining such a bad injury to his ankle he did not play for the rest of the tour. Both of the tour matches before the first Test were drawn – Derbyshire at Derby and Minor Counties at Lord's.

Connie could not secure his release from Nelson for the first Test, despite protracted negotiations between the West Indies management and the Lancashire League

club, as well a last-ditch appeal from Jackie Grant. It was
not just Nelson who had to be considered: 'Other clubs
in the League, hearing that Grant had asked for me, sent
indignant telegrams to Nelson asking them to keep me
for as many games as possible, for their gate receipts were
involved.' If the West Indians had been able to offer financial compensation things might have been different, but
since they were apparently unable to pay each tourist any
more than thirty shillings a week in expenses, that was
clearly impossible. Connie bore Nelson no ill will, reasoning that they were paying him handsomely and were
therefore entitled to demand their money's worth. That the
West Indies board had not sorted the situation out sooner
was undoubtedly a frustration to him, however. Francis had
better fortune with Radcliffe, and played in the side alongside Roach, Barrow, Headley, Hoad, Grant, Da Costa,
Merry, Achong, Martindale and Griffith.

At Lord's, England won the toss and elected to bat but
rain soon intervened and washed out play for much of the
first day. On the Monday resumption the sky was clearer
and conditions were perfect. In the circumstances, the West
Indies did well to keep the England scoring rate down to
around a run a minute and to dismiss the home side for
296. Martindale bowled well, taking four for 85, and got
good support from Griffith, who finished with three for 48.
Pick of the bowlers was Achong, who bowled thirty-five
overs for just 88 runs.

All the good work was then thrown away in a single session. Commencing after tea the West Indies lost Roach,
clean-bowled by Gubby Allen for a duck, and six wickets
fell for 55 before play ended for the day. Despite a fighting knock from Grant, who scored 26 before hitting his
wicket, the West Indies were forced to follow on 199 runs

in arrears. Most of the damage was done – predictably, perhaps, given what had happened against Grimmett – by leg-spinner Walter Robins. When the visitors batted again Roach bagged a pair after shouldering arms to Macaulay, only to see the ball jag back and flatten his stumps. Headley got a half-century, Barrow batted for over an hour to score 12 and Grant and Hoad put on 52 for the fourth wicket, but it was not enough. Macaulay and Verity took eight wickets between them and the visitors lost by an innings and 27 runs.

Their confidence shattered by this crushing defeat, the tourists did not win another game before the second Test. Even the arrival in their party of the talismanic Connie seemed to have little effect. The Trinidadian re-joined his team mates at West Bridgford for the match against Sir Julien Cahn's XI on the philanthropist's private ground. The game was drawn. Connie was dismissed for a duck in the first innings, made 22 in the second and in between took three wickets. He managed to watch a little of the tourists' next match, against Lancashire at Liverpool, but could not play due to League commitments. He was back with them at Harrogate for the game with Yorkshire

On a slow glue-pot of a strip Connie took nine wickets for 94 runs, but his figures were eclipsed by those of slow left-armer Verity, who exploited conditions expertly to finish with match figures of 14–83. Against the great spinner Connie made 0 and 2 and later said that watching Verity bowl to Headley had been 'an education'. The game was notable as the first time on the tour that the West Indians used an actual Bodyline attack. Frustrated by a wicket he felt had been doctored to aid the home side's attack, Grant set a field with just three men on the off-side and a ring of close catchers in the area between silly mid-on

and leg slip. He then ordered Connie and Griffith to bowl
short and fast on the line of leg stump. Later Grant would
declare himself an opponent of Bodyline, though it seems
to have been a late conversion, possibly brought on by the
sight of his brother carried off the field in 1935 after he
had been toppled by a Farnes bumper. Connie, who was
generally unapologetic about bowling bouncers, seems to
have caught the anti-Bodyline mood and when writing of
the game against Yorkshire years later claimed that he was
simply doing as his captain instructed and that it would
have been insubordinate for a professional such as himself
to argue with a gentleman amateur – a line also advanced
by Larwood. Whatever the rights and wrongs of Grant's
tactics, they were unsuited to the conditions. Connie and
Griffith struggled to get the ball above waist height on the
slow, soft pitch; Sutcliffe and Mitchell both cruised to half-
centuries and the home side won by 200 runs.

Connie missed a rain-ruined draw against Nottinghamshire in which Martindale again worked up a head of steam
to take eight for 66 in the home side's first innings. He
returned for the game against Lancashire, but must have
wished he hadn't. After heavy showers, the West Indians
declared on 174 for seven. In reply, Lancashire managed
to reach 39 with two wickets down before the game was
abandoned. Connie scored three and bowled just a handful
of overs.

Weather also spoiled the meeting with Leicestershire,
Connie absent again. He was back for the fixture against
Staffordshire at Stoke-on-Trent and was also available
for the Test match that followed at Old Trafford. The
Staffordshire team included S. F. Barnes, though the great
man had finally fallen prey to the ravages of time. He was
still pro-ing in the Lancashire League, at Rawtenstall,

but that season's return of fifty-four wickets was one of the poorest of his career – hardly surprising, given that he was now sixty.

The weather in Stoke was warm, the wicket flat and dry, and much of the fire seemed to have gone out of Barnes. In the tourists' first innings his eight overs cost 39 runs – a fortune by his own miserly standards. Barrow and Hoad both made runs; Connie was dismissed for nine. Barnes did not bowl in the West Indians' second innings. It was his last match against a touring team, but the game belonged to the visitors, winners by nine wickets, and to Connie, who took 11–72 in the match.

The West Indians travelled up to Manchester by train. Grant used the journey to discuss tactics for the Test match with his leading players. Connie voiced the opinion that few of England's batsmen seemed to enjoy facing the fast rising ball and cited Hammond as an example. (Les Ames agreed with that assessment, saying, 'When we came up against the West Indians, I did detect on Wally's part a slight weakness against the really quick, short stuff. Yes, of course, Martindale and Constantine worried him a bit.')

With Martindale bowling very fast and the strip at Old Trafford likely to be quick, the decision was made to use Bodyline. Connie seems to have been enthusiastic. He had read about the tactic in the press over the winter and thought it would be good for the home side to get a taste of what it felt like. In this he was supported by Don Bradman, who had written in his column in an Australian newspaper that he hoped the West Indies might give a demonstration to the English establishment of what Bodyline looked like.

Grant later claimed that this was the first time that Bodyline had been discussed by the West Indians and that his team had not practised bowling leg theory – a statement that ignores the events across the Pennines earlier on the tour. It should also be noted that Grant's brother Rolph had played for Cambridge University against Oxford University at Lord's a few weeks earlier and witnessed Bodyline first hand. His team mates, the distinctly quick Farnes and the altogether more amiably paced Jahangir Khan, had both bowled short to a packed leg-side field throughout. Farnes in particular caused consternation and outrage as he directed ball after ball at the Oxford batsmen's heads and throats. He finished with seven wickets and a black mark against his name. The match was drawn.

In *Cricket and I* Constantine frankly explained his use of Bodyline, using the term without embarrassment, and his desire to shake up and hurt a batsman without doing him physical injury. It is an attitude that has been expressed by other fast bowlers since – Dennis Lillee and Jeff Thomson most notably, though they did so in slightly more colourful terms than Connie. While Bodyline itself did not sit with Connie's notions of joyous cricket, bouncers certainly did. For the spectator, at least, there can be few sights more thrilling than to watch a batsman take on short-pitched bowling, hooking and pulling daringly and under threat of injury. Connie certainly never complained about being bounced – and he faced the fastest bowlers of his generation, from George John to Keith Miller via Larwood and Voce. His view was and would remain that a batsman had a bat in his hand for a purpose. Those who used it made runs, those who flinched got out.

For the match at Old Trafford the West Indies brought in Connie, Wiles and Valentine for Francis, Griffith and Merry. Grant won the toss and elected to go in on a perfect batting strip. Roach again disappointed, out with the score on just 26. Headley and Barrow then batted magnificently to add 200 for the second wicket. Barrow's innings was streaky and he never looked comfortable, but he showed determination and battled his way to 105, the first West Indian to score a Test century in England. Headley was at his imperious best and never looked in trouble, even when Clark directed a stream of short, high-velocity deliveries at his head. At the close he was 145 not out, the side 333 for six.

On the second day the tourists reached 375, Headley finishing 169 not out. He received some support from Connie, who hit 31. Clark took four wickets and Robins three. Some West Indian writers later suggested that it was Clark who had bowled Bodyline and provoked the West Indians to responding in kind. Herbert Sutcliffe, however, says that England did not bowl actual leg theory and even speculates that Jardine had been warned against deploying it by the MCC. What is certain is that Nobby Clark bowled a lot of bumpers, whether to a plan or not.

When England batted Connie and Martindale soon put the Bodyline plan into operation. England had three very fine players of fast bowling in their line-up – Jardine, Sutcliffe and Bob Wyatt. Unfortunately Sutcliffe ran himself out when he had reached 20 and Wyatt fell to an extraordinary catch when he had made 18. Despite the danger, Sutcliffe seems to have enjoyed the spectacle, describing Connie and Martindale's attack as 'a magnificent sustained barrage'.

England's best strokemaker, Wally Hammond, was less cheerfully disposed to the bumpers and looked uncomfortable from the off. Connie struck his old foe on the shoulder as he ducked away from a short one and then smashed another into his face. Blood sprayed from the gash in Hammond's chin and he was forced to return to the

pavilion for treatment, reputedly leaving the crease mutter-
ing 'If this is what the game has bloody well come to, it's
time I got out.'

Hammond had rejected Bodyline from the off, telling a
group of friends after he had returned from Australia, 'I
found it loathsome and distasteful . . . I was ashamed to be a
part of it.' Now he told his team mates that what was going
on was no more than they deserved: 'We started it, and we
had it coming to us.'

When Hammond returned to resume his innings, his
chin covered with sticking plaster, he walked down the
field and offered his hand to Connie, saying, 'Let's put
an end to this, shall we?' Perhaps the bitter drama of
Bodyline had brought him to a realisation. Connie was
often quick to anger, at times impulsive, but he was also
quick to forgive. As players, he and Hammond had much
in common. They were both sportsmen. Sustaining his
grievance over all those years against a player whose
gifts he admired must have been wearing for Connie.
Forgiveness promised a release from it. He reached out and
shook Hammond's hand warmly. The rage and hurt seem
to have evaporated more or less instantly and the two men
became firm friends. It was a touching moment amidst the
bloodshed.

Hammond fell for an uneasy 34, caught by Martindale
off Connie, and England were four wickets down for 134,
with Macaulay injured in the field and unable to bat. Les
Ames came out to join his captain. Ames was a courageous
player of pace bowling who had once hooked Larwood
for six, but he found it tough going against Connie and
Martindale, and at one point Jardine told him, 'You get
yourself down this end, Les. I'll take care of this bloody
nonsense.'

Connie and Martindale were not as quick as Larwood and Voce, but they were quick enough. Furthermore, they nursed a feeling that the English wickets had been specifically prepared to nullify their threat. (This seems unlikely – English wickets in that period were notorious featherbeds, doctored not to neuter the opposition bowlers but to render all bowlers innocuous.)

The West Indians also had a grudge against Jardine personally because of the incident in 1928 when he'd made the umpire retract a hit-wicket decision given against him. Jardine had been technically correct, but the feeling that he was a cheat persisted. Some England players, including Hammond, had similar feelings about Bradman.

With England in crisis, Jardine played superbly, using his full height to get over the rising ball, even when it was almost head-high. Sutcliffe thought his innings 'a classic and one of the best I have ever seen against such a magnificent attack which was sustained for an incredibly long time'.

Connie, too, was impressed: 'The leg trap stuff did not work ... Mainly because Douglas Jardine played it in the proper manner and stood up to it.' He had a grudging admiration for the unbending Jardine, whose refusal to compromise in some ways mirrored his own. The crowd appear to have been less enamoured of the spectacle, many walking out disgusted or simply bored.

Jardine and Ames took the score to 200, but that signalled the availability of the new ball and Connie and Martindale renewed the assault with vigour. Ames was caught fending a ball off his hip. With the arrival of the next batsman, James Langridge, the leg theory intensified with a fifth fielder brought in to the leg trap. Jardine continued to farm the strike, ducking and weaving when necessary. He brought up his fifty by taking ten off an over from Martindale. Langridge was soon out, but Walter Robins stayed with his skipper until close of play, when the score was 234.

The next morning the West Indies abandoned their Bodyline attack. This was a relief to Connie, who felt it was unsuitable for the surface. He had asked Grant to shift to a more traditional off-stump attack the previous evening, but to his annoyance the captain had rejected the idea. Now, with the score on 374, Connie felt vindicated as he caught Jardine low at point off Martindale. The England captain went slowly and reluctantly, as if suspecting the Connie had grounded the ball, further fuelling West Indies' dislike of him. Jardine had scored 127 in just under five hours. The England captain would see this as reproof to those who claimed that runs could not be made against Bodyline. Stan McCabe, of course, had already demonstrated that fact, and on pitches far quicker than the strip at Old Trafford, against two bowlers who were faster than Connie and Martindale. Nor was Southerton dissuaded from his views, concluding that the England captain's bravery did not make the 'sight of [Bodyline] any more welcome, and most of those who were watching it for the first time must have come to the conclusion that, while strictly within the law, it was not nice'.

Connie felt that if he and Martindale had deployed leg theory on the faster tracks at Lord's and the Oval it would have been a greater struggle for the England skipper. '[He] might have made his hundred but he would have had to adopt different tactics. He would have had to move to the off stump or turn and hook. But to stand up and play defensive strokes as he did at Old Trafford would have been quite impossible.' Since Jardine's initial movement was back and across in the classic manner, it would seem Constantine was suggesting some more exaggerated movement, or the taking of a middle-and-off guard. Clearly he was unaware that when the Australians had tried such an approach the previous winter it had failed.

The following day brought some light relief and an incident that would become part of cricket folklore. Walter Robins had batted gamely to complete his half-century when he danced down the wicket to Ellis 'Puss' Achong, Trinidad's left-arm wrist spinner and the first player of Chinese descent to appear in Tests. The bowler later recalled that 'the ball pitched perfectly and turned back nicely and when Robins saw it coming back at him he opened his legs and the ball went through'. Barrow duly stumped him. Walking past the square-leg umpire on his way back to the pavilion, Robins reputedly spluttered, 'Fancy getting done by a bloody Chinaman', coining the universal term for a left-arm wrist spinner's standard delivery.

In the end England fell just one run short of the tourists' total. With the match already well into the last day there seemed little chance of a definite outcome. But James Langridge bowled so well, taking seven wickets, that, despite a spirited 64 from Roach the visitors were soon 132 for seven. The possibility of defeat was removed by Connie in robust fashion. He clubbed 64 in a little under an hour as the West Indies rallied to 225 all out just before the close to draw the match. It was the first time the West Indies had avoided defeat in a Test in England. England's Tiger Smith claimed that the normally abstemious Headley was so delighted he went out celebrating and got so drunk he could not find the team hotel. True or not, Headley certainly had reason to raise a glass or two: during the course

of the Test he had signed a contract to play for Haslingden
in the Lancashire League in 1934 and 1935. His fee was
five hundred pounds a season.

The repercussions of the Old Trafford Test rumbled
on long after the stumps had been drawn. Warner was
unhappy with what he had seen, as he 'had hoped my
fellow countrymen would avoid a type of bowling which
I believe to be against the best interests of cricket', but
pleased that the British public had at last had a chance
to see Bodyline first hand. *Wisden* would echo Warner's
sentiments, Southerton writing: 'We ... can, at any rate,
be thankful to the West Indies for showing us ... what an
objectionable form of attack this kind of bowling can be.
Most people in England, whichever way they inclined, were
to a large extent ignorant of the effect it had upon cricket,
and there can be no doubt whatever that the exhibition
given at Old Trafford confirmed opponents of it in their
views and caused hundreds who had open minds on the
subject definitely to turn against it.'

The very bowlers who had indirectly inspired Bodyline
had now made a telling contribution to stopping it.

For the final Test at the Oval the West Indies were eager
to retain the services of Connie. They struck a deal with
Nelson that would see all-rounder Stan Nichols of Essex
substituting for Connie in the Saturday League game. It is
claimed that when Jardine learned of this he persuaded his
fellow selectors to scupper the plan by picking Nichols to
play for England for the first time in three years. Whatever
the truth of this, Connie played for Nelson, while Nichols
turned out at the Oval, where he scored 49 and took three
wickets.

Connie's place went to Griffith. Sealy and Merry came
in for Wiles and Hoad. England were led by Wyatt, in for

Jardine who had been injured by a ball smashing into his shin while fielding in a county fixture against Kent. The caretaker captain won the toss on the Saturday and chose to bat. His decision seemed to have backfired as the tourists bowled really well and had four of England's top order back in the pavilion with just 68 on the board. Things would have been worse for the home side had Hammond been caught when he was on nought. Fred Bakewell of Northamptonshire batted beautifully for England, scoring 107 and holding the side together. Charlie Barnett and Nichols put on 95 for the eighth wicket in quick time. England were all out at the end of the day for 312. Martindale was again the pick of the bowlers, taking five for 93 to add to the five for 75 he'd taken at Manchester.

On the Monday the West Indians were a little unlucky as bright sunshine turned to gloom. Rain showers interrupted play and fired up a previously placid wicket. Under the heavy cloud cover the ball moved around in the air. The conditions were distinctly un-Caribbean but even so the West Indies' batting collapse was alarming – they were all out for 100 in two hours. Aside from Sealy, who batted obdurately for 29, the batsmen mixed bafflement with kamikaze shot selection as the hostile Clark (three for 16) and Kent's Irish-born leg-spinner Charles Marriott (five for 37) tore through the innings. The West Indies followed on, 212 runs behind. The second innings began promisingly thanks to one of Roach's sparkling cameos. The opener made batting look a simple business until he was out for 56, struck in just forty-five minutes. At tea the tourists were 137 for three with Da Costa and Headley looking well set. It seemed that the West Indies might yet make a fight of it, but a familiar post-prandial collapse that saw five wickets fall in rapid succession put paid to that. Only a few minutes were needed the following morning to secure England another comprehensive victory. Marriott, a very fine spinner, exposed the West Indies' weakness against accurate slow bowling, taking six for 59 in the second innings to give him match figures of 11 for 96, a remarkable return in what was to be his only Test appearance.

A second Test series in England had ended in abject defeat and the West Indies' standing in the game plummeted. Morale, too, was low after the crushing defeat, so low that the tourists did not win another match.

Connie met his depressed team mates at Blackpool for the game against Sir Lindsay Parkinson's XI. The invitation side, featuring several Lancashire League stars including Arthur Richardson, Fred Root and Ted McDonald, defeated the visitors by seven wickets despite Martindale's eight for 39 in their first innings. Connie made only a minor contribution, scoring 19 runs and bowling thirteen overs without reward. Despite continued wrangling with Nelson it would be his final appearance for the West Indians that summer.

Nine defeats against five victories in first-class matches was a very disappointing record, especially in a summer that was generally hot and sunny – the warmest for over a decade. There were some mitigating factors. Martin was injured early on and ruled out of all remaining matches, while Headley missed several games after an operation to remove a sebaceous cyst – the result of a childhood cycling accident – from his forehead. On top of that, the aunt who had raised him was killed by a freak flood while he was convalescing, causing him a good deal of distress.

Nonetheless, there seemed to have been little advancement made since the 1928 tour. Morale and confidence were major issues, with the team apparently unable to

recover mentally from defeat. That at least was one expla-
nation; perhaps the plainer truth was that aside from
Headley and Martindale – and Connie when available –
the side had no genuinely world-class cricketers and far too
many passengers.

'Inexperienced captaincy and incoherence as a team
were sad drawbacks for us,' Connie noted. 'Once more, the
same old story, some of our best men left behind, not nearly
enough play together before the tour to weld us into a team
(we were more like a mob).'

Connie was critical of Grant's leadership, but purely on
playing terms the captain was at least worth his place in the
side (unlike vice-captain Wiles). The Trinidadian was a very
good close fielder and he finished third in the Test batting
averages behind Headley and Sealy. But that was not really
the issue. The system that had placed Grant in charge was
not only iniquitous, it was also counter-productive. When
the best players in the team had no faith in the captain, the
chances of him doing a decent job, or of his side winning,
were massively reduced. This fact should have been blin-
dingly obvious, but when it came to race and West Indies
cricket, logic would continue to have little place in the argument for a long while to come.

Chapter 9

Cricket in the Shadows

Before he left Jamaica after the triumphant series of 1934–5, Connie had been contacted by the West Indies Board of Control. They were eager to secure his services for the next tour of England. This was four years away, but after losing Connie for much of the previous tour of the British Isles, and almost missing out on his services in the Caribbean that winter, some attempt at forward planning was at last being made.

Euphoric after leading his side to that historic series-winning victory over England at Sabina Park, Connie readily agreed. In early 1938 Harry Mallett got in touch to negotiate the agreement. Connie was still eager to play, but he was a professional nearing the end of his career and would have to give up a lucrative season of League cricket to take part in the tour. While he did not expect the West Indies to be able to match the salary he was on at Rochdale – eight hundred pounds for the twenty-week season, to which collections and benefits would also be added – he did at least expect the gap to be manageable. He was also concerned about the selection policy, believing that on previous trips attempts to appease the interests of the various colonies had weakened the side. Negotiations were protracted, and Connie was forced to travel to Barbados to conclude them. The final arrangements guaranteed him a payment of six hundred pounds for the tour, plus a share of any profits the tour made (as it transpired, there weren't any). Connie was dissatisfied at losing money and made his feelings known. When he discovered that some other players were earning the same as he was, it looked for a moment as if he might not play at all. Eventually his eagerness to be part of the first West Indies team to win a series in England overcame his doubts and he accepted the terms. By the time the tour began he would be approaching forty. It would be the first time he had played a full season of three-day cricket since 1934–5, the biggest test of his stamina and concentration since the epic tour of Australia.

The Inter-Colonial Tournament of 1939, held in Bridgetown, carried added importance as the selection of the tour party was at the forefront of the competitors' minds. The Trinidad side, led by Rolph Grant and including Jeff Stollmeyer and Gerry Gomez, both talented and educated at the island's finest schools, won the Cup with Ben Sealey, Grant and Vic Stollmeyer – Jeff's elder brother – all scoring runs. Elias Constantine, who had travelled to the Caribbean from Rochdale at his own expense in the hope of selection, bowled exceptionally well to take his career-best figures of four for 14 against British Guiana, but it was not deemed enough to earn him a place in the trial matches that followed in Port of Spain. The first of these saw the home side take on Jamaica. Incredibly, this was the first-ever first-class match between the two islands – a sign of how fractured cricket in the Caribbean remained despite nearly four decades of competition. Headley batted

well and received excellent support from a young Ken
Weekes, whose hard hitting had earned him the nickname
Bam-Bam. For Trinidad, Gomez made 161 and Leonard
Harbin – who would go on to play for Gloucestershire after
the war – made 81. Tyrell Johnson, a fast left-arm bowler,
did the damage for Trinidad. Bowling at lightning speed,
he took four for 15 in Jamaica's second innings.

In the second match Jamaica took on a Combined West
Indies side. Johnson again bowled with devastating pace
and took six wickets in Jamaica's first innings. Headley
scored another hundred. In Jamaica's second innings
Weekes drove and pulled spectacularly to compile a not-out
century.

Jackie Grant had retired from cricket and so the selectors' first task was to find his replacement. Sadly, given
the racial politics of the time, there was little chance that
Connie should be allowed to continue in the role he had
filled so splendidly on that final day in Kingston. Though
George Headley, by then skipper of Jamaica, took charge of
the team for one Test in 1948, it was not until 1960, when
Frank Worrell led the West Indies in Australia, that a black
player would be appointed captain of a touring party. In
the circumstances, it was little surprise to anybody that
Rolph Grant was chosen.

Grant was a decent forcing lower-order batsman, a tidy
off-spinner and a brave and athletic close fielder (he had
played as goalkeeper for the England amateur team and
was also Trinidad's heavyweight boxing champion). Grant
had Test experience, had played in England before and
had captained Trinidad successfully. While it is undoubtedly true that others had a greater claim to the captaincy,
Grant's appointment was not such a direct slap in the face
to the veteran black players in the side as the appointment

of his elder brother had been in 1930. That, of course, was small consolation to Connie.

More intriguing and less expected was the choice of vice-captain. John Cameron had been born in Jamaica but brought up in the English West Country where his father – who'd toured the British Isles with the West Indians in 1909 – was a doctor. Cameron was black, but he was light-skinned. Furthermore, he'd been educated at Taunton School and Cambridge University. An uncomplicated attacking batsman and a capable bowler of both wrist and finger spin, he played for Somerset as an amateur. By the sporting definitions of the era Cameron was a gentleman. In cricket, class sometimes trumped race. There had been a great furore over Cec Parkin's call for a professional to captain England, while the news that an Indian, Duleepsinhji, has been appointed to the post at Sussex raised barely a murmur. Duleepsinhji was a prince. Some men were bred to lead, others weren't.

As well as Grant and Cameron, the touring party consisted of Connie, Jeffrey and Victor Stollmeyer, Gomez and Johnson (all from Trinidad); 'Foffie' Williams, Martindale, Derek Sealy and Bertie Clarke of Barbados (the latter pair included at Connie's insistence); Headley, Weekes, Barrow and Hylton of Jamaica and Peter Bayley of British Guiana. The Stollmeyers, Gomez, Johnson, Bayley and Clarke were all young men of limited experience – indeed, Jeff Stollmeyer was still a teenager. Clarke was a gamble. The tall leg-spinner was only twenty-one and had limited first-class experience, but he had impressed George Headley with his bowling in the Inter-Colonial Tournament and it was on the great man's recommendation he was picked ahead of more experienced performers such as Achong. The thinking behind the selection of Barrow as wicketkeeper was more opaque. He had performed decently in the past, but he'd recently moved to America and had not played cricket for some while.

The omission of Elias was a grave disappointment to Connie, whose judgement was perhaps impaired by filial affection. Though Elias had 'played for two or three sea-sons in the Central Lancashire League, where he had put up some fine performances', the idea that he was worth a place in the Test team for 'his fielding alone' seems a little far-fetched. Whatever the misgivings of the side's senior professional, and Jeff Stollmeyer's belief that a place should have been found for the dynamic Rupert Tang Choon, most West Indians regarded the party as the strongest the Caribbean nations had ever sent on tour. Success – at least in the first-class matches – was widely predicted and the feeling amongst West Indian fans was that England would be pushed very close in the Tests, if not actually defeated.

The view in England was altogether different. The success of the West Indies in the home series had failed to convince the hierarchy at Lord's that they were worthy adversaries and the trio of Test matches were allocated just three days apiece instead of the usual five. England fans had every reason to feel confident. A fine collection of young bats-men – Denis Compton, Bill Edrich and Len Hutton – had emerged to complement the mature Hammond. They had amassed huge totals over the preceding ten months, averag-ing 640 in completed innings. The likelihood of the visitors bowling them out twice seemed remote. Especially in nine sessions.

The West Indians arrived to one of the coldest springs in living memory, and the temperature did not improve. 'It was a blue-faced and shivering mob which stepped thankfully off the boat,' Connie observed, 'and once they were here the weather moved steadily back towards mid-winter.' One early net practice was interrupted by a snow storm.

After shivering through two one-day practice matches, the team played their first competitive game against Worcestershire. The county ground had, as seemed traditional, spent several weeks underwater during the winter and the pitch was soft and green. In the chilly grey atmosphere the tourists did well to dismiss the home side for 83. Their own batting failed in the alien environment and they were thrashed in two days.

The next match, against Lancashire at Liverpool, went far better. Headley batted classily and Cameron bowled well as the tourists had by far the better of the draw. Rolph Grant was injured when he was struck by the ball fielding close in and Connie took charge of the side. Batting last, the West Indians needed 247 to win in a little more than three hours. The weather was chilly and the light poor. Contrary to what many might have anticipated, Connie instructed his batsmen to go out and play steadily with a draw in mind. Headley batted brilliantly and when stumps were drawn the tourists had lost just three wickets.

With Grant still injured Connie expected to be in charge of the team against the MCC at Lord's. Shortly before the game, however, he was told that Cameron would be captaining the side. The official reason was that Connie had been too negative in his tactics against Lancashire, but Connie had little doubt as to the real reason – his colour. 'To be brown-skinned, that is to say to have any trace of white blood in one, always gives a man an advantage in the West Indies.'

As it was, the game was ruined by rain. Bad weather also robbed the tourists of a victory against Cambridge

University, Headley scoring the first century of the expedition and Connie bowling with skill and control to take seven for 94. Defeat then followed against Surrey at the Oval, though Connie found form with the bat to hammer a fifty in just under an hour. He was rested for the Oxford University match, which was won by an innings. Connie returned for the fixture with Glamorgan and had a good all-round game, taking six wickets and coming in at nine to score 63, including a mighty six to reach his fifty that struck a spectator, knocking him unconscious.

A team conference was held before they met Essex, in a bid to rally the party. 'We were losing too many matches and though receipts were good so far, there was no doubt that another defeat or two would mean a disastrous attendance at the Tests.'

Whatever was said appeared to work, as the game was won by two wickets. Connie – making up for the diminution in his pace with clever variations of speed and flight – took thirteen wickets for 91 runs. Against Middlesex at Lord's the West Indians won the toss, batted and piled up 665. Connie and Cameron then bowled their side to victory by an innings, Connie deploying a new delivery that 'hung in the air but fizzed off the pitch'; perhaps he had learned a trick or two when facing S. F. Barnes. It was the sort of substantial victory against high-class opponents that was needed to silence those who had again begun to cast doubt on the tourists' qualifications.

For the opening Test at Lord's Grant opted to leave Gomez, Johnson and Williams out of the side. Barrow was included as wicketkeeper despite his rustiness. In the first Test match for which the BBC offered radio listeners ball-by-ball commentary, the West Indians won the toss and took first knock on a track one observer would later describe

as being so easy-going it was positively stupid. A cold wind
blew and storm clouds hung over London, which did not
make for ideal conditions for the West Indians. Nevertheless
they got off to a fast start, Grant making 22 out of 29 before
he failed to get over a lifting ball from Copson and was
caught by Compton at forward short leg. Headley came
in at three and found a partner in the tall and slender Jeff
Stollmeyer, who batted elegantly, favouring the front foot
in a manner not typical of Caribbean batsmen. Lunch
came and went with the pair – veteran and youngster – still
together. When the pair had added 118 Stollmeyer, who
had batted chancelessly for 59, was clean-bowled by Bill
Bowes. Sealy and Weekes both got out after making decent
starts and at tea the tourists were 226 for four with Headley
still at the wicket. During the interval England took the
new ball. Connie played an innings of trademark ingenuity,
cracking three fours off Copson: one to square leg, another
a beautiful glance to fine leg, and a third an amazing hook.
But when he attempted another pull to leg the ball kept low
and he was trapped lbw. It was a shot for a harder, faster
surface. Martindale provided some excitement by smashing
Verity for six into the members' luncheon room, but Bowes
and Copson ripped into the West Indians and the last six
wickets tumbled for 51 runs. Headley was finally caught at
the wicket for 106, one of his finest innings. Copson was
the best of the bowlers with five wickets for 85, while the
bespectacled Bowes got three for 86. They were backed by
superb English fielding. Gimblett and Hutton took England
safely through to the close.

The next morning Lord's was bathed in sunshine.
Twelve thousand spectators had come to watch the day's
play. If they had hoped to escape from the mounting fear
of war they were to be disappointed, the public address

system broadcasting appeals by Wally Hammond for service volunteers during the intervals. The West Indians fought hard to regain the initiative. Cameron in particular bowled tightly during a long spell and Martindale showed some of his old fire. Connie was not at his best, however, and Hutton was immovable, battling on as first Gimblett then Paynter and Hammond fell at the other end. England were 147–3 and wobbling as Compton came to the wicket. The Middlesex batsman was dropped twice in scoring a single, and Hutton offered another chance soon after. Three catches put down was warning enough for these two great batsmen. They proceeded to add 248 for the fourth wicket and effectively bat their opponents out of the match. Compton eventually fell for 120 while the Yorkshireman made 196. In 140 minutes of batting they – along with poor catching – had undone all of the West Indies' good work. On Monday morning, with the score 405–5, Hammond, whose shrewd captaincy impressed Stollmeyer throughout the series, declared.

The West Indies got off to a terrible start when Compson got a ball to kick off a length. It struck Stollmeyer's glove and lobbed into the hands of Verity. Headley came to the wicket with the intention of playing an innings to save the match. He batted with uncharacteristic slowness against tight bowling from the England spinners Hedley Verity and Doug Wright, taking two hours to reach fifty. Sealy, who had put up stiff resistance, was then dismissed. Weekes batted well and appeared comfortable until he was dismissed for 16. The cautious Headley eventually reached his second hundred of the match with a pull off Wright. He was the first player to score a century in each innings of a Test at Lord's. It wasn't until 1990 that Graham Gooch became the second. C. B. Fry in the press room declared that Headley should really be named Atlas because he carried the West Indies on his shoulders. The nickname stuck, at least in the media.

Once the excitement had died away, Headley went back to his task of trying to salvage the match for his team. Unfortunately, in an attempt to farm the strike and with the field positioned to save singles, the Jamaican got taught in two minds, checked a drive that might otherwise have flown to the boundary and lobbed a simple catch to Hutton. With their mainstay gone for 107 the West Indies fell apart, setting England just 99 to win in the final session of the match. Constantine hadn't bowled well in England's first innings but now he came into his own, Warner admiring the way he changed his pace from a 'cleverly flighted slow to an occasional fast ball'. Despite his age, Connie's fielding, Warner noted approvingly, 'remained electric'.

The West Indies bowled accurately and fielded with tenacity but the home side knocked off the runs for the loss of two wickets with just a few minutes to spare, Hammond making the winning hit with a classical off drive. Had Headley or any of the other batsmen stuck around for a few more overs defeat might have been averted. Connie himself did not escape criticism for his part in the second-innings debacle. Stollmeyer later wrote of his dismissal, 'Learie guided an arm ball from Hedley Verity into the safe hands of Wally Hammond at slip, a diabolical stroke undoubtedly conceived in advance and played at the wrong moment. When he came into the dressing room his younger colleagues gathered round and asked the inevitable question, "Learie, what happened?" "Well, it was the in-swinger," he replied vaguely. Every time thereafter one of us got out playing a bad shot and was questioned, our standard answer was, "Well, it was the in-swinger."'

Connie, comfortably the oldest player in the squad, was aware of the breach between his approach to the game and that of the younger generation: 'I was roundly condemned as old-fashioned whenever I tried to put some gunpowder into the game,' he wrote, adding that at times he 'had the impression that I was being slightly indecent, an old barn-stormer amongst refined young actors'. Connie believed the youngsters too often played for safety and that their attitude would ultimately lead to the game becoming embedded in 'competent mediocrity'. Though a professional, Connie had always batted like the most carefree of Edwardian amateurs. Perhaps he overdid it at times. Earlier in the tour he had played a shot against Lancashire in which he hit the ball between his legs. The West Indies were in trouble and he was criticised for being irresponsible. His defence was that he was merely trying to deal a psychological blow to the bowlers – fine if it worked, but disastrous if it didn't. The public still thrilled at the veteran entertainer's style, whether it was à la mode or not, but they were not play-ing alongside him. Connie was often critical of the lack of any sustained plan in the way the West Indies approached matches; whether he would have ever adhered to one that was not of his own devising is another matter.

To the obvious pleasure of Plum Warner, the defeat at Lord's did not destroy the tourists' confidence as it might have done on previous tours. Indeed, it seemed to spur them on and they played better after it than they had before, helped, perhaps, by warmer weather. Early June saw Weekes plunder 123 in a two-day match with Norfolk that ended in a draw, then Nottinghamshire were pum-melled by an innings and 94 runs. Headley scored 234 and Sealy 115 as the pair added 230 for the third wicket; Victor Stollmeyer, despite suffering from the effects of tonsillitis, scored 73. Connie did most of the damage with the ball, taking nine wickets for 117 runs in the match. In July the rain returned, ruining the next five matches, which all ended in draws. When it didn't rain there was sleet. Against Yorkshire on a 'sticky dog', and with Verity at his peak, Headley played an innings of such brilliance that the watching Neville Cardus rated it the finest he'd ever seen in his life, and Connie took three wickets in an over on his way to five for 28 in a match he felt they might have won if icy showers had not wiped out the final day.

Gomez for Weekes and Williams for Barrow were the two changes Grant made for the second Test at Old Trafford. Sealy took over the wicketkeeping duties. The changes baffled many, since they brought the number of bowlers in the side to six, with Grant an additional, occasional and sometimes effective spinner. By Test standards the tail was long – indeed some suggested that it started at number six. While this was a slight to some of the later batsmen, since none of them made double figures in the match it may have had some merit.

England's team at Lord's had been a good one, particularly the bowling, which Warner thought had 'more life and accuracy than any England side for several seasons past'. However, after that victory the selectors elected to experiment. The excellent Verity was dropped, while the experienced and rapid Farnes, who was bowling splendidly for Essex, was not picked at all.

Whether either side's selections were good or bad seemed unlikely to matter when rain and dark skies allowed only half an hour's play on the opening day in Manchester. Grant again won the toss and in the dim light inserted England. In the thirty minutes available Hutton and Arthur Fagg (in for Harold Gimblett) scored 11, Martindale dismissing

Fagg off a no-ball. More rain fell on the rest day, but thanks
to a lot of hard work from the ground staff play was able
to recommence at noon on the Monday. The conditions
were so cold it seemed that winter had come symbolically
early. Hammond made more appeals for military volunteers, Connie commenting with grim humour that 'he was
addressing the right stuff, for only the lion-hearted remained
to watch in the appalling conditions'.

The wicket was heavy and lifeless, though Fagg played
on just before lunch with the score on 34. After the break
Clarke and Grant bowled admirably. They were supported
by fine close catching and England very quickly found
themselves in bother, Hutton and Paynter both out with
the score still on 34, but not before something singular
occurred: the Yorkshireman popped a catch to Connie,
who to his shame dropped it. It was an event so unusual
most newspapers reported it in the manner they might a
triple century. Compton then slipped on the damp turf and
hit his wicket, and though Hammond made a few attacking
shots five wickets were down for 62. The West Indies were
in the hunt, but Joe Hardstaff proved tougher to remove
than his team mates. The Nottinghamshire man batted
with determination for 76 and found support from Wood,
who made 26. When Hardstaff and Wood were dismissed
Hammond declared with England on 164. The termina-
tion of England's innings left the West Indies with an hour
and a quarter to bat through until the close. Grant and Jeff
Stollmeyer opened. Stollmeyer never looked comfortable
and was out for five, but Grant played what was arguably
the innings of his life, striking the ball with fierce power
until he was eventually caught by Fagg off Goddard for
47 out of a total of 56. The Old Trafford crowd gave him
a huge ovation as he walked back to the pavilion. Gomez

failed again, but Sealy and Headley batted adventurously and at close of play the tourists were 85 for three.

On the final day Bowes bowled a magnificent spell and the West Indies' hopes of securing a first-innings lead were dashed as he took six for 33. Only Headley, who fell for 51, seemed to have any idea how to play the Yorkshire paceman, and even he experienced some rare moments of discomfort. Stollmeyer was again irritated by Connie's mode of dismissal: 'He was, when batting, inclined to pre-meditate and decide what he would do before the bowler bowled, not always with the desired results.' When he was bowled behind his back by Bill Bowes in the Old Trafford Test, the next day Neville Cardus wrote that 'Only a clever pedestrian could have got his legs out of the way!'

Despite trailing in a low-scoring match the West Indies were never in danger of defeat. Martindale and Connie both bowled well, quickly knocking over half a dozen England wickets, Connie getting four of them, and Hammond declared on 128 for six, setting the West Indies 160 to win in seventy minutes. It was an impossible target, especially in the gathering gloom, and the tourists had lost four wickets when the game was brought to a premature if welcome end. 'A game to be forgotten,' was Connie's under-standable conclusion.

The hard wicket of the Oval was a blessing and the West Indians enjoyed it thoroughly, beating Surrey by seven wickets. Bam-Bam Weekes blasted 146, Headley made 93 and Clarke took nine for 144. Hampshire were decisively beaten, Clarke adding to his tour haul with thirteen for 107 runs. An innings defeat to Somerset was followed by a two-wicket win over Glamorgan in Swansea. It was a hard-fought match in which Connie took nine wickets for 85 largely by using the heavy atmosphere to swing the ball.

He also produced a couple of those little moments of magic for which he was best remembered, running out Maurice Turnbull who – Stollmeyer recorded – 'played the ball sharply into the gully where Learie was fielding; in one movement he fielded the ball and had the stumps down with Turnbull following the stroke a yard out of his ground'. Then to win the match Connie smacked Cyril Smart for six barely over the head of square leg. The crowd were in raptures over this piece of audacity, but Stollmeyer was less convinced: 'If he had got out, we would probably have been beaten.'

After a draw with Warwickshire the tourists faltered again at Cheltenham, losing the last first-class game before the final Test by seven wickets. Connie, however, won plaudits from the sceptical Stollmeyer: 'Charlie Barnett was beginning to look dangerous. Coming out after lunch, Learie told Manny Martindale "Bowl one short just outside off stump and I will catch him on the cover-point boundary" ... He was prophetic. It happened just as he said. Barnett square cut firmly in the middle of the bat, Learie swallowed the catch and, as he so often used to do, put the ball in his trouser pocket. Fantastic.'

For the final Test at the Oval the West Indies did not repeat the error of playing too many bowlers. Victor Stollmeyer came in for Cameron and Weekes for Williams. The young paceman Johnson also got a start, Hylton – who had lost form badly – making way. The changes strengthened the batting order considerably, with Sealy in at seven. The side also had a balanced attack of five good bowlers. For the first time in a Test in England they seemed to have got the balance right, with specialists in all positions.

Connie had taken the opportunity provided by a rest day before the Test to wander off into the countryside with a packet of sandwiches provided for him by the hotel chef. He needed a break. He had played in practically every game for the simple reason that his name was box office and the West Indies management lived in perpetual fear of losing money. He had not told his team mates what he was up to, missed a team talk and, on his return, was given 'a terrific trouncing by the skipper' for his unexplained absence. The peace and quiet had done him good, though.

The weather was hot and sunny in South London, adding to the sense of anticipation. Connie noted the silvery shapes of barrage balloons floating above the Oval as a precaution against air raids, the aircraft droning overhead and service uniforms speckling the crowd. Tractors pulling anti-aircraft guns joined the red buses passing down the Harleyford Road and everywhere he saw 'hard, frightened faces ... death hovering in the air'.

The field of play at least offered some escape. England won the toss and on a perfect wicket Hammond elected to bat. Hutton played out the first over from Martindale without alarm, but with his first delivery Johnson induced Walter Keeton of Nottinghamshire – making his second Test appearance after a gap of five years – to play on. The lithe and pacey Trinidadian had taken a wicket with his first ball in first-class cricket against Worcestershire in May and now had a wicket with his first ball in Test cricket.

Norman Oldfield, another Test debutant, joined Hutton. The two men batted brilliantly against the pace of Connie, Johnson and Martindale, putting on 131 for the second wicket. But after Hutton went for 73 Oldfield soon followed and Hammond and Compton both failed, the England captain discomfited when Connie switched to bowling medium-paced off-breaks to him. The situation was rescued once again by Hardstaff, who found an excellent partner in Nichols. The two looked to be carrying England to a mammoth total when Connie popped up and broke the partnership. Connie had been bowling well all day, deceiving the batsmen 'with pace and flight variations whose beauties are not advertised by any alteration in action or run', but now it was his astounding fielding that came to the fore. Even at his advanced age he was still, in Warner's estimation, as 'active as the proverbial cat' and showed it now: bounding to collect a shot off his own bowling at cover he shied at the wicket with only one stump to aim for and struck it with a flat, low throw, running out the astonished Nichols by several yards. England had a long tail that was now exposed, and though Hardstaff did his best to farm the strike while hitting everything he could he was finally out for 94. England finished on 352, Connie collecting five wickets for 75.

West Indies had an awkward short spell to bat. They lost Grant almost immediately but Headley and Jeff Stollmeyer played comfortably to the close, which came with the West Indies 27 for one.

The second day was arguably the best the West Indies had enjoyed in England since being given Test status. Headley and Stollmeyer blunted the home attack and took the score to 128 before the Trinidadian opener fell to the bowling of Hutton for 59. He was replaced by his brother Victor, who made his presence felt in a most unfortunate way – running out Headley when the Jamaican looked well set and untroubled on 65. Gomez failed again and four wickets were down for 164. Enter the left-handed Weekes. He was in imperious form and with Vic Stollmeyer added 164 in just a hundred minutes. The experienced England attack of Perks, Goddard, Nichols and Wright could do little to stop the flow of runs. Needing only four for a century on his Test debut, Victor Stollmeyer played forward to Wright and was stumped. England were saved from further punishment when thunder and lightning held up play for an hour after tea. Weekes fell shortly after play resumed for a magnificent 137 struck in 135 minutes. At close of play Connie was at the wicket and the score was 395 for six.

The following morning Connie took charge, batting in an impudent and aggressive style that suggested he was determined to banish the mounting political tension, or at least give the spectators something to look back on fondly during the grim struggle to come. Playing a series of audacious strokes far beyond the imagination, never mind ability, of most batsmen, he crashed his way to 79 out of the 103 that were added for the last four wickets and was the final man out, apparently aiming to belt the ball out of the ground over the head of wicketkeeper Arthur Wood. 'He cut, he drove, he made the most amazing hooks ...' a delighted Warner recalled. 'He also made a few snicks over and through the slips. It was an innings with a strong blend of Jessop in it, combined with a preponderance of Constantine himself.' One shot that lived long in the memory of those watching was a back-foot drive off Perks that was lifted straight back over the bowler's head into the Vauxhall End for six, a prodigious piece of skill and timing. Stollmeyer was full of admiration, noting that Connie 'had the fielders scattered to all corners of the ground. It was the first time I had seen fast bowlers of the calibre of Reg Perks and Maurice Nichols bowling with no slip and all the men in the outfield.' *Wisden* was equally impressed, claiming that Connie had surpassed Bradman 'in his amazing strokeplay', while an excitable C. B. Fry described him as 'an Indian rubberman with double joints'. The batsman left the field to a standing ovation. He had promised friends at the start of the tour that he would make a century in the Test series. He had failed to do so, but in such a glorious fashion that few watching cared.

The West Indies finished with a lead of 146, leaving England with no chance of winning. All that the home side could do was bat for a draw. In Hutton and Hammond they found just the men for the job. The captain made 138 and the Yorkshireman 165 not out as England totalled 366–3.

So the West Indies failed to record a Test victory, but at last they had shown the English cricketing public what they were capable of and – with their scintillating batting – given a hint of what was to come.

The third Test proved to be the last match of the tour. War was coming. Kent had cancelled the fixture that was due to follow the final Test and the West Indies management decided it was best to head home. When Grant told his team of the decision they almost rebelled, so eager were they to play the final six games of the tour.

In twenty-five first-class matches the West Indians had won eight and lost six. It was the first time a West Indian tour party had won more games than it had lost. Some observers felt they might have done even better given the talent in the party, but as in 1933 several had failed to perform at their best and the weight of winning had fallen on a small number of players. Connie was head and shoulders above any other bowler. Coming in off a shorter run to conserve his energy, he had replaced speed with cunning. He took 103 wickets at 17.77 each to finish seventh in the first-class averages, and mixing slower cutters with the occasional much faster delivery he seemed a better bowler than ever. His commitment remained as high as it had always been. He bowled more overs than any of his team mates, *Wisden* describing him as 'the most unflagging member of a very alert side'. Injury to Cameron deprived them of a good all-rounder, though Clarke developed into a top-class spinner as the tour went on and was charmingly wide-eyed about his experience, telling reporters, 'I'd read all about the English stars, the Huttons and the Comptons, and came here on tour with a great feeling of deference. To my amazement I found myself getting these stars out!' Martindale was past his best and took only forty-six wickets at 34 runs each. Hylton was also a disappointment and young Johnson quick but erratic. At his best he was a formidable force and there were signs of what he might have developed into had the Second World War not intervened. The fourth paceman, Williams, was more productive with bat than ball.

The batting once again depended heavily on Headley, who had a fine time scoring 1745 runs at an average of 72.70. Had the tour not ended early he would almost certainly have repeated his feat of 1933 and passed the two-thousand-run mark. The two Stollmeyers were the best of the rest. Jeffrey, in particular, was commendable. He performed consistently well throughout a long and arduous tour. Weekes and Sealy also had their moments of brilliance and Connie had 614 runs at an average of 21.17. Barrow was a total failure, as was Gomez, while Bayly began brightly but then suffered a knee injury from which he never properly recovered.

That the West Indies lost only one of the three Tests showed how much they had improved since that first Test series. In fact, in Warner's estimation, they had performed rather better than South Africa had done the previous summer.

The decision to bring the tour to a premature close proved a sound one. The party went by train to Greenock

to catch the SS *Montrose* bound for Montreal. It docked on
3 September, the day war was declared. The next ship of
the same line to make the Atlantic crossing, SS *Athenia*,
was sunk by a U-boat the day the West Indians arrived in
Canada.

It was to be Connie's final season of first-class cricket. To
mark the departure from the scene of a player whose 'every
movement was a joy to behold', *Wisden* named him as one
of the five Cricketers of the Year. While his team mates
returned to the Caribbean he travelled up to his home in
the North of England. He had a commitment to play for
Windhill in the Bradford League, but his week would begin
with him filling sandbags at Nelson Hospital. It had been a
long, hard summer, but there were greater and more serious
trials ahead.

Chapter 10

Playing Cricket and Beating Hitler

Rochdale's long-running pursuit of Connie had finally ended. They had captured him with a contract worth around eight hundred pounds for a twenty-week engagement. To Connie's pleasure the club also agreed to sign Elias as an amateur. The younger Constantine came over from Trinidad and took up residence in a flat in Manchester Road. Connie continued to live in Meredith Street.

Rochdale was one of the oldest, most successful and wealthiest clubs in Lancashire. Its reputation for big spending could be traced back to the days when the team had been bankrolled by the controversial financier and music-hall impresario Jimmy White, a man whose lavish champagne-and-actresses lifestyle would come to an abrupt end with bankruptcy and suicide in 1927. White had signed Cec Parkin as the club professional and the Lancashire all-rounder was playing at Dane Street when, in 1921, he was called up for England. It was a sign of Rochdale's spending power and ambition that they hired Patsy Hendren as his temporary replacement. Parkin was an eccentric cheeky chappy with a comical bent whose wildly experimental bowling was perfected by trial and error, supposedly in the backyard of his house with his long-suffering wife as the batter. Parkin's personality, like Connie's, shone through on the field and he was a massively popular figure in the leagues. He and Connie would become good friends and Connie would captain his son at Windhill. Parkin was not just a lovable maverick, he was a terrific cricketer too, and a huge success at Rochdale, who won the Central Lancashire League title five years out of six while he was their professional. Parkin's replacement was the infinitely less chirpy S. F. Barnes. Barnes played at Rochdale for two seasons, taking 203 wickets at 7.32 runs, the sort of awe-inspiring figures that were more or less commonplace for him. Connie's West Indies team mate Puss Achong had been Rochdale's professional in 1934, though it is claimed he was only a second choice, brought in at the last minute after negotiations with Don Bradman failed. Achong would stay in Lancashire for many years and take more than a thousand wickets in the leagues.

The Central Lancashire League was founded two years after the Lancashire League, originally as the South-East Lancashire League, and matches were played to much the same format, though those in the CLL began and ended half an hour later. Always considered the junior of the two leagues, in truth there was little between them in terms of quality. Perhaps because it was located in a more densely populated area than the Lancashire League, the CLL attracted larger crowds. It's estimated that in the 1937 season the aggregate attendance at CLL matches was 330,000, around eighty thousand more than in the Lancashire League. Rochdale were the League's best-supported club, though their record home gate – nine thousand for a game against arch-rivals Littleborough during Parkin's heyday – was lower than the crowds that had come to Seedhill to see Connie.

Hedley Verity had been a professional in the CLL and the post-war years would see West Indians of the calibre of Frank Worrell, Garry Sobers and Joel Garner playing in the League. In the thirties, however, most of the pros were Englishmen; Lionel Cranfield, Tommy Simpson, Leslie Warburton and Bill Thornton ranked high amongst them. While they may not have had quite the glamour of the big overseas names who filled the pro ranks in the Lancashire League, most of these men had county experience and a deep knowledge of the game, particularly as it was played in Lancashire. Cranfield, who owned a florist's shop in Middleton, was a former Somerset and Gloucestershire all-rounder and an excellent coach who would later become George Hirst's assistant at Eton, while Leslie Warburton had been called to play in a Test trial by England while still an amateur in the Lancashire League.

Rochdale had joined the CLL the year after it was formed. The club's Dane Street ground was enclosed by huge mills in the centre of the town. On match days, street vendors sold cowheels, the local delicacy, to hungry fans. The ground was surrounded by brick walls that made sighting the ball difficult and because of poor drainage the pitch was notoriously damp and heavy, and favoured the sort of medium-paced cutters that were the specialism of Parkin and Barnes.

For Connie, the season at Rochdale was to be an unhappy one and Dane Street's pudding of a pitch was just one of the things he struggled with. While anything that followed his great final season at Nelson, when he was fêted everywhere he went with bunting and silver bands, was bound to be an anticlimax, the summer of 1938 was something more than that. It was to be marked by rancour and unpleasantness.

Connie arrived at Rochdale to a certain amount of suspicion and resentment. While Connie had always treated his team mates as equals, a preconception that he was a Big-Time Charlie who thought himself a cut above proved obdurately difficult to change. Connie would meet claims that he was if not quite arrogant then certainly a little too full of himself throughout his life. There were some who doubtless agreed with E. W. Swanton's view that 'none could call ... Constantine a modest man'. Certainly there is an element of self-promotion in some of Connie's writing that could lead to that assumption. However, a more sympathetic reading might be that having spent most of his life in a system that constantly and cruelly undervalued him, Connie felt obliged to remind people of his significance. Class, if not race, may also have played a part in Swanton's verdict. Connie was a professional cricketer, and professional cricketers were expected to be unassuming and dignified after the fashion of Jack Hobbs, or comical and self-effacing like Maurice Tate. They certainly weren't expected to draw attention to themselves. Besides, if Connie had been as bumptious as his critics suggested, would he really have been so popular in East Lancashire and the West Riding of Yorkshire, places with a notoriously low tolerance of big-heads?

At least part of the problem at Rochdale was Connie's much-discussed salary. From the start he felt a 'worry that perhaps somebody was paying me too much. I did not feel it, but some people did, and said so.' Just as during his time at Nelson, Connie brought financial benefits wherever he played with Rochdale, 'but you would not have thought so by the manner of some of [the other clubs]'.

Nor was Connie impressed by the attitude of some of the League's cricketers. He felt that many were motivated solely by the prospect of collections, and were quite happy to dawdle their way to a fifty, to the detriment of their side's chances of winning, simply to pick up some cash. 'When a man would rather see his side lose than a miss a chance of turning over an extra pound, the jealous dragons who guard the spirit of cricket ought to eat him up.' Press reports from the time suggest that others felt the same way too.

More damaging than any of this was an incident involving an umpire. Connie had already heard rumours that racially charged comments were being made about him behind his back, so when he was given out by an umpire and, as he walked off, heard the official who had raised the finger make a 'contemptible' comment about him to his colleague at square leg he was furious. Connie asked Rochdale to take the matter up on his behalf. They did so, but quickly found themselves threatened with legal action by the Central Lancashire Umpires Association. Undeterred, the club pressed on. However, when the matter came before the CLL committee they refused to hear any evidence from witnesses and judged that, since the remarks formed part of a private conversation, there were no charges to answer. Naturally Connie was angered and dismayed by a verdict that not only served to sweep the incident under the carpet, but also suggested that the use of racial insults was acceptable.

The season had some highlights, notably a whirlwind innings against Middleton that saw Connie reach 50 in

fourteen minutes and go on to finish on 106 made in just
over half an hour. He followed it by taking five wickets for
21 runs. Rochdale's gate receipts were, predictably, the
highest in the club's history, but for Connie it was a time
best forgotten.

With the German invasion of France the phoney war gave
way to real war. Connie elected not to return to Trinidad,
saying, 'I would have felt like a rat leaving a sinking ship.'
It was a tacit acknowledgement that his home was now in
Lancashire and of the debt he felt he owed Britain, the
country in which he'd made his fortune. After a spell as an
air raid equipment officer he took on work as a billeting
officer with Nelson Council, inspecting and grading local
housing in preparation for the arrival of evacuated children from Manchester and Bradford. The job brought him
face to face with lives of hardship he previously had only
occasionally glimpsed. Later he would write that he 'had
never known the extent of poverty until I came to Nelson'.
Once again he considered how fortunate his own childhood
had been, and how ignorant he had been while living in
the Caribbean of the reality of life for some in the Mother
Country.
    Connie had been preparing for military service when he
heard from the Ministry of Labour and National Service
that his application for the post of welfare officer had been
accepted. As a welfare officer Connie would be responsible for looking after the thousands of West Indians who
had been drafted to work in the factories of the north-
west to help with the war effort. In total around twenty
thousand arrived in Britain during the conflict, mainly to
work in munitions factories. They lived mainly in London,
Liverpool and Cardiff. Far from home, in an alien country,

often doing work for which they were not trained, the immigrants needed someone to act on their behalf and liaise with local authorities, landlords and managers. It was a task for which Connie, with his tact, charm and national reputation, was ideally suited.

Connie began work in the autumn of 1941. Based in Liverpool, he commuted from Nelson when he could and at other times stayed in a hostel. Merseyside had been heavily bombed the previous May. More than three thousand people had been killed, 6500 homes destroyed and 190,000 damaged. The burned outer shell of St Luke's Church close to Connie's office provided a daily reminder of the grim battle ahead.

Connie's job was often a difficult one. The arrivals from the Caribbean were young and predominantly from rural areas. Arriving in an industrial city that had been heavily hit by the Luftwaffe was a disorienting experience for most of them. They had to be found accommodation, and jobs for which they either had the skills or for which they could be trained. They needed help with money, with communicating with their loved ones back in the West Indies and a hundred other things. Connie was sympathetic to their plight, but as a self-sufficient and resourceful man sometimes found himself frustrated by the newcomers' unworldliness. 'We had to do everything for them – as you would for children,' he once declared.

One thing that Connie's new role brought into sharp focus was racial discrimination. He had experienced it himself, of course, but seeing those who had only come to Britain to help fight the Nazis refused housing, turned down for jobs, paid lower wages or simply picked on and bullied couldn't help but make him think more on the matter.

Using all of his considerable powers of persuasion and

working closely with trades unions, Connie helped ease
suspicions on the shop floor and secure parity for black
workers with their white counterparts. When diplomacy
didn't work he could resort to cunning, asking the Ministry
to demand reluctant companies fill orders quickly so that
they would be forced to hire black workers. In other cases
he would tackle problems head-on, as when dealing with a
Greek sea captain who had, during the course of a voyage
and on a variety of spurious pretexts, docked the entire
wages of a West Indian seaman. After a frank and forceful
confrontation with the Greek consul, Connie got the sailor's
wages paid in full.

When it came to racial slurs, Connie generally remained
philosophical, accepting that they were a daily fact of life in
Britain. He said, 'Long ago an old Negro told me: "Learie,
the only thing to do with people with bad manners is to
forgive them; any other way hurts more." He was right.'

One night in a dance hall Connie was shoved by an
American Air Force officer who told him, 'Get out. We
don't allow nigs to mix with white people where I come
from.' Connie politely told the officer to leave him alone,
only to receive the reply: 'Get out, nigger, before I smash
you.' Connie recalled: 'I said to the American, "Come
outside with me," and I had every intention of thrashing
him. I could have done it. I had marked the spot where I
would hit him a formidable blow. But walking the length
of the hall cooled me – I became aware of the newspaper
headlines that would have resulted, and the general inflam-
mation of the black and white problem that it would have
caused, with England at that time filled with black and
white American troops. So, rather sadly, I handed him
over to the porter at the door and he was promptly ordered
outside.'

In many ways this typified Connie's style. He preferred to use decency and dignity rather than aggression to make his point. By acting coolly and with good manners he gave the lie to the popular notion that black people were hot-blooded and intemperate – an accusation that had dogged the West Indies cricket team – while exposing the ugliness and stupidity of those who abused him.

Connie's refusal to be drawn into direct disputes was later criticised by some younger campaigners for racial equality who felt that his wealth and celebrity had made him a 'white Englishman'. It is true that fame perhaps made some people colour-blind, an attitude exemplified in the story of George Headley's days in Haslingden, when it is said that a small boy pointed him out to his mother with the words, 'Look, a black man,' to receive the reply, 'Oh, that is not a black man. That is George Headley, the crick-eter.' Yet this did not work on everyone. Connie suffered abuse ranging from name-calling to ignorant assumptions about his intelligence. His quiet approach to dealing with it served him well, and during a time when it was sometimes difficult to tell the difference between a genuine lack of knowledge about black people and a deliberate slur, it was likely the correct policy.

The fact he was a cricketer helped, naturally. To the West Indian workers he was a national hero and he was an idol to most of Lancashire too – though he was sur-prised to find that some Liverpool cricket fans who had followed his exploits only through newspaper and radio reports were amazed to discover he was black. On numer-ous occasions Connie found that, when trying to settle disputes between the immigrants from the Caribbean and local workers, the whole thing could be eased with a bit of cricket talk. Finding common ground was often the key to forging lasting understanding. Years later another great West Indian cricketer, Rohan Kanhai, would find his passage in the Northumberland pit village of Ashington, where he had gone to play as a professional, was greatly eased when the locals discovered that, like them, the Guyanese batsman was a keen dominoes player.

There is little doubt that the job of welfare officer was a difficult one, and that Connie did it well. Certainly it was appreciated by the people he worked with and around. Bessie Braddock, the firebrand Labour MP for Liverpool Exchange, said Connie had shown 'all the tact in the world, and common sense as well' in discharging his role. One thing of which he was keenly aware was that such a senior civil service position would have been denied to him in Trinidad simply because of the darkness of his skin.

Connie's involvement with the League of Coloured Peoples – formed by Harold Moody, a Jamaican who had moved to London in 1904 to pursue his medical studies – had begun in the thirties. In terms of Connie's political awakening, this was an important period and began with a visit to Nelson by C. L. R. James. James had attended the prestigious Queen's Royal College in Port of Spain on a scholarship and played cricket for Maple, the club of predominantly light-skinned middle-class black Trinidadians. The future historian and Marxist activist came to stay with the Constantines in May 1932 after a short spell in London hanging around on the fringes of the Bloomsbury set. He found Lancashire more to his liking than the capital and lodged at Meredith Street for a year, even playing a couple of games for Nelson's second XI.

Connie had originally contacted James about the

possibility of them collaborating in writing his auto-biography. James was excited by the idea and duly helped Connie complete *Cricket and I*. But while the two men enjoyed many long conversations about cricket – some of which would find their way into James's classic *Beyond a Boundary* – it was their discussions of the political situation in the Caribbean which had the most profound effect on both of them. 'Within five weeks we had unearthed the politician in each other,' said James. 'Within five months we were supplementing each other in a working partner-ship which had West Indies' self-government as its goal.'

At that point there was growing agitation in the West Indies against the ruling class. The Great Depression that had brought such misery to the Lancashire cotton towns had had a similar effect across the Caribbean. There was a fall in demand for sugar, cocoa and other exports, a rise in unemployment and a drop in living standards for the working class. The fact that a white minority monopolised political and economic power increasingly became a source of anger.

Chatting by the fire in Connie's snug sitting room the men began to feel that they might be able to use their influ-ence to effect a change; to, in James's words, 'initiate the West Indian renaissance, not only in cricket but in politics, history and writing'. Connie was aware that the majority of British people had little or no idea about what life was like in the Caribbean. With the encouragement and support of James, he could do something about that. At the same time he could, by his example both on the cricket field and off it, demonstrate that West Indians were just as capable of self-government as Australians or Canadians.

This was an important point as, even amongst those of a generally liberal bent, there was still a good deal of

racial theorising as far as West Indies cricket was concerned. This was often couched in comments about the
effect the hot Caribbean weather had on the temperament
of the players. Paradoxically, the equally hot Antipodean
temperatures seemed to have no such 'mercurial effect' on
white Australians, or none anyone felt moved to comment
on.

Jack Hobbs – as decent a man as it was possible to meet
and a huge admirer of Connie's – offered the view that
the West Indians were 'just big boys'. Moreover, their temperament meant that they were 'very high up in the air
one minute, very down in the mouth the next'. The great
Neville Cardus likewise felt moved to observe that the
'erratic quality of West Indian cricket is surely true to racial
type', before going on to say that the West Indies would
never produce good slow bowlers because, like schoolboys,
the West Indians all wanted to bowl fast. Ironically, the
West Indies' first Test victory in England would be the
result of brilliant bowling by Sonny Ramadhin and Alf
Valentine, both spinners.

Connie had already begun to give occasional talks
around Nelson to Rotary clubs and church groups.
Enthused by James, he now began taking on more and
more public-speaking engagements. Connie's local popularity ensured large audiences and, while cricket was
generally the main topic, he found people were also fasci-
nated to hear about life in Trinidad. James observed that
Connie's charm and grace made it possible for him to
speak about nationalism and race without causing alarm
amongst the more conservative elements in the audience.
Always aware that he was a professional sportsman not a
professional politician, Connie did not push too far. While
James spent his days in Nelson Library reading about

the Russian Revolution and gradually moving towards
Trotskyism, he never became a true radical. Yet he got
his point across. James often spoke at the same meetings
and was touched by the positive response he encountered.
He felt that converts were being made and bonds forged.
It helped that the cotton towns had a history of political
radicalism – part of the Puritan tradition that had nurtured
Gerrard Winstanley and sheltered George Fox, the founder
of Quakerism, who had spoken out against the tyranny
of the clergy from Pendle Hill, which overlooked Nelson
Cricket Club. Nelson itself was sometimes referred to as
Little Moscow and the socialist policies of the Independent
Labour Party-dominated town council so impressed James
that he joined the local branch of the ILP – which had
been disaffiliated from the official Labour Party a year or
so earlier over its hard-left ideas, such as the nationalisation
of banking.

Like the majority of sportsmen, Connie was at heart
politically conservative. The left-leaning part of him
was entirely that which concerned race and his native
Trinidad. He believed that 'they are no better than
we', but took the idea little further. The equality of the
races concerned him; the equality of all people did not.
Perhaps this is because the world Connie inhabited as
a professional cricketer was – within certain limits – a
meritocracy. He and James might discuss the iniquity of
some of the selections for the West Indies tour parties –
James was particularly dubious about the talents of the
white Trinidadian wicketkeeper George Dewhurst – and
the injustice of the white captaincy policy, but ultimately
Connie's was a profession in which talent, so unevenly and
unfairly distributed, generally won out.

But while Connie would never embrace James's hard-left

beliefs,* or approve of his lifestyle (James was a notorious womaniser) the two men had similar views on the self-determination of the West Indian colonies and the politics of race. To this end both joined the League of Coloured Peoples not long after it had been formed. Connie also paid for the publication, in pamphlet form, of one of James's essays, 'The Case for West Indian Self-Government', an important text in the developing independence movement.

After James had left Lancashire for London, where he began – with Connie's help – to build a career as a successful writer, Connie continued to give talks and lectures around the north of England, though not so frequently. It had become plain during James's time with him that politics distracted him from his main occupation – cricket. Not only was the game his livelihood, it also remained Connie's best means of getting his point across. After watching him in glorious action only the most hardened bigot could have gone away believing that black people were inherently inferior to whites.

The political consciousness that had been kept in the background while he was playing was reawakened and refreshed during the war years. As well as bringing him into contact with West Indians from all parts of the Caribbean, Connie's work also saw him meeting and dealing with the problems of immigrant workers from Africa too, which widened horizons that had previously been focused solely on his native region. Connie began to see things in more global terms and he became more involved with the League of Coloured Peoples, often referring cases

* Connie's upbringing as a Roman Catholic must have militated against this, though he had broken with the Church following an incident during his trip to New York, when he and Norma had kneeled to pray in the front pew of a church, only to be interrupted by the verger yelling 'Niggers at the back!'

of discrimination to them when he became frustrated by his employer the Ministry of Labour's inability or unwillingness to deal with them. Connie also became concerned with the problems facing mixed-race children born to white women after affairs with West Indian workers or black US service personnel. Many such children were abandoned and Connie organised charity cricket matches in the hope of raising money for a children's home in which they could be looked after. The home was never built – the money went to the Liverpool Royal Infirmary and other good causes instead – but Connie's campaign brought him into much greater contact with Harold Moody.

Moody was lucid, self-controlled, practical and diligent, and his moderate approach to racial politics closely resembled Connie's own. During the war the League of Coloured Peoples became increasingly important. Its membership was swelled by new immigrants and the political role it might play in shaping the post-war world became clearer. Like Connie, Moody believed that the British Empire should be at the forefront of promoting racial equality in the world. To Moody, if the British government failed to address discrimination at home then there was a danger of it 'carrying on the *Herrenvolk* idea against which we are fighting'. The founder's work and writing would continue to have a profound influence on Connie's thinking for many years, and when Moody died in 1947 Connie briefly took over as chairman of the organisation, sitting on an executive committee that included Hastings Banda, a deeply conservative GP who would later become president of Malawi. Without Moody's guiding presence, however, the League of Coloured Peoples gradually fell from importance and folded in 1951.

In the summer of 1944 the League drew up its 'Charter

for Coloured People', which called for self-government in
the colonies and demanded equal opportunities for all men
and women regardless of colour, and that discrimination in
'employment, in places of public entertainment and refresh-
ment, or in other public places' be made illegal. This last
point would prove to have a particular, cruel relevance to
Connie.

While working as a welfare officer Connie had been encouraged to carry on giving the sort of talks that had been a
feature of his life when playing for Nelson. His brief was
wider and he gave talks about the West Indies to service personnel as a means of promoting understanding between the
many different groups from across the Empire who were now
fighting together. He also spoke in schools and to youth clubs,
to religious organisations and in hospitals. Unsurprisingly,
perhaps, Connie had also found time to move into broadcasting – a natural place for an eloquent man with what one
reviewer described as a 'rich, musical voice'. One of his early
talks on the BBC addressed his experiences as a black man
in England, perhaps the first that ever tackled the topic. For
most listeners his descriptions of the prejudices he and his
family had encountered were eye-opening and shocking,
though as usual his charm and obvious lack of bitterness
shone through. Not long afterwards Connie was invited to
appear on the BBC's *Brains Trust* discussion programme, a
first for a sportsman. He would go on to appear regularly
on radio and television until the mid-sixties, speaking on
politics, race and of course cricket, and spent a spell as a
commentator, usually on limited-overs matches, a form of
cricket he had long supported and for which his own game
might have been ideally suited.

Disillusioned after his season in the Central Lancashire

League, Connie found faith and equilibrium restored on the other side of the Pennines. He signed for Windhill of the Bradford League in 1939. Connie said this was the biggest contract of his career, which it was – in theory at least. The Yorkshire club's committee were a canny bunch and put in various clauses that reduced the contract's value in the event of the war they knew was coming. Nevertheless, at twenty-five pounds a week it was considerable – almost treble what top-flight footballers were earning at that time.

The Bradford League was founded in 1903. All the clubs that played in it hailed from within a ten-mile radius of Bradford Town Hall. If anything, it was even more parochial than the Lancashire League, and yet it commanded huge respect, because in many ways the Bradford League epitomised Yorkshire cricket. Just about every great player the county had produced had played in it at some point in his career. It had attracted a host of big-name pros from outside the county too, mainly because it had refused to shut down during the First World War despite an outcry from Lord's. The Bradford League differed from the Lancashire League in its approach to payments. The Lancashire clubs were limited to one professional, but in the Bradford League they could have up to four. In the years before Connie arrived dozens of Test cricketers had appeared in the League, including Jack Hobbs, S. F. Barnes, Maurice Leyland, Wilfred Rhodes, Herbert Sutcliffe, Charlie Llewellyn, Stewie Dempster and Connie's old West Indies team mate Edwin St Hill.

Connie was impressed with the organisation of the Bradford League and found the standard of the cricket, even with war on the horizon, exceedingly high. In fact, he believed that the Bradford League was the bedrock on which the cricketing success of Yorkshire was built.

Of the professionals who had graced the League Connie wrote: 'These are the players who have appeared regularly before Yorkshire crowds, and whose style has been sedulously copied by Yorkshiremen and boys who will, in the future, emulate them to the discomfort of cricket counties further south.'

He had 'never found more keenness than in the Bradford League' and wondered why, since Yorkshire – whose style and spirit he much admired – used it as the basis for their Championship-winning teams, there had been no move to organise proper league cricket in the South of England. The simple answer was that southern cricket was still dominated by the amateur ethos – even in working-class areas. Competitive league cricket was thought to be detrimental to the spirit of the game, even by John Arlott, a man who generally championed the cause of professional cricketers.

Windhill Cricket Club had been founded in 1863 and joined the Bradford League in 1905, first winning the League title in 1911. The club had employed a number of top-class professionals down the years including Charlie Parker, one of county cricket's greatest slow left-armers. Parker played a single season for Windhill before moving on to Gloucestershire, for whom he took more than three thousand first-class wickets.

Windhill's ground in Busy Lane had been bought by the club in 1923 with the proceeds of a well-organised bazaar. In those years they employed the South African Test all-rounder Bert Vogler and Alf Morris, a bowler from Hartlepool who had once taken seven wickets in a match against Syd Gregory's touring Australians for an England representative XI

It was a strong side that also included the all-rounder Fred Berry, who later played for Surrey, and the bowlers Squire Render, a doggedly accurate medium-pacer, and Johnny Lawrence, a talented if notably slow leg-spinner who would go on to appear in over two hundred first-class matches for Somerset and later, as a coach back in Yorkshire, would nurture the talent of the young Geoffrey Boycott. Cec Parkin's son Reg was another team mate.

These high-class cricketers had helped Windhill lift the League title in 1937, and then repeated the feat in 1938 and 1939. Connie joined them in 1940 and did not disappoint. His first season saw him make 366 runs, including a blistering hundred against Brighouse in under an hour, and take seventy-six wickets at an average of 11.80, including a hat-trick against Spen Victoria. Windhill landed the title again.

At the end of his first season Connie was selected to play for the Bradford League XI against Yorkshire in a match to raise money for the Red Cross. The match drew a crowd of seven thousand to the old Park Avenue ground in Bradford. The League side, which also included Eddie Paynter and Manny Martindale, had first knock and Connie was at his whirlwind best, belting a century – including three sixes and fourteen fours – in just shy of an hour. His batting allowed the League XI to declare on 259 for seven. For Yorkshire, the veteran Herbert Sutcliffe responded with a century of his own, though it came at a slightly more sedate pace, and saved the match for the county, who closed on 209 for six. Sutcliffe later commented that 'Constantine's innings was a real gem and he batted far better than ever I've seen him.'

The following season Windhill won their fifth title on the bounce, fending off the challenge of Idle by just one point.

Connie became the second player in Bradford League history to take four wickets in four balls in a match against Lidget Green.

In 1942 Windhill once again claimed the title, with Connie taking sixty-eight wickets and hitting 322 runs. By now he was playing as an amateur.

Connie's war service meant he would not return to Windhill until 1945, the club making up for his absence by signing two Derbyshire cricketers, Alf Pope and Bill Copson. Later they added Les Ames to the line-up.

Leaving Windhill did not put an end to Connie's cricket, however. He played occasionally in the Liverpool and District League and in charity matches that raised hundreds of thousands of pounds for the war effort. In many of the games West Indian cricketers in Britain combined to play as a side. In August 1940 they took on an English XI raised by Sir Pelham Warner at Lord's. The West Indian team included Connie, Martindale, Edwin St Hill and Bertie Clarke. Warner's side was also a strong one and included Hutton and Compton. They ran out winners by 117 runs. Denis Compton was man of the match, scoring 73 and then taking three wickets for no runs with his leg-breaks. For the West Indians Ernest Eytle, a barrister from British Guiana whose brother, Les, would become Mayor of Lewisham, batted well for 47 and Clarke took five wickets for 68.*

Highlights of the West Indians' wartime schedule included a game at Lord's in 1943 against a very powerful England

---

* Clarke had stayed on in England after the 1939 tour to pursue his medical studies at Guy's Hospital. Over the six summers of the conflict he took 665 wickets. When peace came he practised medicine and played county cricket for Northants and Essex. An enthusiastic contributor on cricket for the World Service, he'd play for various BBC teams until he was well into his seventies.

XI, which attracted twenty thousand paying spectators. The West Indies batted first. Alec Bedser gave a hint of what he was capable of by taking six for 27 as Connie's team were bowled out for 120. Connie nipped out the England openers but then Les Ames made 72 and Jack Robertson 80 to guide their side home by eight wickets. With play prematurely ended a beer match was quickly arranged, Connie starring with 59 not out in forty-five minutes, including two massive sixes off leg-spinner Doug Wright.

Connie, Martindale and Clarke were then called up to play alongside cricketers from Australia, New Zealand and South Africa in a Dominions side for a two-day game against England at Lord's. England scored 324 and bowled the Dominions out cheaply. They then scored quickly to declare at lunch on the second day, leaving the Dominions to score 360 in two sessions for victory. Stewie Dempster of New Zealand made 113, Clarke a half-century and Connie blasted 21 before falling to a cheeky catch by Compton on the boundary, the Middlesex man bracing himself against the fence with one hand to ensure he didn't step across the boundary rope and collecting the ball with the other. In a thrilling finish in front of fourteen thousand spectators England emerged the victors by 8 runs.

In 1944 five games were arranged for England at Lord's. Hammond captained the side who took on Australia (a side made up entirely of Royal Australian Air Force personnel), the West Indies, the Rest of the World and the Dominions.

On Saturdays and bank holidays the games drew crowds of over twenty thousand; indeed thirty thousand saw the Whit Monday one-day game with Australia. They were broadcast live on the radio and raised four thousand pounds for charity. Connie captained the side and hit a brisk 42 that included a six into the members' stand, but it was Hammond who got most of the plaudits, scoring a century on a day of blazing sunshine. Anyone thinking the war was already over had a rude awakening three days later when the first flying bomb struck the capital. Within a month the V-1 rockets had killed six thousand people.

In the last summer of the war Connie was selected to play for the Dominions against England at Lord's. Germany had by now surrendered and large crowds gathered, eager to be entertained. They were not disappointed. The match proved to be a momentous one. Lindsay Hassett, the schoolboy who had defied the West Indies bowling in Australia more than a decade earlier, was now a Test crick-eter and was chosen to captain the side. On the morning of the match, however, he fell ill. Plum Warner, who was managing the Dominions, now had a decision to make. As far as he was concerned Constantine, 'who was the senior international cricketer on the side' and had been captaining the West Indians, was the obvious choice. Warner would later comment, 'In this country, certainly on the cricket field, colour does not excite the feeling and prejudice that exists in some parts of the Empire. It was, however, neces-sary to secure both the consent and co-operation of the rest of the Dominions side, and I went into the dressing-room. I chose my words with care, referring to [Constantine's] seniority and position in the cricket world. I think I sensed that for a moment there was a slight hesitation, but after a very prominent member of the side had agreed that it was the proper choice one and all fell into line.'

Connie proudly led this very fine team, in which he was the only non-white player, onto the field to a standing ova-tion. It was to be an exceptional game of cricket. Indeed *Wisden* described it as 'one of the greatest games ever pro-duced'. For the Dominions Keith Miller bludgeoned 185, including eight sixes, and Martin Donnelly an elegant 133, while Hammond momentarily rediscovered his youth to score a century in each innings for the home side against an attack that included the leg-spinning all-rounder Cec Pepper, a player whose reputation in League cricket would soon match Connie's own. Doug Wright, the unorthodox England leg-spinner for whom Connie had great respect, bagged five wickets in each innings. Connie made 40 in a partnership with Miller that was worth 117 and even now, in his forties, his fielding was still a joy to behold. With his customary panache he ran out Lancashire's Eddie Phillipson thanks to a throw Hammond described as 'one of the finest returns I have ever been thrilled to see'. Connie recalled the moment vividly: 'I had picked up the ball 30 yards from the wicket, my hand shot out as in youthful days, and I saw Phillipson's wicket jump all ways into the air.'

The match swung to and fro throughout the three days, but in the end Connie got the better of Hammond and his side won by 45 runs, with eight minutes remaining. It was Connie's last first-class appearance, and a fitting end to a remarkable career.

Connie had never captained the West Indies in a Test, but he had shown that he would have been more than capable of doing so. Denzil Batchelor wrote that his captaincy 'had subtlety, skill and enthusiasm for the game which infected every ball bowled, every stop in the outfield'.

By the end of that week Japan had surrendered. The dark clouds had rolled away. Cricket could come out into the sunlight once again.

The curtain had, however, come down on Connie's first-class career. He would continue working as a welfare officer until the summer of 1946, dealing with everything from helping repatriate unemployed West Indians to dealing with an uprising on a Caribbean-bound ship when the black passengers had been given hammocks instead of the bunk beds for which they had tickets. In May 1947 Connie was awarded the MBE in recognition of his service.

Connie had turned out for Windhill occasionally during the war and had even made a few appearances as an amateur for his beloved Nelson. He returned to the Bradford League full time in 1946 and was asked to captain the Windhill side.

At Windhill Connie was joined by George Dawkes, who had appeared for Leicestershire before the war and would go on to play close to four hundred matches for Derbyshire and be selected for an MCC tour to Pakistan, and his old West Indian Test colleague Manny Martindale, who topped the Bradford League bowling averages in his first season, taking fifty-six wickets at only 9.80 each.

In 1947 Connie took fifty wickets, topping the bowling averages. He was the leading bowler again in 1948 with forty-five wickets at 10.48. His most memorable innings that season came in a Priestley Cup match against Queensbury, when he cracked eight sixes and ten fours in scoring 101, with twenty-eight of the runs coming in a single over.

This was Connie's last season in the Bradford League. He played his final game for the club on 11 September against a strong Keighley side at Busy Lane. Keighley batted first and Connie took four wickets, including the final one. He then made 69 not out to guide his side to victory, hitting the boundary that won the match and the League Championship. It was a typical flourish with which to end his career as a League professional.

*

To people back in the West Indies it had seemed strange that Connie was considered quite capable of captaining a team of white players in Yorkshire, but not on his native island. The issue had been a vexed one ever since the West Indies had been given Test status and C. L. R. James, for one, had railed against it in print. Certainly there is evidence that the denial of any kind of leadership role in the international team for great cricketers such as Connie contributed to anti-imperialist sentiment across the Caribbean. Such feelings were exacerbated when highly respected white West Indian cricketers such as Harold Austin spoke out against the notion of self-government.

Writing in the fifties, Connie put the case for ending the 'white captain' fiasco. 'The colour question affects every player's chances of selection and above all it causes some very strange choices of captain for touring sides.' He commented that 'better players have made way for worse ones with white or near-white-skins' and expressed his belief that the full potential of West Indies cricket would never be realised until the practice was dropped. When it was, with the appointment of Frank Worrell in 1960, the West Indies did indeed become a dominant force in Test cricket.

When in 1943 Connie had been selected to play for the Dominions at Lord's he booked rooms for Norma, Gloria and himself at the Imperial Hotel in Russell Square for four nights. He had paid a deposit for the rooms by cheque and told the hotel that he and his wife and daughter were black. The family had once been refused the rooms they had booked at a hotel in Brighton because of their race and Connie had no wish to repeat that unhappy incident.

On arriving at the hotel on the evening of 30 July Connie

was told that they could have the rooms for just one night, and would have to find another hotel for the remainder of their time in London. The problem seemed to stem from the presence in the hotel of a number of white US Army officers. The US Army, like much of America in those days, was strictly segregated and service personnel had even been warned before coming to Britain that they must expect to see black people drinking in bars and eating in restaurants alongside whites. The message did not always get through.

Apparently worried that the presence of the Constantines might antagonise their American guests, the hotel manager, Margaret O'Sullivan, decided to cut short their stay. Connie overheard someone say, 'The hotel is coming to something if you are going to take niggers in.' He was enraged. Arnold Watson, a friend of his from the Ministry of Labour, was present and calmed him, persuading Connie that in the interests of his family he should leave. Connie did so, but he resolved to take the matter further. He had been subjected to racism of both the casual, abusive kind on the cricket field and of the institutional variety that prevented a black player captaining the West Indies. He had spoken out with restraint and dignity against both. On this occasion the blow was doubly wounding, firstly because it affected Norma and Gloria and secondly because the juxtaposition of the attitude of the hotel and the crowd that would greet him rapturously at Lord's seemed once again to bring up the notion of first-class cricketer and third-class citizen. Connie believed deeply that the British Empire could have a major role in bringing people of different races, religions and cultures together – the Dominions team and the war effort seemed to confirm his view. The actions of the staff of the Imperial Hotel stood in opposition to all he believed in. It was time to make his feelings public via the courts.

In June 1944 the case of Constantine v Imperial Hotels Ltd was heard before Mr Justice Birkett. Connie was represented by Sir Patrick Hastings, a King's Counsel who had been involved in many high-profile cases including defending John Williams in what became known as the Case of the Hooded Man, and Rose Heilbron, one of Britain's first female barristers.

At the time there was no legislation in Britain outlawing racial discrimination in the provision of services, and so the complaint had to be brought as a breach of contract case. Connie told the court that he had booked the rooms by telephone and informed the manager who took the booking that he was black. He was told this was not a problem and the deposit of two pounds was accepted. When Connie and his family arrived they were shown to their rooms, but then a porter came and asked Connie to return to the reception desk. Here he met a work colleague (possibly Sam Morris) who told him that the manager of the hotel had said they 'could not have niggers in the hotel because of the Americans' and that several complaints had already been lodged by guests who had seen him signing in. O'Sullivan told him that though he, Norma and Gloria could stay the night, the following morning their luggage would be put out and their rooms locked. An argument broke out, in which it was pointed out that Connie was a British subject and a civil servant. The manager replied that, nevertheless, he was 'still a nigger'. Though indignant, Connie was persuaded that, in the interests of his wife and daughter, he should accept the offer of rooms at one of the company's other hotels, the Bedford, which was a couple of minutes' walk away.

The defence argued that since the Constantines had left

voluntarily and been housed in another of its hotels the company had discharged its contractual obligations.

Mr Justice Birkett rejected the idea that an alternative hotel was the same as the one that had been booked. He pointed out that rooms were available at the Imperial, and that Connie was 'a man of high character' and that nothing in his behaviour or that of his family had given the hotel any cause to refuse him the rooms he had booked. He praised Connie's evidence, found that he had suffered 'much unjustifiable humiliation and distress' and awarded him damages of five guineas. The damages were, because of the nature of the case, nominal, but there was little doubt that Connie had scored an important and resounding victory. He received hundreds of letters of congratulation from around Britain, questions were asked in the House of Commons, and the *Evening Standard*'s David Low drew a famous cartoon pointing to the irony of Connie's treatment in a nation that was fighting for freedom and liberty against a racist foreign power.

Connie might have pushed the matter further – there was a sound case for a defamation action – but he chose not to: 'I was content to have drawn the particular nature of the affront before the wider judgement of the British public in the hope that its sense of fair play might help to protect people of my colour in England in the future.'

It was a typically moderate response and reflected Connie's belief in the essential decency of humanity. His case would not end racial discrimination in British hotels, restaurants and boarding houses, but it established a precedent. Henceforward people who were discriminated against knew that they had a case for damages on grounds of distress. In highlighting the lack of legislation to prevent discrimination, Connie had also paved the way for legislation that did address the issue. *Constantine v Imperial Hotels Ltd* was an important legal milestone on the way to the 1965 Race Relations Act. His actions on the cricket field would gradually fade from memory, but those few days in court would be his lasting legacy.

Chapter 11

Insults and Ermine

For many great athletes, life after retirement from sport often has a sense of the dying fall. For Connie, however, there was to be no long twilight of golf, newspaper columns and after-dinner speaking. He spent much of his post-cricket career putting into practice the ideas he and C. L. R. James had discussed sitting by the fire in Meredith Street. Self-government for the Caribbean colonies would come quicker perhaps than either man expected. Connie would play a significant part in both hurrying forward Trinidadian independence and guiding the fledgling nation through its first few years. And if drawing up legislation to control the taxi ranks of Port of Spain did not draw quite the same levels of applause or awestruck commentary as a six struck into the Mound Stand at Lord's, a cartwheeling middle stump or a diving catch, that is not to say it lacked a greater significance.

Connie would go on playing cricket occasionally, particularly in Scotland and the Republic of Ireland, where he coached at Trinity College, St Mary's College and Leinster Cricket Club, for most of the rest of his life. In Scotland he played infrequently for the Colonial Cricket Club in Edinburgh, lining up alongside West Indian students who had not been born when he made his Test debut.

He wrote books about the game too. *Cricket in the Sun*, an autobiography, was published in 1947. It covered some of the same material as *Cricket and I*, but in more uncompromising style, Connie giving short shrift to anything he felt stood in the way of his enjoyment of the game he loved. He referred to the autocratic Lord Hawke as 'Hitlerian' (Cec Parkin would surely have chuckled at that), attacked deliberate slow play (what would he have made of the over rates of the all-conquering West Indian teams of the seventies and eighties?) and what he already recognised as the foolishly outmoded gentleman/player divide. Other works followed: *Cricketers' Carnival*, *Cricket Crackers* and *Cricketers' Cricket*, a coaching manual that ends with an unexpected comparison between the reactionary authorities controlling the game and the floundering of post-war Western society, with its 'yelling newspapers and yodelling political gang-leaders'. He became a radio commentator on the BBC, sitting alongside Rex Alston and covering the joyful West Indies 1950 tour when John Goddard's team pulled off a momentous victory at Lord's. Later he'd work with John Arlott, who enjoyed his company and simple, direct style.

Connie also continued in his rather laboured legal studies. Distracted by cricket, broadcasting and public speaking, he found studying hard and it was clearly less lucrative than his other pursuits, nor anywhere near as much fun as his busy social life. Norma, as always, was supportive, encouraging him to stick to the task while trying to weed out those who genuinely wanted his friendship from others who simply hoped to exploit him, either directly or by association. Connie had always been a man who valued money but he was also generous, especially to members of the West Indian community, and sometimes suffered losses as a consequence.

Progress with his legal studies was slow. He had entered himself as a law student at the Middle Temple in 1944, but his experience as a law clerk in Trinidad and the brief time he had spent at the legal practice in Nelson now seemed a distant memory. His pursuit of qualifications was, it seems, partly connected to status – he could certainly have earned better money doing something else – and a need to prove himself in the eyes of the world, and most specifically to the establishment in Trinidad. Certainly becoming a barrister in London would pave his way to returning to Port of Spain, an ambition he had nursed for some while. Connie passed the first of his Bar exams in 1947. Two years later he and Norma reluctantly decided to leave Nelson for London so that he could better focus on his studies. They settled in Earl's Court.

In London, as a result of his position as a member of the Colonial Social Welfare Advisory Committee, Connie found himself heavily involved in the Seretse Khama affair: the marriage between a tribal chieftain from the South African protectorate of Bechuanaland and a white Englishwoman, Ruth Williams. The marriage had upset the apartheid government in Pretoria, who protested to Whitehall. Instead of telling them to mind their own business, Clement Attlee's officials, terrified of jeopardising trade links with gold-rich South Africa, summoned Khama to London and told him he was no longer recognised as a chief and that he would not be allowed to go back to Bechuanaland. The case became a media *cause célèbre* involving everyone from theatrical designer Oliver Messel to West Indian-born sprinter McDonald Bailey, via Tony Benn, Alec Guinness and Augustus John. (The story of Khama and Williams's marriage was made into an acclaimed film, *A United Kingdom*, released in 2016.) Connie joined the committee that campaigned for Khama's reinstatement and return. The couple had, however, suffered problems in Bechuanaland – Williams was treated with hostility and suspicion by both the local white and black populations – and decided reluctantly to stay in England. It was a decision with which Connie, always a man prepared to fight his corner, vocally disagreed.

In 1954, at the age of fifty-three, Connie finally passed the last of his Bar exams. He was plainly proud of his achievement; so too was his former home town, the *Nelson Leader* running the news under the headline LOCAL BOY MAKES GOOD.

His position as a barrister-at-law allowed his long-intended return to Trinidad. His former employer, Trinidad Leaseholds, had generously offered to keep a job open when he first left for Nelson back in 1929. Now, finally, he could return to them, not as a lowly clerk but as assistant legal adviser, a position that paid seven hundred pounds per year. Gloria had now qualified as a teacher and was engaged to be married to a Trinidadian barrister, André Valere, she had met in London while training. The couple had moved back to Port of Spain. They married in December 1954.

Connie and Norma had lived a quarter of a century in England and their return to their native island, where the white minority still ruled, was something both approached with a certain amount of trepidation. Indeed to Connie it appeared almost more daunting a task than when he had left for Nelson twenty-five years earlier.

His departure was marked by the publication of *Colour Bar*. Written in collaboration with journalist Frank Stuart, this was a frank and at times withering look at racial politics in Britain, a country that Connie felt was 'only a little less intolerant than segregated America or South Africa'. He related numerous incidents in which he had been slighted and insulted, detailed his adoption of what he called 'negro-in-England manners', and angrily criticised Britain's colonial policies, particularly in Africa where 'the excuse is always, "The African is not ready for responsibility." But nothing is done to make him ready, everything is done to prevent the majority of Africans from making themselves ready.'

It was the first time Connie had moved away from his usual measured approach to a subject about which he felt so passionately. Unsurprisingly, given the climate of the fifties, *Colour Bar* received a mixed reception in Britain and some black commentators, including his former friend James, were underwhelmed. Connie was accused of being a communist, or being ungrateful, and of getting his facts wrong. To the modern reader there are certainly some jarringly odd passages in it – including an assertion that the better educated people become the less they are interested in 'sex excitement' – but the sincerity of it cannot be doubted. In many ways it was Connie's most personal book, a cry from the heart born of hurt and frustration with a country he at once loved and yet by which he felt disappointed and oftentimes rejected. Britain was, after all, the Mother Country, and who would want to be treated by a parent in so callous and uncaring a manner?

Connie had hoped that his return to Trinidad would allow him to pay back a debt to the island of his birth. 'I owe something to them,' he told the BBC radio audience in a broadcast delivered shortly before he set sail, 'coming back there and trying to teach them something of what I have learned and perhaps learning myself a little bit of the progress they have made.'

Back in the Caribbean and now a senior figure at Trinidad Leaseholds, Connie found himself moving in the upper-class white circles that had once excluded him. He and Norma moved into a company bungalow in Pointe-à-Pierre and received a brochure, designed for expatriates, which advised them against travelling on local buses and trains. That his employer was effectively cautioning Connie against mixing with his own people may explain why his time with the company was to prove short-lived. There was also the difficulty of readjusting to life in Trinidad. Connie had been away a long time and some of his fellow countrymen seemed to nurture a resentment against him. His proclaimed intention of 'teaching them' perhaps came across as condescending, and then there was the old accusation of his apparent Englishness. These attitudes were reflected in the events that had followed the passing of the British Nationality Act in 1948. This had made citizens of the colonies effectively British subjects and immigration to Britain from the Caribbean became far easier. To help the new arrivals a guidebook, *A West Indian in Britain*, was commissioned. With his experience as an author and as a West Indian who at that time had lived in Britain for twenty years, Connie might have seemed the obvious person to write it, but he was rejected because it was felt people in the Caribbean would view him as 'too Anglicised'. Though Connie might have railed against the racial injustices of the Empire he had accepted an MBE. To some in the Caribbean Connie, now living in his bungalow and attending functions at elite social clubs, appeared to have become a member of the white establishment.

It was something of which he became increasingly and painfully aware. 'I didn't see eye to eye with my country-men on so many things. As far as they were concerned I had been abroad for twenty-five years living it up, while they had been suffering in conditions where the feeling of oppression was never far away. There was a feeling of depression and an understandable frustration about which so many grumbled but took no action.'

This latter comment seems rather unjust. During the thirties Trinidad had been the scene of strikes and labour riots that had seen leading black trades unionists jailed. In response, the British government had instituted a series of wide-ranging reforms that set Trinidad and other West Indian colonies on the path to independence. Action had been taken, but Connie had played little part in it.

Upset by his reception and unhappy with his working environment, Connie briefly considered moving to Ghana and taking up a position as a barrister in Accra. Cricket at least provided a refuge. Though now in his fifties, Connie still played sporadically. More importantly, he coached youngsters at local schools and helped develop Trinidad Leaseholds' ground at Guaracara Park sufficiently for Trinidad's first-class matches to occasionally be played there.

Connie had generally kept away from party politics. During the Khama affair he'd been invited to stand as the Liberal candidate in Shipley, Yorkshire, not far from Windhill. Though the Liberal Party's policies on race chimed more closely with his own than those of Labour (Connie had met Attlee several times and felt that the public school-educated prime minister regarded himself as rather above the affairs of 'coloured' people), after con-sideration Connie turned the offer down, feeling he could do more good as a citizen than an MP. The Liberal Party would approach him again in 1968, when a by-election was held in Nelson. Again the offer was declined. In Trinidad, however, he gradually began to get directly involved. The People's National Movement was a new political party. Broadly leftward-leaning, it had been founded shortly after Connie arrived back in Trinidad by Dr Eric Williams. A brilliant school student, he too had left for England, to take up a scholarship at Oxford. While there he and Connie had become friends and Williams had stayed in Meredith Street on several occasions. Connie later recalled how the future prime minister of Trinidad and Tobago insisted on drinking only German beer, and since none was available in Nelson had to be driven to Clitheroe whenever he wanted a pint. At Oxford Williams had earned his doctorate with a thesis on the slave trade which argued that its abolition within the British Empire was for economic rather than humanitarian reasons (an opinion he shared with C. L. R. James). Williams later moved to the United States and became a professor at Howard University and the deputy chairman of the Anglo-American Caribbean Commission. He returned to Trinidad after losing the latter job. A forceful and at times aggressive man, Williams was brusque, inscrutable and deep – a very different character from the ebullient and open former cricketer. He was also a charismatic and brilliant public speaker. Williams launched his new party in June 1955 with a call for constitutional and educational reform, and the redistribution of wealth.

Williams's political stance of 'pragmatic socialism', anti-corruption and nationalism appealed to Connie. He was also familiar with a number of Williams's close associates, including Patrick Solomon and Winston Mahabir, doctors he'd met in London, where they were training.

Mahabir was of Indian descent and would later fall out with Williams over what he felt was the PNM's hostility to Trinidad's Indian minority. Arguments over the truth or otherwise of this accusation rumble on to this day.

Williams was keen to recruit Connie to the PNM, not only because of his celebrity but because his generally moderate views would widen the party's appeal amongst those who feared radicalism. Connie's presence would also help mollify Trinidad's British-owned newspaper industry, which was generally hostile to independence but susceptible to celebrity. After discussions with his employer, Connie agreed to join Williams and, at the PNM's inaugural conference, was elected party chairman for a five-year term. Working at weekends, in the mornings before he began work and in the evenings after he was finished, Connie laboured to build up the party organisation from scratch. It is testament to his diligence that within a year the PNM was the most efficiently run political party on Trinidad. Amazingly, despite his incredible workload Connie also found time to pen cricket articles for the party newspaper and to lead a team of PNM international cricketers (including Victor Stollmeyer, Andy Ganteaume and Puss Achong) in a charity match on the Savannah. After the years with Trinidad Leaseholds during which his life seemed to have entered the doldrums of middle age, Connie was once again fired up by the sort of energy he had shown on the cricket field. The exhilaration of being involved in front-line politics for the first time, the feeling that he was at last at the forefront in the Caribbean renaissance he and James had discussed in Nelson, filled Connie with the sort of hope and expectation he had felt on the ship to England in 1929. A new, brighter future seemed within not only his grasp, but of all of the peoples of the Caribbean. Caught up in the whirl of the PNM's rise, he agreed to stand in the forthcoming election for Trinidad's Legislative Council, even though Trinidad Leaseholds had made it plain that if he succeeded he would have to resign his job.

Connie found himself running against the Mayor of Port of Spain for the seat of Tunapuna. He launched his campaign in front of a crowd of seven thousand people in August 1956, speaking with inspirational zeal. It was a tough fight against a candidate with huge personal support amongst the local Indian population, but Connie triumphed at the polls by a tiny margin, 6622 votes to 6443. It was a highlight of what proved a marvellous day for the PNM. They won thirteen of the Legislative Council's twenty-four seats. Trinidad's Governor, Sir Edward Beetham, called on Williams to form a government. Though self-rule was another six years away, it was the first time in history Trinidad's black majority had held any kind of power on the island.

Connie was triumphant, congratulated by his party colleagues for pulling off what many had thought an impossible task. He immediately resigned his post at Trinidad Leaseholds, determined to focus on politics full-time. As a reward for his hard work, Williams appointed Connie as his Minister for Communications, Works and Public Utilities. It was a key position. The departmental budget accounted for half of all public spending, and Williams believed that by delivering a better and more efficient infrastructure to Trinidad he could convince the British that the islanders were ready for independence.

For Connie, the brief was wide-ranging. His department controlled everything from the weather forecast to the water supply via the postal service. Undaunted, Connie formulated a five-year plan to expand the road system and the electricity supply, build more schools and improve harbour and airport facilities with a view to developing the tourist trade and reducing the island's dependence on the fluctuating prices of sugar and cocoa. Preparing Trinidad for the latter half of the twentieth century was a major job – in the post-war years technological advances were coming at a greater rate than ever before. Connie supervised the increased provision of streetlights, the introduction of driving legislation and parking restrictions and an extensive bridge-building programme. He was also compelled briefly to become the Caribbean equivalent of Thomas Beeching and begin the closure of Trinidad's steam railway, a process he would eventually reverse after the failure of various bus companies to deliver a reliable replacement service.

In the main, Connie handled his new role with his usual tact and aplomb, but politics is a dirtier business than cricket – even the Bodyline version of the game – and Connie soon found himself enmeshed in a scandal. The seven-hour shipping route between Trinidad and Tobago was plied by two steamers, the SS *Trinidad* and the SS *Tobago*. By 1958 it was plain that both were perilously close to the end of their working life. Connie sold off the two old ships, commissioned the building of replacement vessels and in the meantime chartered a single, larger ship, the *City of Port of Spain*, to ferry passengers and cargo between the islands. In his view, it was a cheap and neat solution. In the Legislative Assembly, however, opposition members seized on certain aspects of the deal and suggested, noisily, that either incompetence or corruption had been involved. The two old steamers had been sold for eight thousand pounds. This was, the accusers claimed, far below their market value. The implication of some kind of kickback was clear – certainly to Connie. At the parliamentary debate on the budget he launched an impassioned counter-attack: 'I have travelled five continents and I have been respected and looked upon as a man of integrity, a man that is honest, and I shall be loath to stand in this council and have members make insinuations and charges against me without registering a solid word of protest.'

Perhaps if he had left it there things might have gone better for him, but Connie continued, 'I hope I may not be immodest when I say that many people never knew of the West Indies until they got to know of Constantine, and if this is the thanks I am going to get from the country for the service I have rendered abroad, then I hope I will live long enough to regret the day that I entered into politics.'

Connie had always been a man who prided himself on acting honestly both on the field of play and in life generally, so to have his honour publicly impugned with so little evidence was plainly upsetting. But that is politics. Instead of dispelling the rumours, the vehemence of Connie's reaction served only to fuel them. Why was he so angry if there was no truth to what was being said? The final part of his speech, meanwhile, carried more than a hint of the arrogance of which some had long suspected him. The suggestion that he alone had brought Trinidad into the consciousness of other nations was insulting. And when a sportsman or politician refers to himself in the third person, no matter what the context, the public are apt to think him a pompous ass.

The reaction to Connie's outburst, even amongst his party colleagues, was not favourable. He was perceived as thin-skinned, a man too used to being fêted and adored to last long in the less reverential world of politics, particularly on an island with a long tradition of enjoying insulting jokes directed at those in power. It was true that Connie often spoke or acted instinctively – that, after all, was how he'd played cricket – but there were times when he ought to have stepped back and considered his next move, to play the situation not his own game. This was definitely one of them.

For Connie, the experience was bitterly disillusioning. Invoking parliamentary privilege, opponents could say things in debates that if uttered outside the Legislative Assembly would have been slanderous and actionable. And now they had seen how easy it was to provoke him the opposition continued their attacks with increased fervour until Connie came to dread the regular Friday question-time sessions.

There was little relief to be found in the game Connie loved. Caribbean cricket was undergoing violent upheavals. The 1959–60 MCC tour of the West Indies was rancorous – England wasted time continually, slowing over rates to a crawl, and there was a controversy over the action of a couple of West Indies bowlers. When Connie attended the Trinidad Test at Port of Spain the game was held up by rioting that greeted the controversial dismissal of local batsman Charran Singh. Connie was called into action, catching a bottle that had been hurled at the Governor before it could strike him on the head. British cricket writers blamed the disturbances on alcohol. But Connie and other Caribbean observers believed it had been fuelled by mounting frustration at the slow progress towards self-government and the continuing insistence of the West Indies Cricket Board that the team must be captained by a white player (in this instance, the Cambridge-educated wicketkeeper Gerry Alexander). Connie had warned that the vexed issue of the captaincy would end in violence, and now it had come to pass.

Though it was damaging to West Indies cricket, in many ways the WICB's stance on the captaincy played into the hands of independence campaigners such as Connie, Williams and James. In the cricket-mad Caribbean, here was an obvious example of racial oppression. James believed the reactionaries had actually done the self-rule movement a good turn, handing their opponents a wonderful opportunity to exploit and, as first George Headley and then other talented black players were passed over for the captaincy, they did so with greater and greater effect. That John Goddard, Jeff Stollmeyer and Gerry Gomez, some of the best-known white cricketers, had caused controversy on a tour of Australia by having a massive argument on the field during a Test hardly bolstered the WICB's cause. For James, the focus became the Barbadian Frank Worrell, a fluently elegant batsman who, like Connie, had played league cricket in Lancashire and used his spare time to take a degree in economics at Manchester University. Worrell had been offered the captaincy after John Goddard's retirement but turned it down to focus on his studies, and the job went instead to Alexander. James now lobbied hard on Worrell's behalf, as did others. With an increasing number of black politicians now holding ministerial posts, the WICB's position became increasingly untenable. When England won the series in the Caribbean 1–0 they could resist no more. The unfortunate Alexander, a decent man caught in a political row that was not of his making, resigned. The following autumn Worrell was appointed captain for the West Indies' tour of Australia. Alexander kept his place in the team and scored a vital century in the Sydney Test, in a series that is widely regarded as one of the greatest of all time.

With the question of the captaincy at last resolved,

Connie turned his mind to another of the problems besetting West Indies cricket – the talent drain. Ever since
he had made good in Nelson, top cricketers from the
Caribbean had been making the trip to England and the
leagues. The post-war years had seen Everton Weekes,
Clyde Walcott and Worrell all playing in Lancashire and
they were soon joined by Garry Sobers, Collie Smith,
Lance Gibbs and a host of others. Because of contractual
obligations most did not return for the winter unless the
West Indies had a Test series. Connie believed that watching such great players in regular action in the inter-colonial
competition and for club sides would inspire a younger
generation. Walter Hammond had expressed a similar view
about Connie and Headley.

Taking time out from the continuing arguments about
steam ships, his resurrection of the railways and attempts to
resolve the problems of Trinidad's erratic public bus system,
Connie chaired a committee to look into ways of reversing
the trend and ensuring that the best West Indian cricketers stayed in the Caribbean. The obvious method was to
offer them professional contracts on a par with those in
the leagues. Connie felt that the WICB should put aside a
tranche of the profits from Test series at home and abroad
in order to provide what would effectively have been an
early version of the central contracts system England use
today. Sadly the idea got no further and the best Caribbean
cricketers would continue to play in England for league
sides, and increasingly for counties, for the next thirty
years.

Connie himself was not to stay in Trinidad much longer.
He had served the PNM and Williams well, discharging his
duties smoothly and efficiently. His department was dynamic
and well run, and he was popular with those who worked for

him. Moreover, he had proved by the way he had managed the budget, while improving the island's infrastructure, that Trinidad was more than ready for independence. Politics, however, was not a natural field for Connie. He was too sensitive to criticism, resented the remorseless scrutiny and constant questioning of his motives and disliked the confrontational style of political debates. Nor was he a deep political thinker. His opinions were personal, pragmatic and at times a little eccentric. He did what he sincerely thought was for the best of his country rather than slavishly following an ideology. At times his attitudes put him at odds with his party colleagues, yet despite that he remained not only respected but broadly liked. In an environment of big egos that alone was a considerable achievement

After the early problems, and the furore over the steam ships, Connie's return to Trinidad could be considered a success. Despite his love for the island, however, he found himself bridling against the isolation of his life there. It was time to move on. When prime minister Williams came to appoint Trinidad and Tobago's first High Commissioner to Great Britain, Connie   with his reputation and his wide-ranging contacts in England – was the obvious choice for the role. He and Norma would return to London.

Connie's new post began officially in June 1961, though Trinidad and Tobago were not yet fully independent. Initially his brief was a narrow one, to act as a senior public relations officer for the islands to encourage British investment and tourism. Gradually the role expanded. Connie was particularly concerned with looking out for the interests of his fellow countrymen who had lately immigrated to Britain. In many ways it was a resumption of the task that had faced him as a war-time welfare officer. By now the minor uproar surrounding *Colour Bar* had died away and Connie was welcomed back with pleasure. Thanks to his broadcasts on the BBC and his cricket commentary he remained a well-known and popular figure in Britain. He had been back in England for less than a year when he was awarded a knighthood by Harold Macmillan's government. Though the honour was in recognition of Connie's political service, he nevertheless became one of a select band of professional cricketers to receive such an honour – Sir Jack Hobbs and Sir Len Hutton being the other two at that time.

A year later Connie received another popular distinction, by becoming the subject of an episode of ITV's *This Is Your Life*. Surprised in a Shepherd's Bush cinema by the programme's proverbially avuncular presenter Eamonn Andrews, the half-hour that followed brought together significant figures from Connie's past, both political and sporting. It was certainly a wide-ranging cast of characters, the boogie-woogie pianist Winifred Atwell rubbing shoulders with Bessie Braddock, MP, Gene Lawrence and his Triniana Quintet, and Ian Peebles.

Shortly afterwards there would be the BBC equivalent: an appearance with Roy Plomley on *Desert Island Discs*;* and in between he'd receive the freedom of Nelson, Alderman John Shepherd stating in his address that Connie's success was 'never won at the expense of honour, justice, integrity, nor by the sacrifice of a single principle'. If only the opposition parties in Trinidad had been listening.

On top of all that, the publication of C. L. R. James's cricket masterpiece, *Beyond a Boundary*, brought Connie's cricket career back into prominence. He and James might have drifted apart and the writer–historian not been entirely

---

* Connie's favourite selection was 'De Li'l Pickaninny's Gone to Sleep' by Paul Robeson, his book was *The Old Curiosity Shop* and his luxury item a cricket bat.

complimentary about some of Connie's forays into politics, but there was no doubting his belief in his countryman's genius on the cricket field and it shone through in a book in which Connie was one of, if not the, central figures.

Connie's life in London was not all public acclaim, however. At times his high profile was not an easy fit with the discretion required of a diplomat. When he returned to London there were around 115,000 West Indians living in Britain, the majority in the poorer neighbourhoods of the larger cities. Racial tensions had mounted and occasionally flared into violence. The 1958 Notting Hill Riots, which lasted for several days and largely involved gangs of white youths, many of them Teddy Boys, attacking Caribbean immigrants and their white friends, brought into the public eye problems which the government had previously chosen to ignore. Connie felt a moral duty to involve himself in racial issues in Britain, but as High Commissioner he needed to work behind the scenes. He did this in a number of ways, mainly by offering legal advice to innocent West Indians who had found themselves arrested or harassed by the police. When in 1963 it emerged that Bristol's main bus operator – the Bristol Omnibus Company – had instituted a policy against hiring black workers (such discrimination was within the law at that time), Connie broke cover. Visiting Bristol to watch the touring West Indians play Gloucestershire, he made a public statement about the matter, which had by now escalated into a battle between the company and local activists who had organised a boycott and were picketing the bus depot. He also appeared on the BBC to speak about it, had private talks with the Mayor of Bristol and with officials from the Transport and General Workers Union, and wrote a piece for a local newspaper about discrimination in the workplace.

Connie's intervention, alongside the work of the unions, racial-equality campaigners and the MP Tony Benn, eventually led to the Bristol Omnibus Company dropping the policy. Like the Imperial Hotels case, it was an important milestone, shaking the political establishment out of its complacency and convincing the Labour leader Harold Wilson that legislation was necessary to prevent such discrimination in future.

Connie was justifiably pleased with his work in resolving the affair. However, it rapidly became apparent that others were not. High amongst those he had displeased was Eric Williams.

Aware that Williams believed he had overstepped the mark in interfering in a matter that – officially at least – was not his concern, Connie made the mistake of following his instincts and immediately flying to Trinidad to put his case before the prime minister. That he had not sought permission to leave his post only compounded the situation. Williams was a tough man with a reputation for being uncompromising in his treatment of those who went against his wishes, contradicted him or seemed to threaten his position. Over the years he would dismiss or discard many of those who had helped him achieve power as he gradually became more and more solitary and reclusive. Now he simply refused to speak to his former friend and minister. Perplexed and hurt, Connie returned to London. Aware, no doubt, of Williams's unrelenting character, he decided that the chances of his appointment as High Commissioner being renewed were slim and announced that he would be standing down from the post when his current term expired. Williams made no move to dissuade him, and if Connie held hopes that their friendship might one day be repaired he was to be cruelly disappointed. Williams remained intractable on the matter, and when he wrote an account of his political career chose not to mention Connie at all. If Connie had felt politics was a nasty business before, he surely knew it now.

Ironically, Connie's intervention in Bristol attracted no censure or complaint from the British government, and when she heard of his resignation as High Commissioner the Queen sent him a note expressing her regret and enclosed a signed photo of herself and the Duke of Edinburgh as a memento. Not for the first time in his life Connie could be forgiven for thinking he was better appreciated in his adopted country than he was in the land of his birth.

Now comfortably off, Connie and Norma moved out of the official residence and into a large and well-appointed apartment in Brondesbury, North London. Connie was sixty-two, still athletically built but a little wider round the middle and more creased about the eyes and mouth. Laughter still came easily to him, but in repose his face conveyed a certain sadness. The loss of his role in Trinidadian life and his cold treatment by Williams had hurt him deeply. For the first time he found himself on the fringes. Old age too was catching up with him.

Without a fixed job, Connie's life diversified into many areas that reflected his interests and his varied career. He opened his own law practice, served on the Race Relations Board, the Sports Council and the Board of Governors of the BBC, was a judge at the Miss World contest and was also elected the first black rector of the University of St Andrews. He continued to broadcast on the BBC and wrote a couple more cricket books, including one with his long-time admirer Denzil Batchelor. In *The Changing Face of Cricket* Connie returned to some of his favourite topics: the caution he felt was destroying cricket and turning Test matches into 'a war of attrition', the need to persuade news-papers not to publish batting and bowling averages and spectators to stop applauding maiden overs. Like most vet-eran sportsmen, Connie could not help but feel that things had been better in his day and amongst other things called for a return of the back foot no-ball rule, the repeal of the 1937 amendments to the lbw law, a reintroduction of the two-hundred-run new ball rule and the abandonment of mass coaching of youngsters. Surprisingly, given this last belief, his previous book, *The Young Cricketer's Companion*, had been a coaching manual aimed at children. Connie's own experience of what he felt was the wrong sort of coaching – the sort of by-the-book method that was widely adopted in British schools – went back to the 1923 tour when, during sessions arranged for him at Lord's cricket school by Warner and Hobbs, he had been persuaded to change his batting stance and play more orthodoxly by a coach named Young. The results had not been good, and Connie soon reverted back to his old ways.

Connie's involvement with cricket continued as he was called on to commentate on television coverage of the newly introduced one-day competitions of which he had long been an advocate. He still played the game very occasionally too, appearing for the Authors XI and, in what was to be his final ever appearance on the cricket field, for the BBC World Service team in a match at Herongate in Essex.

Increasingly beset by health problems that affected his breathing, Connie gradually stepped back from public life as the sixties came to an end, though his maiden speech in the House of Lords, an impassioned attack on the Commonwealth Immigrants Act, so impressed the Liberal leader Jeremy Thorpe he considered offering him a role within his party.

Shortly before he had stepped down as High Commissioner, Harold Wilson had put Connie at the top of a list of eight nominations for a life peerage. As part of the fall-out from the Bristol bus affair the appointment was delayed, finally arriving in the New Year's Honours of 1969. Connie would take the title of Baron Constantine of Maraval in Trinidad and Nelson in the County Palatine of Lancaster, and become the first black person to sit in the House of Lords. For Connie, it was the crowning moment of his life and career. That the peerage was not just significant to him but to all black citizens of the Commonwealth was not lost on him. In a letter to a cousin, Hubert Andrews, he wrote, 'I am proud of this honour and feel that it is another opportunity to serve my fellow countrymen.'

In 1971, with his bronchial problems worsening, Connie decided he should move back to the Caribbean for the good of his health. He announced his decision to the press in June. Sadly the plan came to nothing. Connie died of a heart attack at his home in North London on 1 July. A state funeral was held in Port of Spain. Eric Williams emerged from his residence to sit in the front row of mourners. Norma, Connie's steadfast and beloved companion, died two months later.

Some in the Caribbean had mocked Connie for accepting his honours, the old charges of his being a black-whiteman resurfacing. For the younger generation, honours seemed part of the old order, something to be swept away. As time wore on, however, the significance of Connie's elevation to the peerage would come to be recognised. As a cricketer he had been a pioneer, the first black player to become a star in England. He had blazed a trail that others – including Frank Worrell, the first black captain of the West Indies, and Garry Sobers, an all-rounder who surpassed even Connie in his gifts – could follow. The same was true in politics. Connie had made it easier for all who came after him. He had changed Britain not through revolution but by small and significant increments. At times it was frustrating for him, at times it may have left him bitter, but he persisted. It was the sort of steady progress with which some were impatient, but it was the sort that lasts.

As a cricketer it might be argued – certainly by statisticians – that Connie's reputation as one of history's great players is exaggerated. There can be little doubt, however, about his greatness and significance as a man. The country we live in would be a much diminished place had he stayed in Trinidad. White or black, we are in his debt.

Notes

Introduction

2 *'he must be made . . .'*: John Arlott, 'Lord Learie Constantine: The Spontaneous Cricketer', *Wisden* (1972).

2 'He brought the nature . . .': Manley, *A History of West Indies Cricket*.

2 'prodigious': Alec Douglas-Home, quoted in Howat, *Learie Constantine*.

2 'a genius': Neville Cardus, *Cardus on Cricket: A Selection from the Cricket Writings of Sir Neville Cardus* (London: Souvenir Press, 2000)

2 'Next to Donald Bradman . . .': Warner, *The Book of Cricket*.

2 'The most exciting . . .': Raymond Robertson-Glasgow, *Cricket Prints: Some Batsmen and Bowlers, 1920–1940* (London: T. Werner, 1943).

5 'Constantine is not a Test cricketer . . .': James, *Beyond a Boundary*.

5 'He revolted against the revolting . . .': Ibid.

6 'Nearly all the prejudice . . .': Constantine, *Cricket in the Sun*.

6 'firm but free of acrimony': Arlott, 'Lord Learie Constantine'.

Chapter 1: Sipping Nectar with the Gods

13 'Only matches against Australia . . .': Tate, *My Cricket Reminiscences*.

16 'real pig': Farnes, *Tours and Tests*.

17 'as fine a piece of bowling . . .': Ibid.

17 'the man who lost us the Test match': Wyatt, *Three Straight Sticks*.

19 'barefoot people who have paid good money': Constantine, *Cricket in the Sun*.

19 'made the subject of a speech . . .':Farnes, *Tours and Tests*.

20 'calm, unforced and unorthodox': Wyatt, *Three Straight Sticks*.

22 'It was just one of those days . . .': Constantine, *Cricket in the Sun*.

24 'in a fit of pique': Farnes, *Tours and Tests*.

25 'felt as if I could . . .': Constantine, *Cricket in the Sun*.

25 'the loving care a mother . . .': Ibid.

25 'right on their toes': Farnes, *Tours and Tests*.

26 'like a meteor': Ibid.

27 'Every tree instantly deposited . . .': Hammond, *Cricket My Destiny*.

27 'It was one of those moments . . .': Constantine, *Cricket in the Sun*.

28 'washing day somewhere . . .': Farnes, *Tours and Tests*.

30 'a gibbet': Ibid.

31 'We're going to win at a common canter . . .': 'Reggie', quoted in Constantine, *Cricket in the Sun*.

31 'Graceful, swift, exact': Constantine, *Cricket in the Sun*.

32 'far faster than he had . . .': Farnes, *Tours and Tests*.

32 'It was like being hit . . .': Wyatt, *Three Straight Sticks*.

32 'You could hear the crack . . .': Farnes, *Tours and Tests*

33 'like a bullet': Ibid., quoting Hendren.

34 'the sort of innings . . .': Constantine, *Cricket in the Sun*.

Chapter 2: A Cushion for the Life Ahead

41 'the most loved and respected . . .': James, *Beyond a Boundary*.

42 'well up to the standard . . .': *Wisden* (1896).

44 'Cumberbatch and Woods . . .': Leveson Gower, *Off and On the Field*.

45 'In the competition . . .': Ibid.

47 'dashing and faultless display': Pelham Warner, *Cricket in Many Climes* (London: Heinemann, 1900).

48 'The black members of the team ...': Ibid.
49 'On the return home ...': Quoted in Beckles and Stoddart (eds), *Liberation Cricket*.
49 'very quickly fallen ...': Quoted in ibid.
51 'the natural captain ...': James, *Beyond a Boundary*.
53 'As children we had never ...': Constantine, *Cricket in the Sun*.
54 'Off the fastest bowlers ...': Ibid.
56 'just as he bowled ...': Ibid.
57 'My father knew the dictum ...': Ibid.
57 'A happy childhood ...': Ibid.
59 'A thickset, rather slow boy': James, *Beyond a Boundary*.
59 'from a kind of flour bag': Constantine, *Cricket in the Sun*.
60 'Magnificent ...': Leveson Gower, *Off and On the Field*.
61 'flat expanse of yellow ...': Farnes, *Tours and Tests*.
62 'as if they knew they represented ...': James, *Beyond a Boundary*.
63 'stuff which one could ...': Ibid.
63 'You ought to be at school ...': George John, quoted in Constantine, *Cricket in the Sun*.
64 'as a potential fifth columnist': James, *Beyond a Boundary*.

Chapter 3: The Chilly Embrace of the Mother Country

66–7 'It is so much harder ...': Constantine, *Cricket in the Sun*.
68 'the Hobbs and Hammond ...': Ibid.
68 'turned into a terrific ...': Ibid.
73 'I recall miserable journeys ...': Ibid.
76 'That is cricket cunning ...': Ibid.
76 'perfect, far different ...': Constantine, *Cricket and I*.
76 'The West Indies enjoyed ...': Warner, *Cricket between Two Wars*.
77 'bulldog fighters ...': Constantine, *Cricket in the Sun*.
79 'The West Indians were cheered ...': Leveson Gower, *Off and On the Field*.
79 'We felt we had put   ': Constantine, *Cricket in the Sun*.
80 'unorthodox to the point ...': John Arlott, 'Lord Learie Constantine: The Spontaneous Cricketer', *Wisden* (1972).
80 'A piece of fielding by Constantine ...': Warner, *Long Innings*.

80 'In the deep he picked up ...': Arlott, 'Lord Learie Constantine'.
81 'We returned home elated ...': Constantine, *Cricket in the Sun*.
82 'recognised the game ...': Arlott, 'Lord Learie Constantine'.
83 'To put it plainly ...': Constantine, *Cricket in the Sun*.
85 'The best wickets are like ...': Root, *A Cricket Pro's Lot*.
86 'We'd been good pals ...': Constantine, *Cricket in the Sun*
86 'He liked a shag': Eddie Paynter, quoted in Foot, *Wally Hammond*.
87 'Constantine himself, on his first ...': Hammond, *Cricket My Destiny*.
89 'was among the five best ...': Root, *A Cricket Pro's Lot*.
90 '"Stop it, Learie," we told him ...': James, *Beyond a Boundary*.

Chapter 4: A Man of Steel Springs and India Rubber

95 'bow-legged and bright-eyed': Lawrence, *Masterclass*.
95 'I have seen Trumper ...': Ibid., quoting Tennyson.
97 'he had possessed ...': Warner, *Cricket between Two Wars*.
98 'We used to beg him to settle down ...': James, *Beyond a Boundary*.
98 'When I landed in England ...': Constantine, *Cricket and I*.
99 'I ought to have been careful ...': Constantine, *Cricket in the Sun*.
99 'if he wanted to get me out': Ibid.
105 'waiting for the newspapers ...': Ibid.
110 'Two of his strokes ...': Warner, *Cricket between Two Wars*.
114 'he was well over fifty ...': Constantine, *Cricket and I*.
116 'No, no, they are no better than we': Renton, *C. L. R. James*.
118 'never faced fast bowling': Quoted in Warner, *Cricket between Two Wars*.
118 'far over his head' Maurice Tate, *My Cricket Reminiscences*.
118 'which they never seemed to master': Wyatt, *Three Straight Sticks*.
119 'somewhat mercurial temperament': Warner, *Cricket between Two Wars*.
119 'the biggest personality on the side': Ibid.

Chapter 5: Cricket for the Atomic Age

122 'Please let it be cricket . . .': Giuseppi, *A Look at Learie Constantine.*

122 'comrade, adviser and inspiration': Constantine, *Cricket in the Sun*, dedication.

125 'For every one insult . . .': Ibid.

125 'as pretty a ground . . .': James, *Beyond a Boundary.*

127 'indiscreet', 'the most impertinent . . .': From Brian Heywood, 'Ashes cricketers and the Lancashire League', *Sport in Society*, 15:8 (2012).

128 'a cricketer is just a cricketer . . .': Constantine, *Cricket in the Sun.*

130–1 'This trafficking in foreign players . . .': Ibid., quoting Tennyson.

133 'a shrewd chap who thought it paid to clown': Quoted in Mike Huggins and Jack Williams, *Sport and the English, 1918–1939* (London: Taylor & Francis, 2006).

134 'leered at Carrick . . .': Root, *A Cricket Pro's Lot.*

134 'cricket as I understand . . .': Ibid.

135 'disregarding any MCC rule . . .': Ibid.

135 'shed blood for the cause': Basil D'Oliveira with Patrick Murphy, *Time to Declare: An Autobiography* (London: Dent, 1980).

135 'Any first-class cricketer . . .': Constantine, *Cricket and I.*

136 'On any fine afternoon . . .': Ibid.

137 'he never bowled a full toss . . .': Constantine, *Cricket in the Sun.*

137 'doing a bit either way . . .': Kay, *Cricket in the Leagues.*

138 'I'm a great admirer of your cricket . . .': Quoted in Williams, *Cricket and Race.*

139 'Look what that bloody pro . . .': Ibid.

139 'meant to wound': Constantine, *Cricket in the Sun.*

140 'It may be "cricket" . . .': Ibid.

141 'This surely . . .': Genders, *League Cricket in England.*

143 'He set two men in the gully . . .': Constantine, *Cricket in the Sun.*

144 'Constantine deserves it . . .': Root, *A Cricket Pro's Lot.*

144 'the job of a professional . . .': Constantine, *Cricket in the Sun.*

145 'always looking around the horizon . . .': Ibid.

145 'Get some, Connie . . .': Ibid., quoting Barnes.

147 'I could not find my pace . . .': Ibid.

149 'costing pounds per minute': From Patrick Pringle (ed.), *The Boys' Book of Cricket* (London: Evans Bros, 1949).

149 '£250 was not too great a sum . . .': Edmundson, *See the Conquering Hero*.

149–50 'I was given a suite of rooms . . .': Constantine, *Cricket in the Sun*.

155 'he would be a strong candidate . . .': Warner, *The Book of Cricket*.

155 'there is no better bowler . . .': Hutton, *Cricket Is My Life*.

155 'It was really great bowling . . .': Constantine, *Cricket in the Sun*.

156 'certain members of the Lancashire Board . . .': Ibid.

156 'a coloured chap . . .': Quoted in Williams, *Cricket and Race*.

157 'Promises are always fulfilled . . .': Root, *A Cricket Pro's Lot*.

158 'Many times I have been criticized . . .': Constantine, *Cricket in the Sun*.

159 'Constantine is not leaving . . .': Ibid.

159 'I could not walk a mile . . .': Ibid.

160 'never gave the club . . .': Howat, *Learie Constantine*.

160 'perfect citizen of Nelson . . .': John Kay, *Manchester Evening News*.

161 'I am a better person . . .': Constantine, broadcast on BBC *Light Programme*, March 1954.

Chapter 6: Bubbles with a Dash of Brandy

164 'There was nothing else to do . . .': Constantine, *Cricket in the Sun*.

166 'Play within your limitations . . .': Quoted in Lawrence, *Masterclass*.

166–7 'bowled at lightning pace . . .': Wyatt, *Three Straight Sticks*.

167 'Champagne cocktail': Denzil Batchelor, *A Gallery of Great Players from W. G. Grace to the Present Day* (London: Collins, 1952).

167 'four short legs and two deep': Wyatt, *Three Straight Sticks*.

167 'edge out of his wicket': Constantine, *Cricket in the Sun*.

167 'shut up and bat': Ibid.
169 'laugh with delight': Ibid.
169–70 'it was obvious the English captain . . .': Ibid.
173 'simply far too good for us': Wyatt, *Three Straight Sticks*.
174 'some of the most extraordinary . . .': Ibid.
175 'They are fine natural players . . .': Ibid.
176 'very long arms': Ibid.
176 'The West Indies's weakness . . .': Constantine, *Cricket in the Sun*.

Chapter 7: A Mob Down Under

178 'Whatever they taught him at Cambridge . . .': Constantine, *Cricket in the Sun*.
179 'the most solidly welded . . .': Ibid.
180 'Throughout that tour . . .': Ibid.
181 'a young Bradman': *Australian Cricketer*, quoted in Bassano and Smith, *The West Indies in Australia 1930–31.*
181 'a brilliant player . . .': Ibid.
182 'We were more like a mob': Constantine, *Cricket in the Sun*.
183 'hard-boiled, tough . . .': Ibid.
184 'felt very pleased': Ibid.
185 'to make a hole . . .': Ibid.
185 'certainly unique in everything': Monty Noble, quoted in Bassano and Smith, *The West Indies in Australia 1930 31.*
186 'Everything is tabulated . . .': Constantine, *Cricket in the Sun.*
187 'batted all day against Grimmett . . .': Ibid.
197 'The game did not look so bad for us': Ibid.
198 'We could not get together . . .': Ibid.
199 'The man was said to have . . .': Ibid.
201 'I went indoors . . .': Ibid.
202 'It was obvious . . .': Ibid.
204–5 'Alpha and Omega, the Beginning . . .': Ibid.
205 'Some very bitter things . . .': Ibid.
211 'our fielding was terrible . . .': Ibid.
216 'to play cricket, without regard . . .': Ibid.
219 'We suffered badly from umpiring . . .': Ibid.
221 'You could hear their voices . . .': Ibid.
221 'who were horribly nervous and strung up': Ibid.

222 'Never have I been frightened . . .': Ibid.
223 'I scratch it down with the tips . . .': Ibid.
224 'There are moments a man . . .': Ibid.
224 'sure that not only the cricket . . .': 'Bradman On Our Cricketers in Australia', *Kingston Gleaner*, 29 April 1931.
225 'As young players we used . . .': Stollmeyer, *Everything under the Sun*.

Chapter 8: The Whiff of Gunpowder

229 '1933 was not . . . a happy season . . .': Warner, *Cricket between Two Wars*.
232 'Hendren's three-peak cap . . .', 'ridiculous . . .': Quoted in Abhishek Mukherjee, 'Patsy Hendren wears the first "helmet" in cricket', cricketcountry.com, 22 May 2016, <http://www.cricketcountry.com/articles/patsy-hendren-wears-the-first-helmet-in-cricket-294641>.
232–3 'The people can say what they like . . .': Ibid.
234 'Bodyline was gunpowder in those days . . .': Constantine, *Cricket in the Sun*.
236 'Other clubs in the League . . .': Ibid.
237 'an education': Ibid.
239 'When we came up against . . .': Quoted in Foot, *Wally Hammond*.
241 'a magnificent sustained barrage': Quoted in Hill, *Herbert Sutcliffe*.
242 'I found it loathsome . . .': Frith, *Bodyline Autopsy*.
243 'The leg trap stuff did not work . . .': Constantine, *Cricket in the Sun*.
244 'sight of [Bodyline] any more welcome . . .': Sydney Southerton, '1933 – England v West Indies (Second Test): Own Medicine', *Wisden* (1934).
244 '[He] might have made his hundred . . .': Constantine, *Cricket in the Sun*.
245 'the ball pitched perfectly . . .': Quoted in Kim Johnson, *Descendants of the Dragon: The Chinese in Trinidad 1806–2006* (Kingston: Ian Randle, 2007).
246 'had hoped my fellow countrymen . . .': Warner, *Cricket between Two Wars*.

246 'We … can, at any rate …': Sydney Southerton, 'The West
      Indies team in England 1933', *Wisden* (1934).
249 'Inexperienced captaincy and incoherence …': Constantine,
      Cricket in the Sun.

Chapter 9: Cricket in the Shadows

254 'played for two or three seasons …': Constantine, *Cricket in
      the Sun.*
254–5 'It was a blue-faced and shivering mob …': Ibid.
255 'To be brown-skinned …': Ibid.
256 'We were losing too many matches …': Ibid.
256 'hung in the air but fizzed off the pitch': Ibid.
259 'cleverly flighted slow to an occasional …': Warner, *Cricket
      between Two Wars.*
259 'Learie guided an arm ball …': Stollmeyer, *Everything under
      the Sun.*
260 'I was roundly condemned …': Constantine, *Cricket in the
      Sun.*
261 'more life and accuracy …': Warner, *Cricket between Two
      Wars.*
262 'he was addressing the right stuff …': Constantine, *Cricket in
      the Sun.*
263 'He was, when batting …': Stollmeyer, *Everything under the
      Sun.*
263 'Only a clever pedestrian …': Ibid., quoting Neville Cardus,
      Manchester Guardian.
263 'A game to be forgotten': Constantine, *Cricket in the Sun.*
264 'played the ball sharply …': Stollmeyer, *Everything under the
      Sun.*
265 'hard, frightened faces …': Constantine, *Cricket in the Sun.*
266 'with pace and flight variations …': Ibid.
266 'active as the proverbial cat': Warner, *Cricket between Two
      Wars.*
267 'He cut, he drove …': Ibid.
267 'had the fielders scattered …': Stollmeyer, *Everything under the
      Sun.*
267 'an Indian rubberman with double joints': C. B. Fry, *London
      Evening Standard.*

268–9 'the most unflagging member . . .': 'The West Indian team
in England 1939', *Wisden* (1940).
269 'I'd read all about the English stars . . .': Quoted in Bridgette
Lawrence and Reg Scarlett, *100 Great West Indian Test
Cricketers: From Challenor to Richards* (London: Hansib, 1987).
269 'every movement was a joy to behold': 'Cricketer of the
Year – 1940: Learie Constantine', *Wisden* (1940).

Chapter 10: Playing Cricket and Beating Hitler

274 'none could call Constantine . . .': E. W. Swanton, *Cricketers of
My Time* (London: André Deutsch, 1999).
274 'worry that perhaps . . .': Constantine, *Cricket in the Sun*.
275 'but you would not have thought so . . .': Ibid.
275 'When a man would rather see his side . . .': Ibid.
276 'I would have felt like a rat . . .': Ibid.
278 'Long ago an old Negro told me . . .': Ibid.
280 'all the tact in the world . . .': Quoted in Mason, *Learie
Constantine*.
281 'Within five weeks we had unearthed . . .': Quoted in
Renton, *C. L. R. James*.
281 'initiate the West Indian renaissance . . .': James, *Beyond a
Boundary*.
282 'just big boys': Quoted in McKinstry, *Jack Hobbs*.
282 'erratic quality of West Indian cricket . . .': Quoted in
Williams, *Cricket and Race*.
283 'they are no better than we': Quoted in Renton, *C. L. R. James*.
285 'carrying on the *Herrenvolk* idea . . .': Harold Moody, quoted
in Howat, *Learie Constantine*.
286 'rich, musical voice': 'A Spectator's Notebook', *Spectator*, 9
September 1943.
288 'These are the players who have . . .': Constantine, *Cricket in
the Sun*.
289 'Constantine's innings was a real gem . . .': Quoted in Hill,
Herbert Sutcliffe.
292 'who was the senior international . . .': Warner, *Long Innings*.
292 'In this country . . .': Ibid.
293 'one of the finest returns I have . . .': Hammond, *Cricket My
Destiny*.

293 'I had picked up the ball . . .': Constantine, *Cricket in the Sun*.

293 'had subtlety, skill and enthusiasm . . .': Denzil Batchelor, *A Gallery of Great Players from W. G. Grace to the Present Day* (London: Collins, 1952).

295 'The colour question affects . . .': Constantine, *Cricket in the Sun*.

298 'a man of high character': *Constantine v Imperial Hotels Ltd* (1944) KB 693.

298 'I was content to have drawn . . .': Constantine, *Cricket in the Sun*.

Chapter 11: Insults and Ermine

301 'yelling newspapers and yodelling . . .': Constantine, *Cricketers' Cricket*.

304 'only a little less intolerant . . .': Constantine, *Colour Bar*.

304–5 'I owe something to them . . .': BBC radio broadcast, 1954.

306 'I didn't see eye to eye . . .': Howat, *Learie Constantine*.

311 'I have travelled five continents . . .': Ibid.

316 'never won at the expense of honour . . .': Ibid., quoting *Nelson Leader*.

321 'I am proud of this honour . . .': Quoted in Giuseppi, *A Look at Learie Constantine*.

Bibliography

Andrews, Gordon, *The Datasport Book of Wartime Cricket 1940–45* (Shipston-on-Stour: Datasport, 1990)

Barker, Ralph, *Ten Great Innings* (London: Chatto & Windus, 1964)

Bassano, Brian and Rick Smith, *The West Indies in Australia 1930–31* (Tasmania: Apple Books, 1990)

Batchelor, Denzil (ed.), *Great Cricketers* (London: Eyre & Spottiswoode, 1970)

Beckles, Hilary, *A Nation Imagined: First West Indies Test Team, The 1928 Tour* (Kingston: Ian Randle, 2003)

———— (ed.), *An Area of Conquest: Popular Democracy and West Indies Cricket Supremacy* (Kingston: Ian Randle, 1994)

———— and Brian Stoddart (eds), *Liberation Cricket: West Indies Cricket Culture* (Kingston: Ian Randle, 1995)

Birbalsingh, Frank, *The Rise of West Indian Cricket: from Colony to Nation* (Hertford: Hansib, 1996)

Bose, Mihir, *A History of Indian Cricket* (London: André Deutsch, 1990)

Bowes, Bill, *Express Deliveries* (London: Stanley Paul, 1949)

Constantine, Learie, *Cricket and I* (London: Philip Allan, 1933)

————, *Cricket in the Sun* (London: Stanley Paul, 1946)

————, *Cricketers' Carnival* (London: Stanley Paul, 1948)

————, *Cricketers' Cricket* (London: Eyre & Spottiswoode, 1949)

————, *Cricket Crackers* (London: Stanley Paul, 1950)

————, *Colour Bar* (London: Stanley Paul, 1954)

————, *The Young Cricketer's Companion: The Theory and Practice of Joyful Cricket* (London: Souvenir Press, 1964)

———— and Denzil Batchelor, *The Changing Face of Cricket* (London: Eyre & Spottiswoode, 1966)

Douglas, Christopher, *Douglas Jardine: Spartan Cricketer* (London: Allen & Unwin, 1984)

Duckworth, Leslie, *S. F. Barnes – Master Bowler* (London: Hutchinson, 1967)

Edmundson, David, *See the Conquering Hero: The Story of the Lancashire League 1892–1991* (Altham: Mike McLeod Litho, 1992)

Farnes, Kenneth, *Tours and Tests* (London: Lutterworth Press, 1940)

Foot, David, *Wally Hammond: The Reasons Why – A Biography* (London: Robson, 1996)

Frith, David, *Bodyline Autopsy: The Full Story of the Most Sensational Test Cricket Series – Australia v England 1932–33* (London: Aurum Press, 2002)

Genders, Roy, *League Cricket in England* (London: Werner Laurie, 1952)

Giuseppi, Undine, *A Look at Learie Constantine* (London: Thomas Nelson & Sons, 1974)

Guha, Ramachandra, *A Corner of a Foreign Field: The Indian History of a British Sport* (London: Picador, 2002)

Hammond, Walter R., *Cricket My Destiny* (London: Stanley Paul, 1945)

Hill, Alan, *Herbert Sutcliffe: Cricket Maestro* (London: Simon & Schuster, 1991)

Howat, Gerald, *Learie Constantine* (London: Allen & Unwin, 1975)

————, *Walter Hammond* (London: Allen & Unwin, 1984)

Hutton, Leonard, *Cricket Is My Life* (London: Hutchinson, 1949)

James, C. L. R., *Beyond a Boundary* (London: Hutchinson, 1963)

Kay, John, *Cricket in the Leagues* (London: Eyre & Spottiswoode, 1970)

Lawrence, Bridgette, *Masterclass: The Biography of George Headley* (Leicester: Polar, 1995)

────── and Ray Goble, *The Complete Record of West Indian Test Cricketers* (Leicester: ACL & Polar, 1991)

Leveson Gower, Henry, *Off and On the Field* (London: Stanley Paul, 1953)

Manley, Michael, *A History of West Indies Cricket* (London: André Deutsch, 1995)

Mason, Peter, *Learie Constantine* (Oxford: Macmillan, 2008)

McKinstry, Leo, *Jack Hobbs: England's Greatest Cricketer* (London: Yellow Jersey, 2011)

Nelson Cricket Club 1878–1978: Centenary Brochure (Nelson: Nelson Cricket Club, 1978)

Nicole, Christopher, *West Indian Cricket: The Story of Cricket in the West Indies – with Complete Records* (London: Phoenix Sports Books, 1957)

Phillips, Mike and Trevor Phillips, *Windrush: The Irresistible Rise of Multi-racial Britain* (London: HarperCollins, 1999)

Pilkington, Edward, *Beyond the Mother Country: West Indians and the Notting Hill White Riots* (London: I. B. Tauris, 1988)

Renton, Dave, *C. L. R. James: Cricket's Philosopher King* (London: Haus, 2007)

Root, Fred, *A Cricket Pro's Lot* (London: Edward Arnold & Co, 1937)

Stollmeyer, Jeff, *Everything under the Sun: My Life in West Indies Cricket* (London: Stanley Paul, 1983)

Tate, Maurice, *My Cricket Reminiscences* (London: Stanley Paul, 1934)

Warner, P. F., *Cricket between Two Wars* (London: Chatto & Windus, 1942)

──────, *The Book of Cricket* (London: Sporting Handbooks, 1945, 4th edn)

──────, *Long Innings: The Autobiography of Sir Pelham Warner* (London: Harrap, 1951)

Wild, Noel, *The Greatest Show on Turf: To Commemorate the Centenary of the Lancashire Cricket League* (Nelson: Hendon, 1992)

Wilkinson, Geoff (ed.), *A Century of Bradford League Cricket 1903–2003* (Bradford: Bradford League, 2003)

Williams, Jack, *Cricket and Race* (Oxford: Berg, 2001)

Wyatt, R. E. S., *Three Straight Sticks* (London: Stanley Paul, 1951)

Index

Also by Harry Pearson

The Trundlers

Some men are born medium-paced, some achieve medium-pace, and some have medium-pace thrust upon them.

Bowlers who take wickets not with pace or spin, but – at speeds between 65 and 85mph – by nagging accuracy are the commonest in cricket. So far, however, nobody has paid them any attention. Yet seam bowling remains one of cricket's most mysterious arts. George Hirst, one of the best early exponents of swerve, was as puzzled by it as his opponents. 'Sometimes it works,' he said, 'and sometimes it doesn't.'

Examining the history of medium-pace bowling, explaining how swing both normal and reverse actually works, and telling the story of some of the great and not-so-great dobbers such as Shackleton ('His bowling, like his hair, never less than immaculate,' noted *Wisden* approvingly), *Trundlers* will bring bread-and-butter bowlers who 'do a bit off the seam', 'wobble the odd one about' or simply 'nag away at off-stump' out into the limelight for the first time.

Warm, affectionate and told with Harry Pearson's trademark humour, *Trundlers* celebrates dobbers in all their sleeves-rolled-up, uncomplaining workaday glory.

Slipless in Settle

Slipless in Settle is a sentimental journey around club cricket in the north of England, a world far removed from the clichéd lengthening-shadows-on-the-village-green image of the summer game. This is hardcore cricket played in former pit villages and mill towns. Winner of the 2011 MCC Cricket Book of the Year, it is about the little clubs that have, down the years, produced some of the greatest players Britain has ever seen, and at one time spent a fortune on importing the biggest names in the international game to boost their battle for local supremacy.

Slipless in Settle is a warm, affectionate and outrageously funny sporting odyssey in which Andrew Flintoff and Learie Constantine rub shoulders with Asbo-tag-wearing all-rounders, there's hot-pot pie and mushy peas at the tea bar, two types of mild in the clubhouse, and a batsman is banned for a month for wearing a fireman's helmet when going out to face Joel Garner . . .

To buy any of our books and to find out
more about Abacus and Little, Brown, our authors
and titles, as well as events and book clubs,
visit our website

www.littlebrown.co.uk

and follow us on Twitter

@AbacusBooks
@LittleBrownUK

To order any Abacus titles p & p free in the UK,
please contact our mail order supplier on:

+ 44 (0)1832 737525

Customers not based in the UK should contact
the same number for appropriate postage
and packing costs.